WORD 2002

in easy steps

SCOTT BASHAM

In easy steps is an imprint of Computer Step
Southfield Road . Southam
Warwickshire CV47 0FB . England

http://www.ineasysteps.com

Notice of Liability

Every effort has been made to ensure that this book contains accurate and current information. However, Computer Step and the author shall not be liable for any loss or damage suffered by readers as a result of any information contained herein.

Trademarks

Microsoft® and Windows® are registered trademarks of Microsoft Corporation. All other trademarks are acknowledged as belonging to their respective companies.

Printed and bound in the United Kingdom

ISBN 1-84078-141-6

Table of Contents

4 Working with a Document 47

5 Styles and Themes 63

6 Using Speech Recognition 77

7 Tabulation 81

Getting to Know Word

This chapter gets you started with Word 2002 quickly. It explains the screen layout, and introduces the various viewing modes that you can use to display your documents. It looks at new Word 2002 features such as the Task Pane, personalised menus, docking toolbars, and the extensive Help facilities.

Covers

Chapter One

Introduction

Word-processing was one of the first popular applications for the modern personal computer. In the early days it provided little more than the ability to enter and change text on a computer monitor. As time went on software and hardware improved, and features such as spell-checking and various typographical effects were added. The number of users increased.

Microsoft Word 2002 for Windows is widely acknowledged as a leader in its field, and is one of the best selling packages in any software category.

Let's face it, with Word 2002 we're talking about a *big* package. It has retained the position as market leader by stuffing itself full of useful features, taking it from word-processing into the realms of graphical and data-oriented documents, and adding the capacity for easy to use web publishing. At first it may seem to contain a bewildering array of options and controls, but many are there to make life easier – providing quick access to the most commonly used features.

A big package inevitably comes with a depressingly large amount of reference material, which will describe each and every function in minute detail. This book is not intended to replace Microsoft's documentation; instead you should view it as a more graphical teaching guide. Wherever possible, pictures and examples are used rather than pages of text to explain and demonstrate the concepts covered.

To gain maximum benefit from this book:

- Make sure that you are first familiar with the Windows operating environment (i.e. using a mouse, icons, menus, dialog boxes etc.).
- It is important to experiment using your own examples; like many things you will find that practice is the key to competence.

In the past, only programs (not individual windows within programs) displayed on the Windows Taskbar. With Word 2002, however, all open windows display as separate buttons:

Log of main Word 20... | Word 2002 - chec...

Click a Word window to launch it

This feature is called Quick File Switching. In order to use Quick File Switching you need to be using:

- *Windows 98/2000/Me/XP, or:*
- *Windows 95 with Internet Explorer 4.0 (or a later version)*

The Word 2002 Screen

Start Word by selecting Programs>Microsoft Word from the Start menu. You should see the following screen.

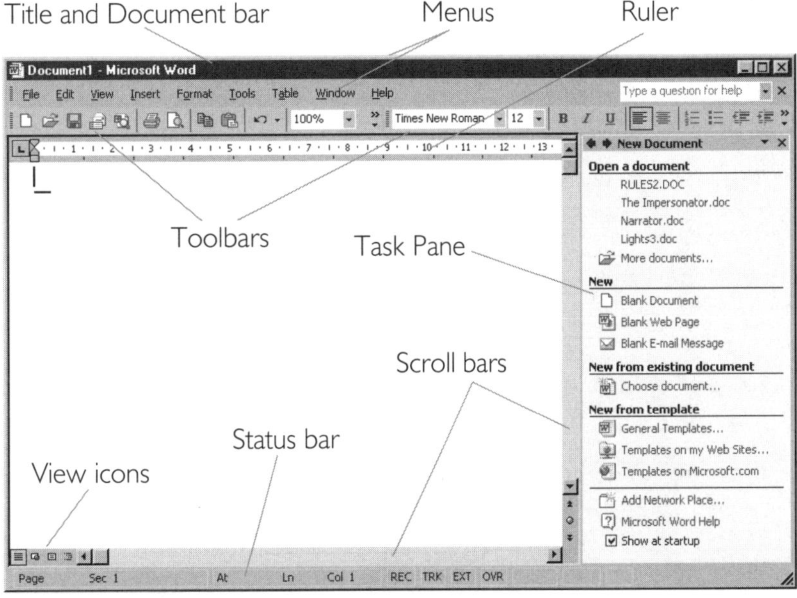

To quickly activate a toolbar, right-click the mouse on any currently visible toolbar to display a shortcut menu. Check the toolbar of your choice.

To deactivate a toolbar, follow the same procedure, but instead uncheck the toolbar in the menu.

Don't worry if the screen you see has extra items or things missing; you'll see in a moment that it's possible to configure the Word 2002 screen in different ways.

Toolbars

Toolbars can appear at the top of the screen, at the bottom, or as floating palettes. They give you instant access to features without the need to search through menus and dialog boxes. There are sixteen toolbars but we usually only require several at any time.

For more on toolbars, see pages 12 and 16.

Task Pane

The Task Pane (classed as a toolbar) is a handy pane from which you can undertake a wide variety of jobs. The advantage of the Task Pane is that, unlike a dialog box, it stays on-screen as long as you want; you don't keep having to launch it.

Page Views

There are four different ways of viewing the page, which you can select from the top section of the View menu: *Normal, Web Layout, Print Layout, and Outline.*

The quickest way to switch views is to use the icons in the bottom left corner of the screen.

Normal View

This view allows fast editing, previewing most text effects, but does not display images and other objects.

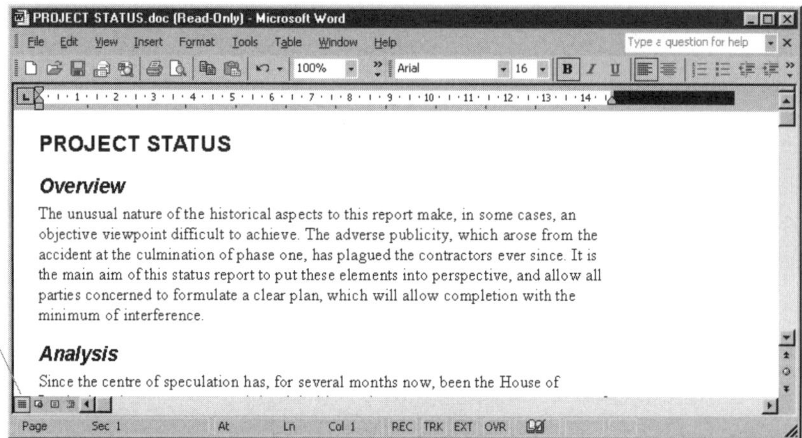

Web Layout View

This makes online reading easier by displaying text larger than it would necessarily print, and by displaying the Document Map, a tool you can use to move easily through your document.

In any of these views, paragraph symbols (markers denoting carriage returns, spaces, etc.) are by default not visible. To display them, click on the Paragraph Symbols icon normally displayed in the Standard toolbar:

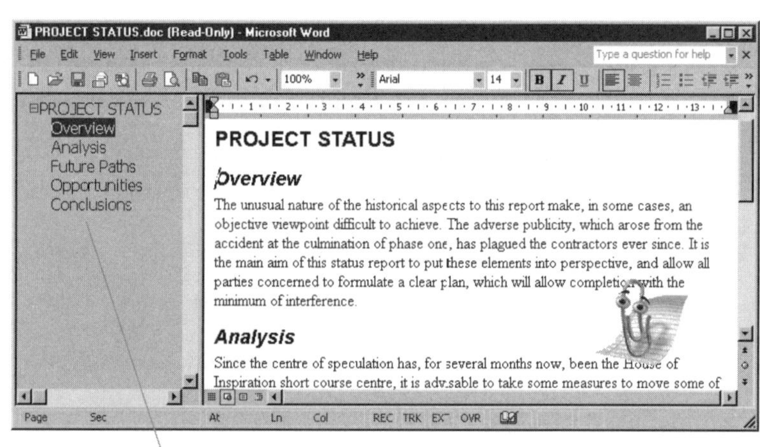

Document Map

Print Layout View

This view displays your document as actual pages, previewing text and graphics effects.

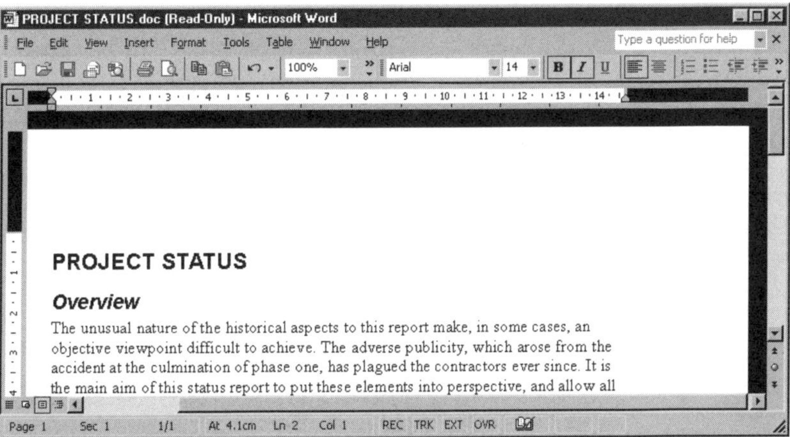

Outline View

The structure of a document can be rearranged from Outline view by dragging the plus and minus signs to another part of the document.

This allows you to view your text as a structured outline. Each major heading is marked with a plus sign; subordinate headings are marked with a minus sign. To collapse a heading so that subordinate headings are not displayed, double-click on the plus sign.

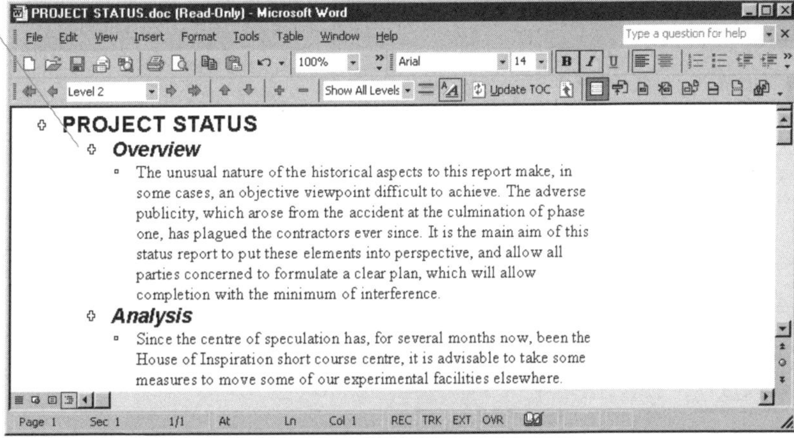

In previous versions of Word (before Word 2000), there was an additional Master Document View. Now this has been merged with Outline View.

Toolbars

To add a new button to a toolbar, right-click over the toolbar. Click Customize. In the dialog which launches, click the Commands tab. In the Categories field, click a category (a group of associated icons). In the Commands box, drag a button onto the toolbar in the open document. Finally, click Close.

To move a toolbar, click the left edge and drag to another location. (Dragging to the main page area makes the toolbar freestanding.)

See page 16 for how to access toolbar buttons which are currently off-screen.

To resize a toolbar, drag on its right-hand edge.

The Task Pane is a toolbar. To hide or show it, untick or tick the Task Pane entry.

Toolbars are important components in Word 2002. A toolbar is an on-screen bar which contains shortcut buttons. These symbolise and allow easy access to often-used commands which would normally have to be invoked via one or more menus.

For example, Word 2002's Standard toolbar lets you:

- create, open, save and print documents
- perform copy & paste and cut & paste operations
- undo editing actions
- insert a hyperlink

by simply clicking on the relevant button.

Specifying which toolbars are displayed

Pull down the View menu and click Toolbars. Now do the following:

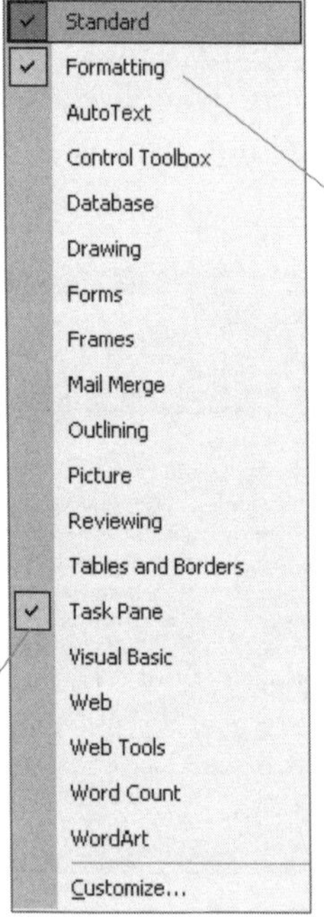

Click the toolbar you want to be visible – a ✔ appears against it. (Repeat to hide a toolbar – the tick disappears)

Repeat this procedure for as many toolbars as necessary.

Adjusting the Page Setup

Go to the File menu and choose Page Setup. The Page Setup dialog box appears. Like many of Word's dialog boxes, it is *tabbed*, i.e. subdivided into sections. You can select your required section by clicking on the appropriate tab at the top of the box.

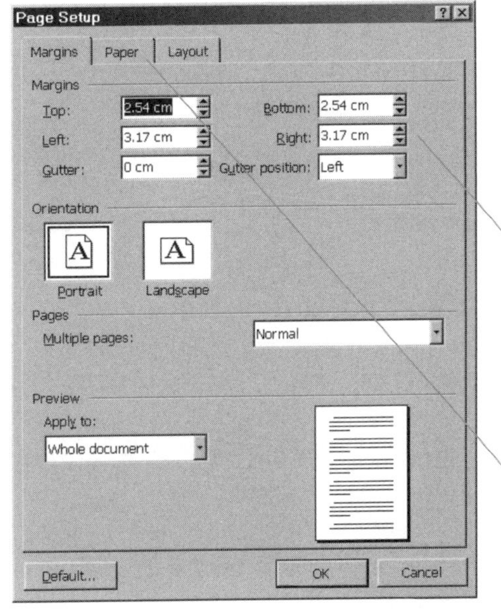

1 Make sure the Margins tab is selected.

2 Type in any required changes to the margin or header/ footer dimensions.

3 Click on the Paper tab.

You can also select tabs by pressing the Alt key together with the underlined letter in the tab name.

Alternatively, pressing Control together with the Tab key itself will cycle through each tab in turn.

4 Select a paper size from the drop-down list, or enter custom values in the Width and Height boxes.

5 Make any necessary changes in the Layout tab.

6 Click OK to apply your changes.

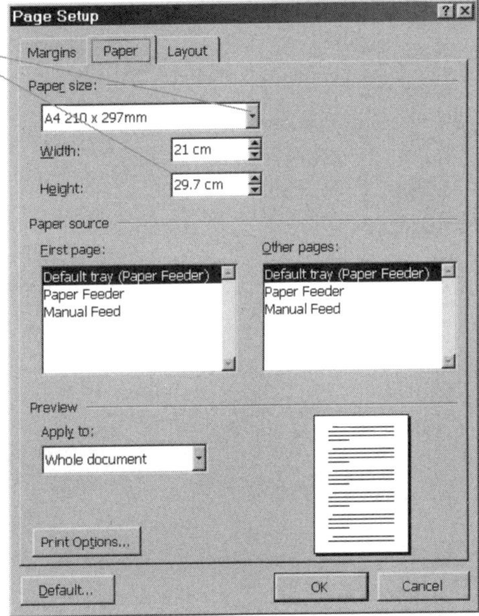

Help

Word 2002 features several basic ways of offering you help. In increasing order of sophistication, these are Help boxes, context sensitive help, and Ask-a-Question.

Help Boxes

If you allow your mouse pointer to rest over an icon for a moment, a Help box will appear. This gives you a brief explanation of the icon's function.

Help box

Context Sensitive Help

1. Go to the Help menu and choose What's This?

The pointer turns into an arrow with a question mark attached until the next time you click.

2. Move your pointer to the element in which you're interested, then click.

The keyboard shortcut for context sensitive help is Shift + F1.

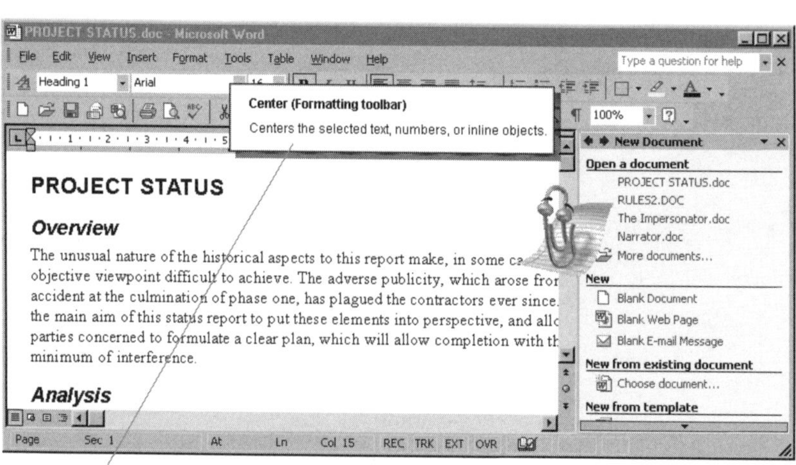

A pop-up box will appear, with a description of the item or menu option.

Ask-a-Question

In Word 2000, users had to run the Office Assistant (see the tip) to get answers to plain-English questions. In Word 2002, however, this isn't the case. Simply do the following:

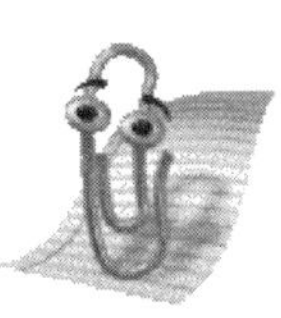

The Office Assistant (shown in a few of the illustrations in this chapter) is turned off by default. To turn it on, pull down the Help menu and click Show Office Assistant.

The Assistant is an animated (and frequently unpopular) helper which answers questions, but you can achieve the same effect more easily with Ask-a-Question.

1 Type in your question here and press Enter

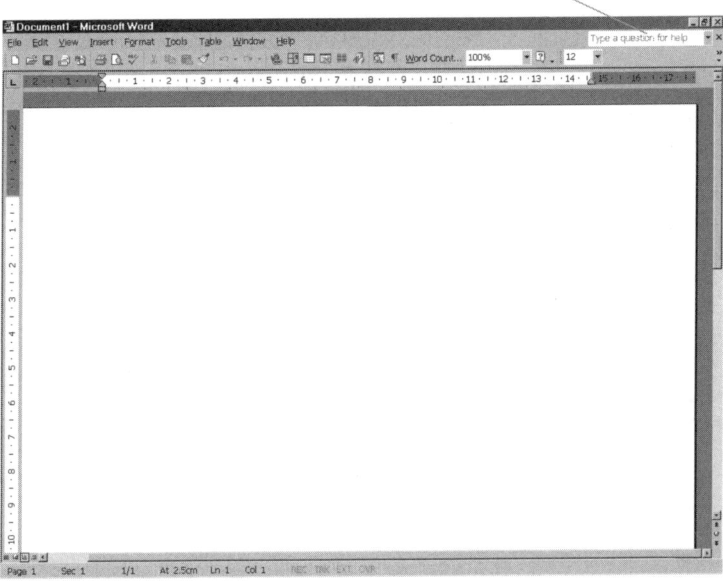

After step 2, use the Contents and Index tabs as you would in any other program.

- Troubleshoot formatting worksheets
- Copy formats from one cell to another
- Clear cell formats
- CELL worksheet function
- About formatting worksheets and data
- See more...

2 Click a relevant entry (or See more, for more topics)

3 Optional – in the next window (not shown) click Show All to display all sub-topics

Automatic Customisation

Individual features are dynamically promoted or demoted in the relevant menus.

This means menus are continually evolving...

Word 2002 menus expand automatically. Simply pull down the required menu, (which will at first be abbreviated) then wait a few seconds: it expands to display the full menu.

However, to expand them manually, click here on the chevrons at the bottom of the menu:

Automatic customisation also applies to toolbars. Note the following:

- *if possible, they display on a single row*
- *they overlap when there isn't enough room on-screen*
- *icons are 'promoted' and 'demoted' like menu entries*
- *demoted icons are shown in a separate fly-out, reached by clicking:*

Until Word 2000, it was true that, although different users use different features, no allowance had been made for this: the same features displayed on everyone's menus and toolbars...

Now, however, menus and toolbars are self-customising in Word 2002.

Personalised menus

When you first use Word 2002, its menus display the features which Microsoft believes are used 95% of the time. Features which are infrequently used are not immediately visible. This is made clear in the illustrations below:

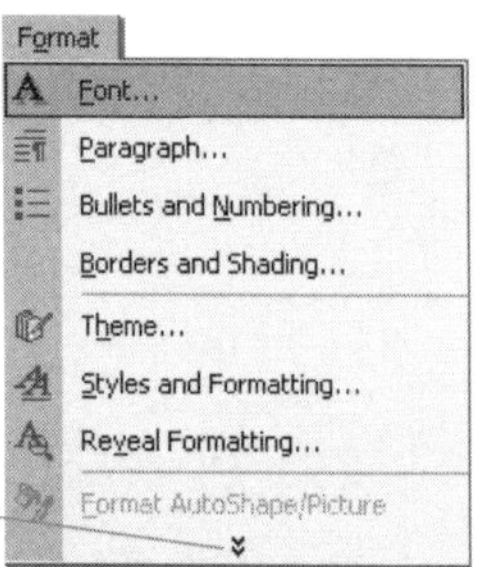

Word 2002's Format menu, as it first appears...

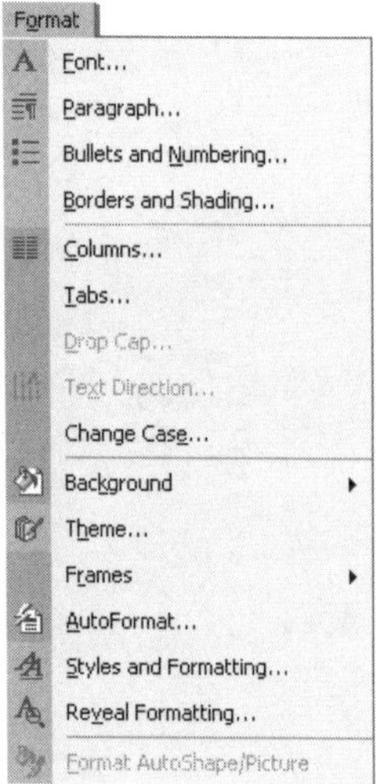

...the expanded menu

Using Smart Tags

You can disable Smart Tags. In the Tools menu click AutoCorrect Options. In the dialog, select the Smart Tags tab. Untick Label text with smart tags.

Re step 2 – choose Keep Source Formatting to retain the pasted text's original format, or Match Destination Formatting to make it conform to the host text.

Types of data Word applies Smart Tags to include the following:

- *dates/times*
- *places/addresses*
- *Outlook email recipients*

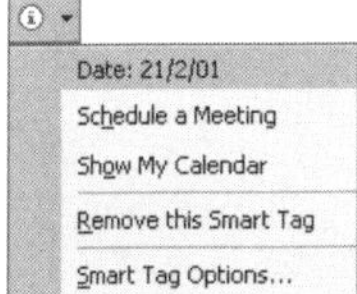

Options for a date Smart Tag

Here, you can opt to have the AutoCorrect correction undone just this once (Change back to "bu") or you can stop the correction being made in future (Stop automatically correcting "bu").

Word 2002 recognises certain types of data and underlines them with a dotted purple underline or a small blue box. When you move the mouse pointer over the line/box an 'action button' appears which provides access to commands which would otherwise have to be accessed from menus/toolbars or other programs.

The Paste Options button

1 'Button' has been copied and the Paste command (Shift+Insert) issued...

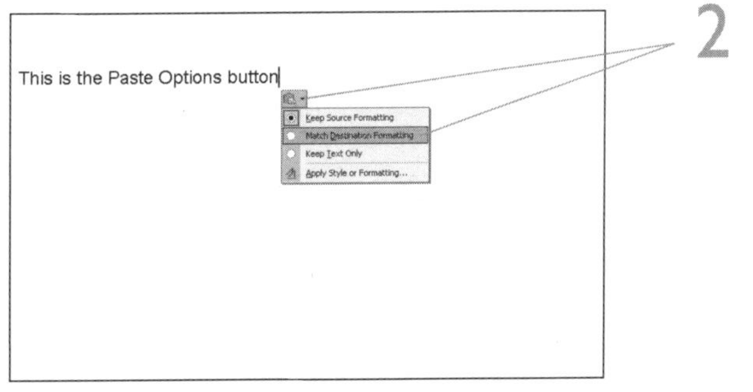

2 Clicking the arrow launches a menu – make a choice

The AutoCorrect button

1 An AutoCorrect entry has been set up which replaces 'bu' with 'button'

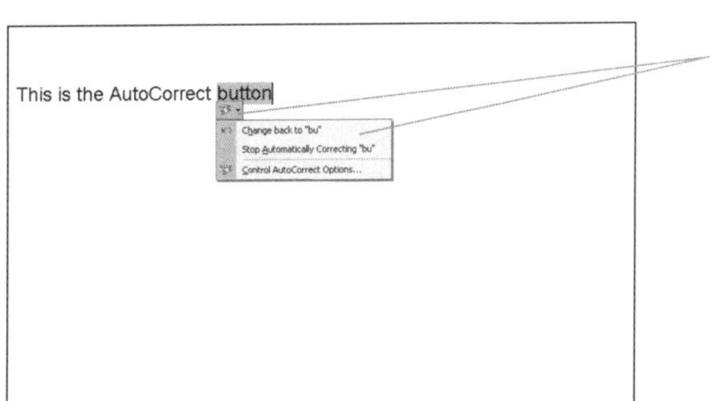

2 Clicking the arrow launches a menu – make a choice

Saving Configuration Settings

You could save configuration details on your website, as a handy backup.

The Save My Settings wizard saves all your Office XP settings, not just Word's.

Not closing all Office programs can result in faulty configuration details being written.

You can use a special wizard – the Save My Settings Wizard – to save configuration details in a special file (with the extension .ops). You can then restore the details in the file as a way of transferring your settings to another machine, or as a backup for your existing PC.

Using the Save My Settings Wizard

1 Close Word (and all other Office programs)

2 Click Start, Programs, Microsoft Office Tools, Save My Settings Wizard

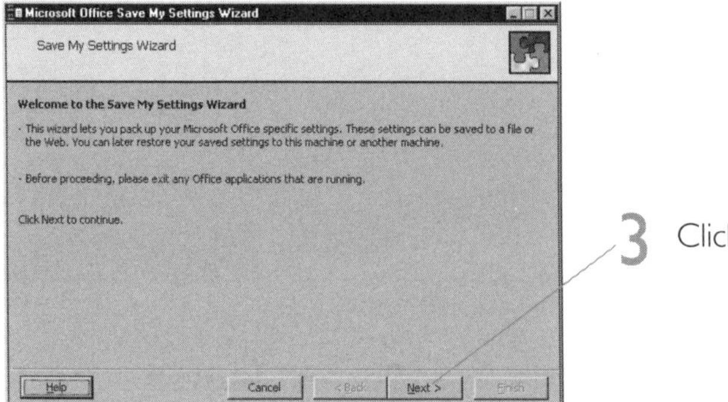

3 Click Next

4 Click Save... to save configuration details, or Restore... to implement previously saved settings

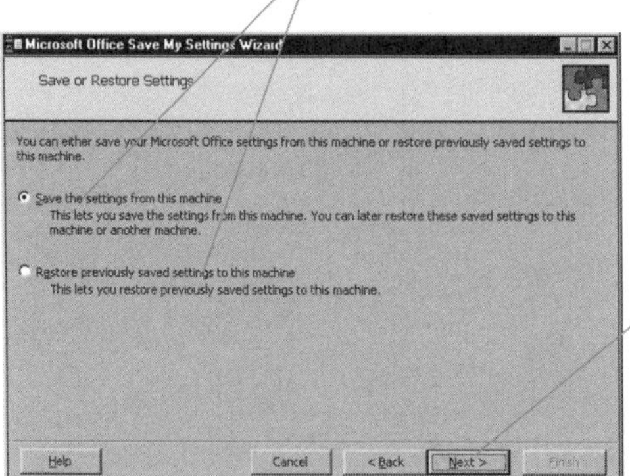

5 Click Next and complete the subsequent dialogs

Basic Text Manipulation

This chapter helps you start entering and manipulating text on the screen. It looks at different ways of editing and formatting type, as well as saving and printing your work.

Covers

Chapter Two

The Document Window

Note that the New Document icon looks like this:

1. If there is no Document window, then create a new one by clicking on the New icon in the top left of the standard toolbar.

2. Enter a sentence of example text.

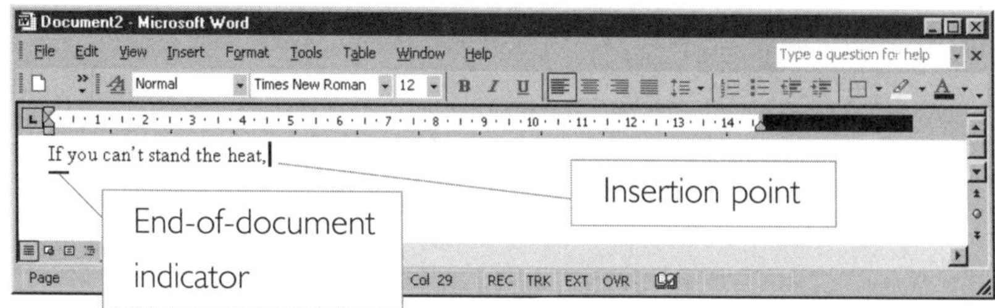

The vertical line is your *insertion point*, indicating where new text will appear. You can move the insertion point by:

- Using the cursor (arrow) keys.
- Clicking a new position with the mouse.

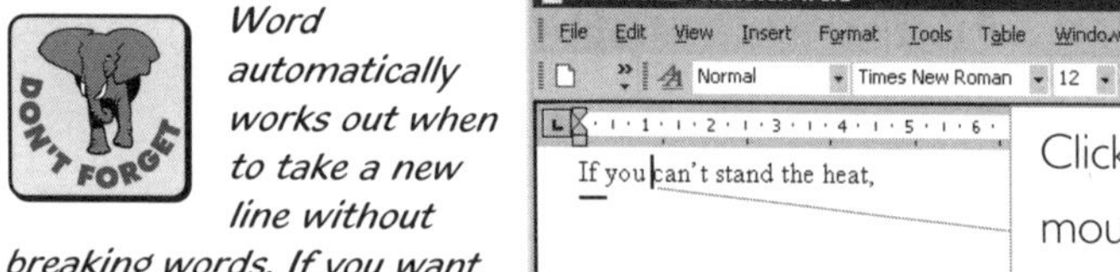

Word automatically works out when to take a new line without breaking words. If you want to start a new paragraph, press the Return or Enter key.

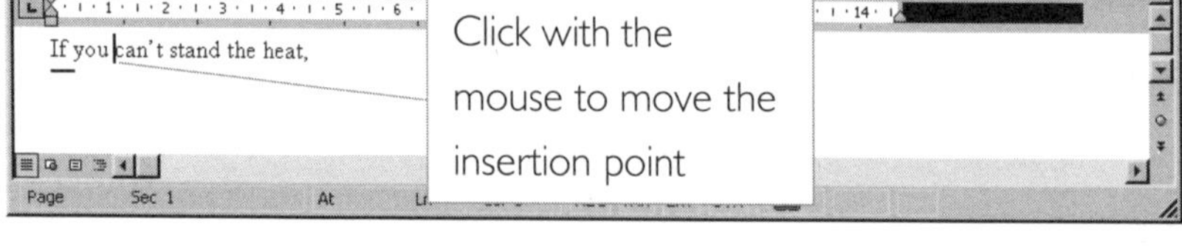

Inserting Text

1. Move the insertion point to where you'd like to add more text.

2. Type the text. It will appear at the insertion point.

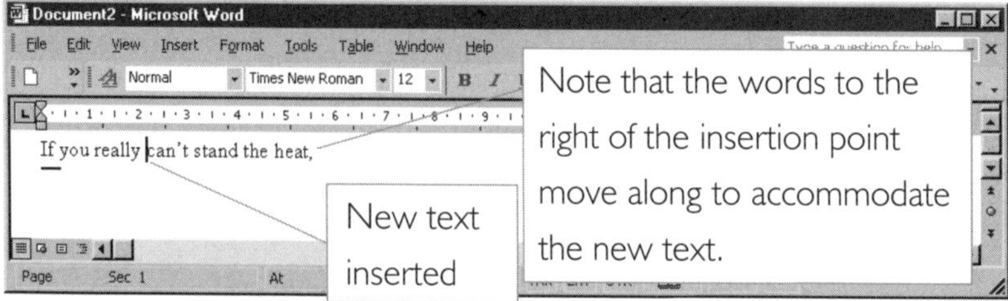

Deleting Text with the Backspace Key

1. Place the insertion point directly after the text you want to delete.

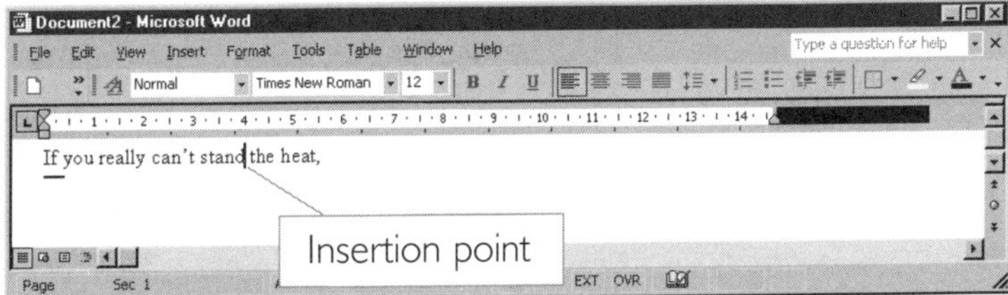

2. Press the Backspace key once to erase each character to the *left* of the insertion point.

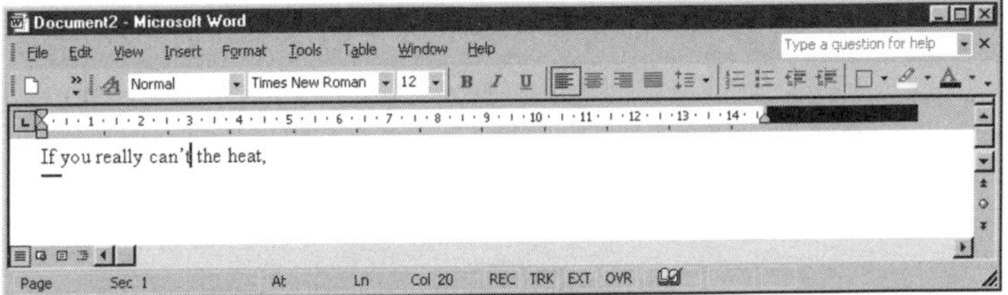

Deleting Text with the Delete Key

1. This time move the insertion point before the text to be deleted.

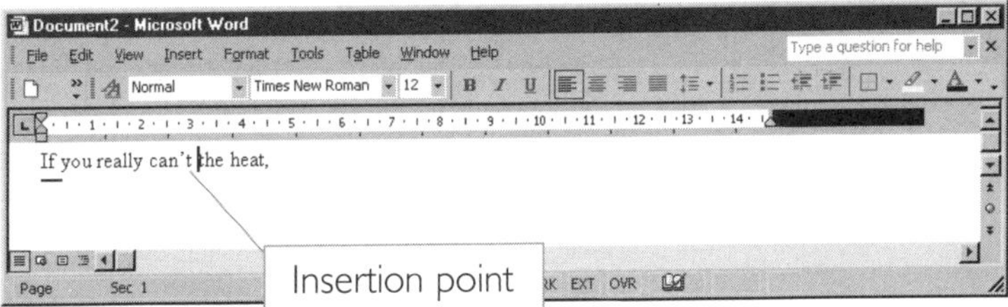

2. Press the Delete key once to erase each character to the *right* of the insertion point.

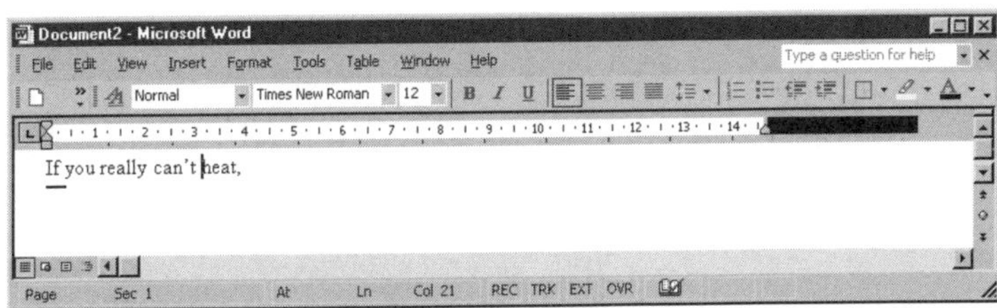

Selecting Text

Select text by dragging horizontally across it, while holding down the left mouse button.

By default, Word is in Insert mode. This means that when you add new text, existing text makes room for it. However, Word also has an alternative mode called Overtype. In Overtype mode, new text replaces any text to the right of the insertion point.

To enter (or leave) Overtype mode, press the Insert key.

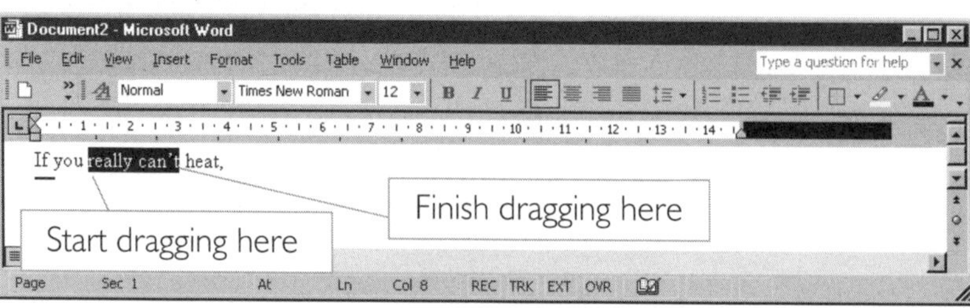

Replacing Selected Text

Anything you type will replace the currently selected text.

Adding More Text to the End of the Document

To select all text within a document, press Control+A.

1 Make sure the insertion point is at the end of the document text.

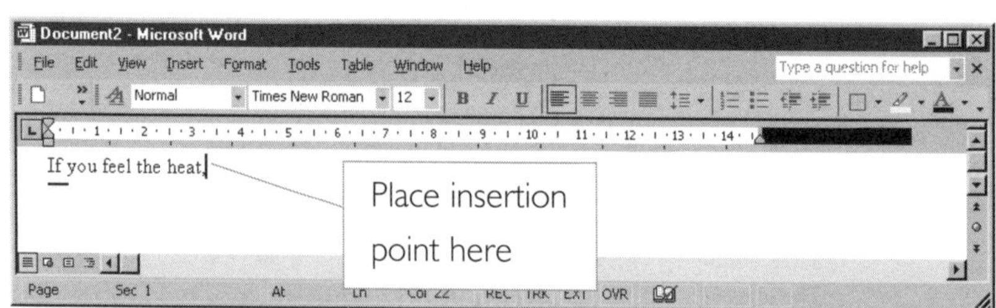

2 Add the text:

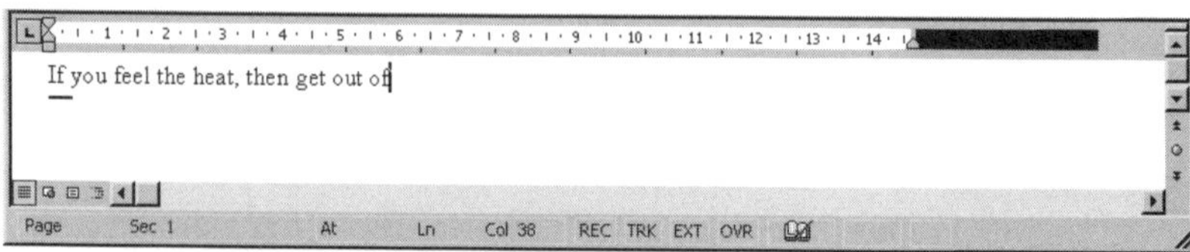

Changing the Appearance of Text

1. Select the text, open the Size drop-down menu from the toolbar, and increase the point size to around twice the previous value.

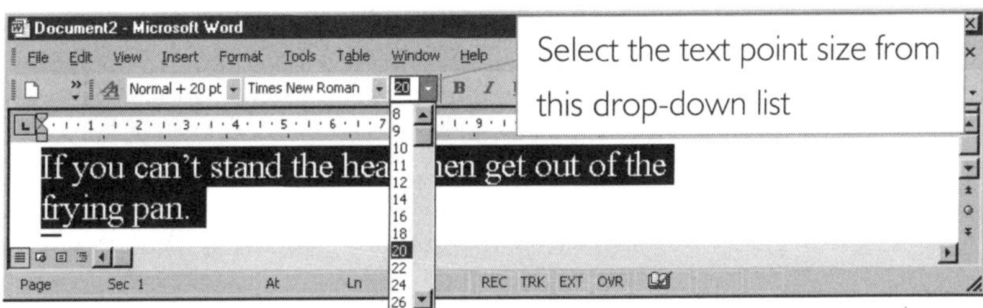

2. Select a single word and use the toolbar to choose Bold.

The keyboard shortcut for Bold is Control+B.

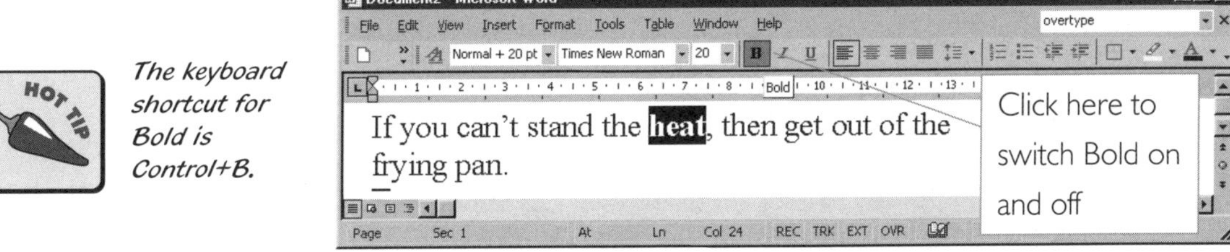

3. To select text over more than one line, drag over the area:

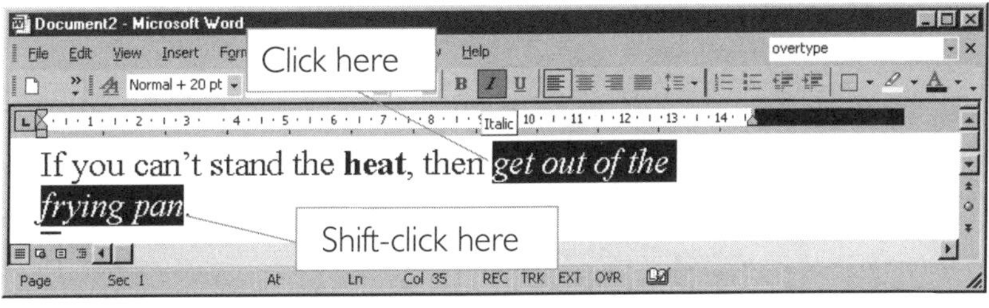

4. You can also select whole lines of text by dragging vertically over the area within the left margin.

Drag vertically within this margin area (note the different-angled mouse pointer)

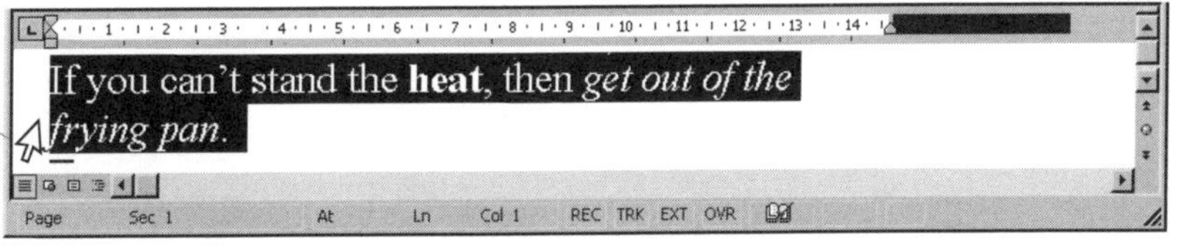

5 Alternatively, you can double-click to select a single word, or triple-click to select an entire paragraph.

6 If you click an insertion point and then type more text, the new text takes its attributes (appearance) from the previous character:

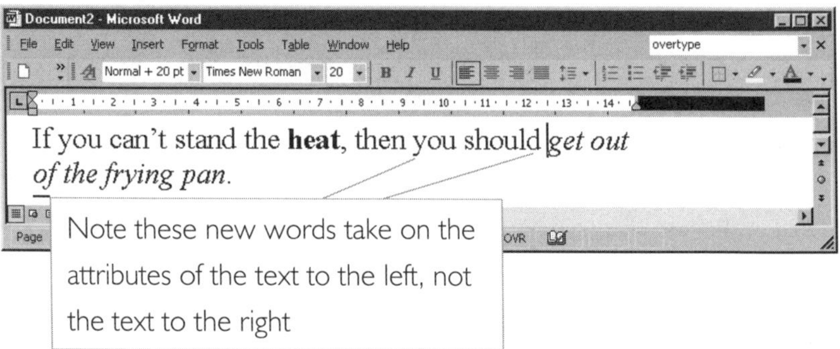

Click and Type

In Print Layout or Web Layout view you can add text virtually anywhere on the page. Double-click to establish an insertion point.

If Click and Type doesn't appear to work then first make sure that you're in Print Layout or Web Layout view. Then open the Tools menu and choose Options. Select the Edit tab and make sure that Click and Type is activated.

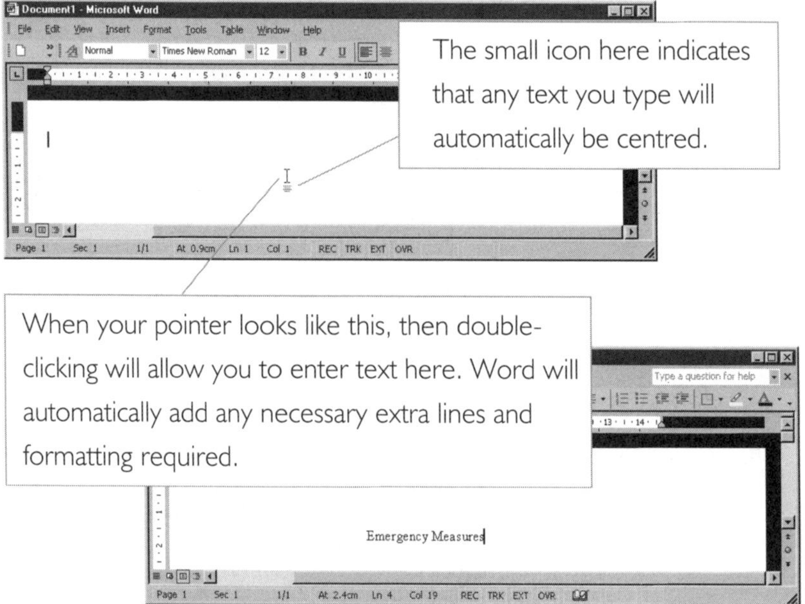

Multiple Text Selection

It is now possible to select discontinuous blocks of text.

1 Make the first selection in the normal way.

2 Hold down the Control key to select a second block of text without deselecting the first.

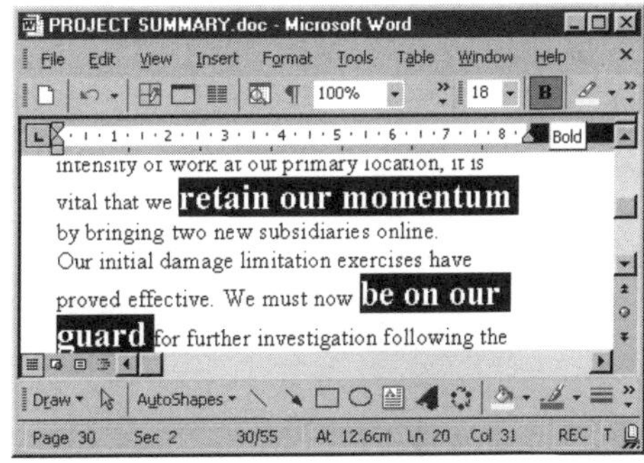

3 Repeat this process for any additional blocks of text. You can then apply formatting to everything which has been selected.

Auto Recover

1 Once your computer is up and running again, restart Word 2002.

If your machine has problems which cause Word 2002 to crash or otherwise terminate unexpectedly, Auto Recovery (an automatic document recovery) can rescue your most recent work.

2 The Document Recovery options will appear automatically. These give you the opportunity to view two versions of your document: the one you last saved, and the one Word recovered and attempted to repair when it terminated.

Don't assume that the recovered/repaired version of your document is always the one you should use. Carefully check both versions before you decide which is better.

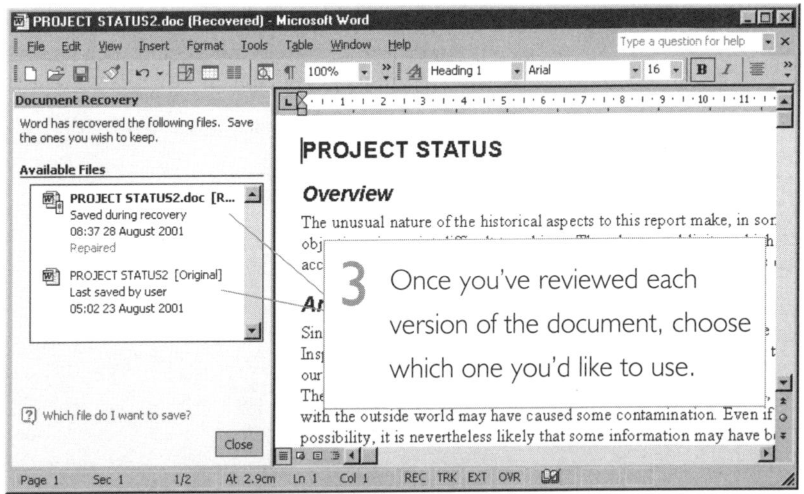

3 Once you've reviewed each version of the document, choose which one you'd like to use.

Handwriting Text

To use handwriting recognition for the first time, you have to perform a custom install. Do this in the usual way but select Office Shared Features/Alternative User Input in Office's installer.

You can import handwritten notes made on a Handheld or Pocket PC into Word – see the device's documentation.

Re step 2 – click Write Anywhere to write directly on-screen, or On-Screen Standard Keyboard to use a virtual keyboard to enter text.

You can write with special devices (e.g. graphics tablets) or with the mouse.

By default, Word converts handwriting to text. However, you can have it entered as handwriting (which can be formatted in the normal way). Click this button in the Writing Pad:

You can handwrite text into a special writing pad and have Word convert it into standard text. You can also use a virtual keyboard to enter text.

1. If the Language Bar isn't visible or minimised on the Taskbar, go to Control Panel. Double-click Text Services. In the dialog, click Language Bar. Select Show the Language bar on the desktop. Click OK twice.

2. Click Handwriting.

3. Select Writing Pad.

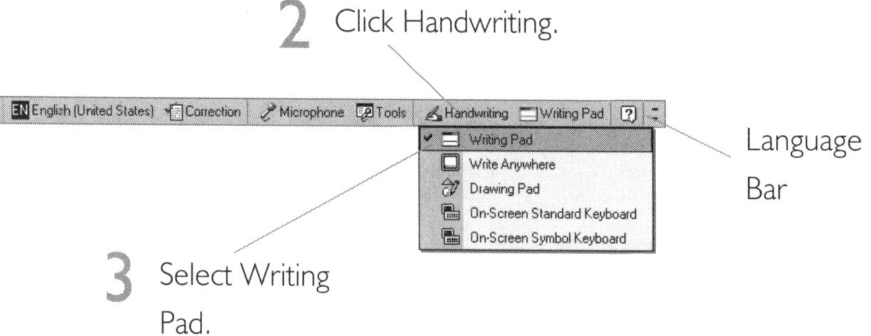

4. Handwrite text on the line in the Writing Pad (don't pause between letters but do leave a space after words) – Word enters the text as soon as it recognizes it.

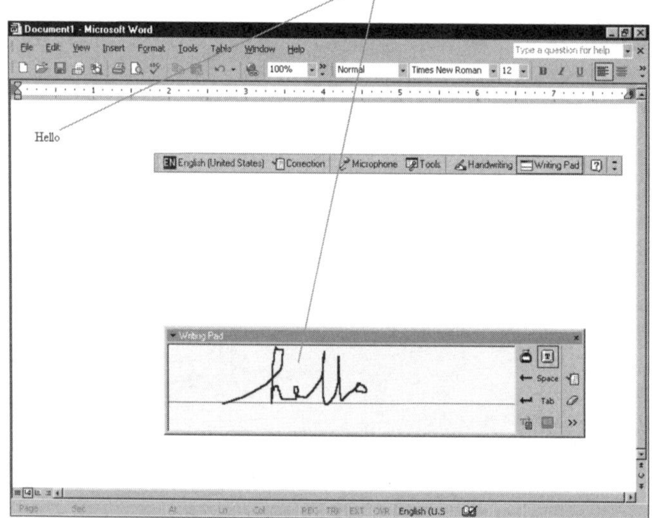

The Task Pane

New to Word 2002, the Task Pane is a useful way of manipulating settings without going into a series of dialog boxes. The benefit of this is clear: you can try out options and immediately see the effect on your document, without having to wait until you've exited a dialog box by clicking OK.

The Task Pane can be used to show different sets of controls, including Clipboard, Search, Clip Art, Styles and Formatting and Mail Merge facilities.

1 Ensure the Task Pane is active by ticking its entry in the View menu.

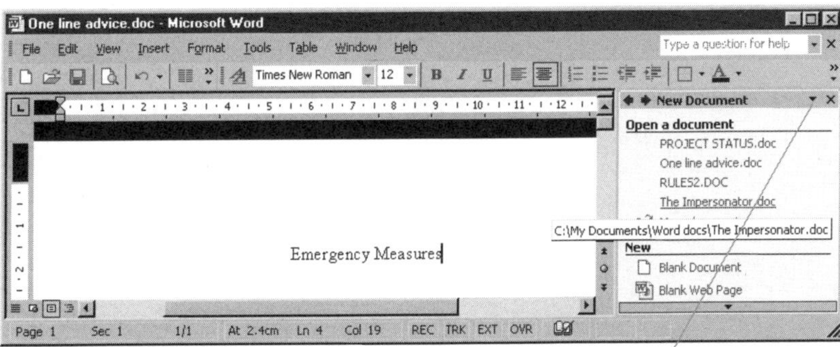

Like toolbars, the Task Pane can be undocked from the main window. To do this, simply drag on its Title bar towards the centre of the screen, until the Task Pane becomes 'free floating'.

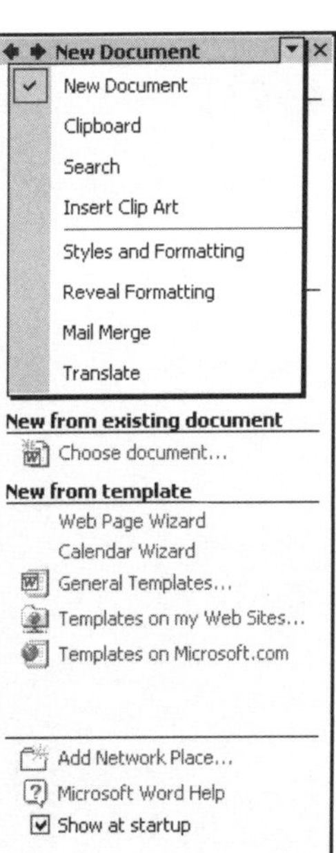

2 If the New Document controls are not visible, then select New Document from the drop-down menu in the Task Pane's top right corner.

3 You can now choose to open a recently-used document, or start a new document from scratch. The More documents... option will take you to the general Open dialog box.

New Document

4 The left and right black arrows at the top of the Task Pane let you cycle through the sets of controls currently open.

Saving a Document

1 To Save your work either choose Save from the File menu, or click on the Save icon in the toolbar.

Note that the Save icon looks like this:

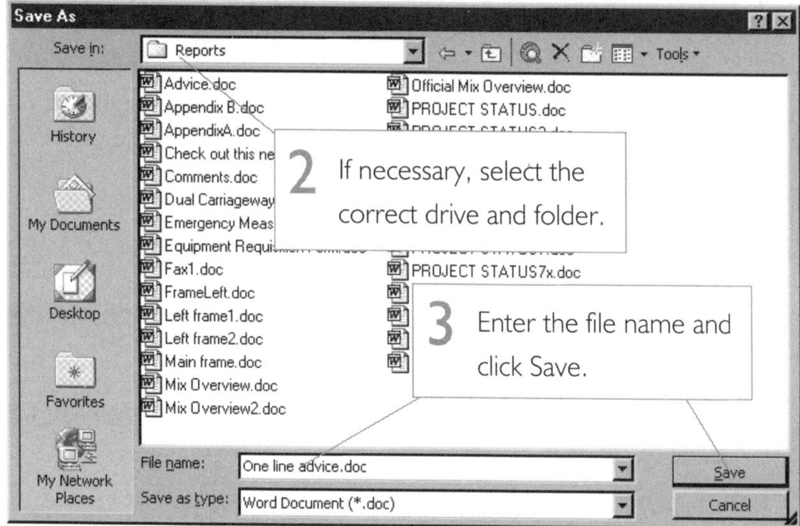

4 If you have finished with the document, choose Close from the File menu.

Opening a Document

Either:

- Choose Open from the File menu or click on the Open icon:

Or:

- The last few files used are listed in the lower section of the File menu, and can be selected directly.

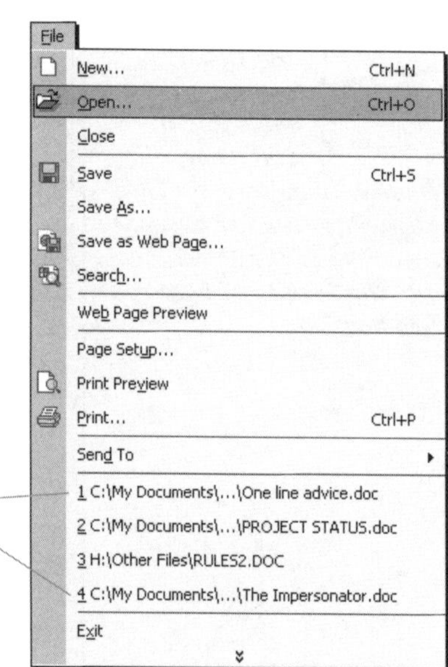

Print Preview

Note that the Print Preview icon looks like this:

Before you print a document, you may wish to check it on screen, in order to eliminate any errors that were not spotted at the basic text-proofing stage. Word 2002 offers a facility, Print Preview, which shows you all the pages of your document exactly as they will print, with none of the modifications made by the normal Word views. To access this special view, select Print Preview from the File menu, or select the corresponding icon from the Toolbar.

The following screen appears:

To edit the text in Print Preview, click here: (the cursor changes back to its normal text-editing shape). Then click in the text and make your changes.

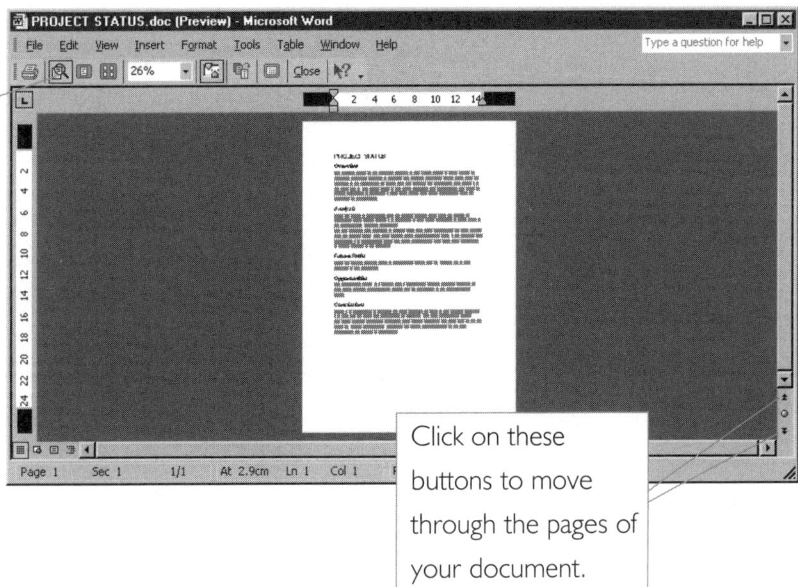

Note that the cursor is initially in the shape of a magnifying glass. To zoom in to a particular area of the page, click over it with the left mouse button; to zoom out, click a second time.

If you are satisfied with your document, select Print from the File menu, or click the Print icon:

(see the following page). If you want to continue editing, click Close instead.

Printing a Document

1 Choose Print from the File menu.

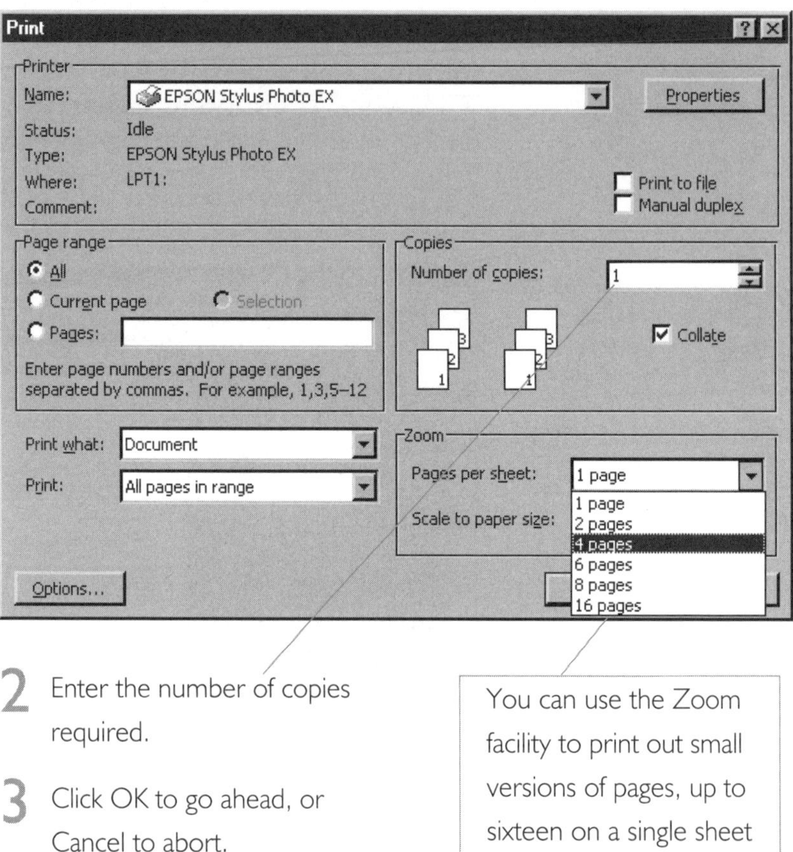

2 Enter the number of copies required.

3 Click OK to go ahead, or Cancel to abort.

You can use the Zoom facility to print out small versions of pages, up to sixteen on a single sheet

The method detailed above allows you the greatest control over how your document is printed. If, however, you do not need to make any refinements to the printing method, there is a much quicker way to print: simply click the Print icon in the Toolbar:

This begins to print immediately, bypassing the Print dialog box and using the default print settings.

Formatting Text

This chapter looks at ways in which you can change the appearance of your text. You'll start by examining what you can change on a character level. Then you'll see what you can control on a paragraph-by-paragraph basis.

Covers

Chapter Three

Character-level Formatting

What does 'character-level' mean?

Character-level attributes include font name, size, emboldening, underlining plus all sorts of other effects which can be applied to individual characters. If required, every single character could be given different attributes (although this would tend to make your document look a little like a ransom letter).

Using the Formatting Toolbar

1 Select the text which you want to format.

2 Choose the font required from the toolbar drop-down menu:

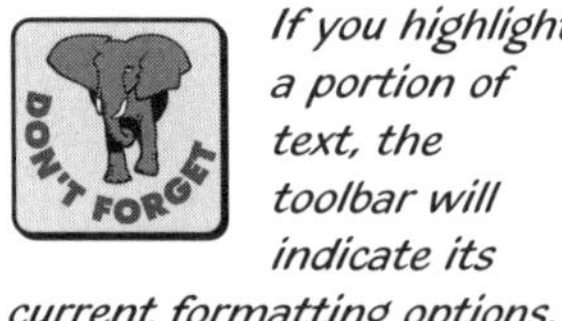

If you highlight a portion of text, the toolbar will indicate its current formatting options.

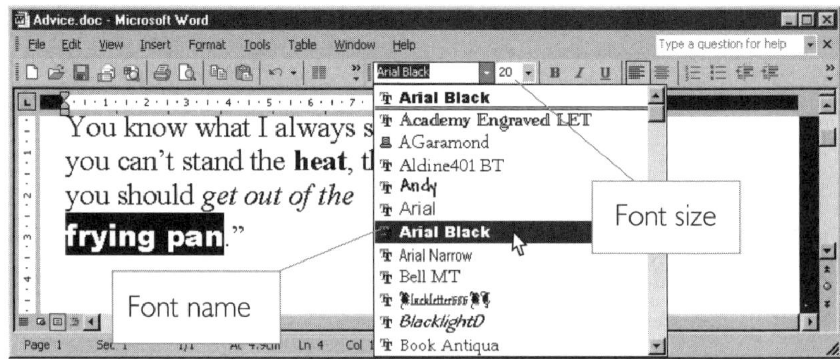

A font is a collection of characters with a particular visual style. Common fonts include:

Times or Times New Roman (useful for main text)

Arial (useful for headings)

Courier (the typewriter font)

3 Look at the font names in the drop-down list:

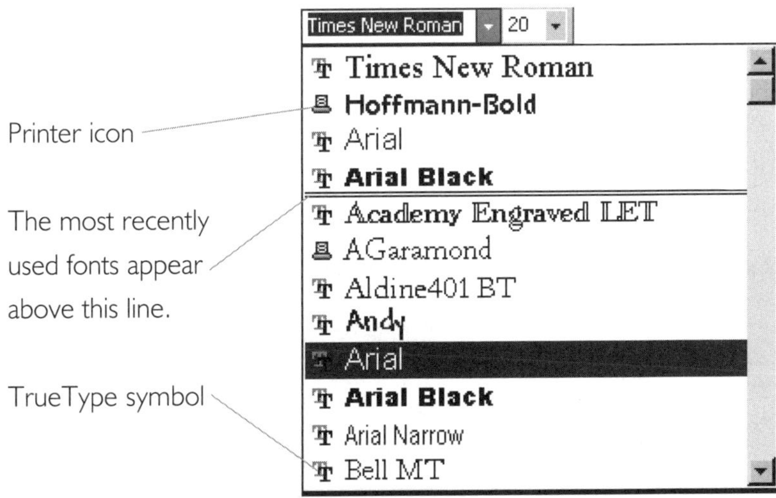

- A printer icon beside the name indicates a printer font. Your machine will use the closest available screen font (which may not match the printed output exactly).
- A double T symbol indicates a TrueType font, which is used for both screen display and printing.
- No symbol beside the font name shows a screen font. Check your printer can reproduce this to a high enough quality.

4 You can use the buttons on this toolbar to add effects such as Bold, Italic, and Underline:

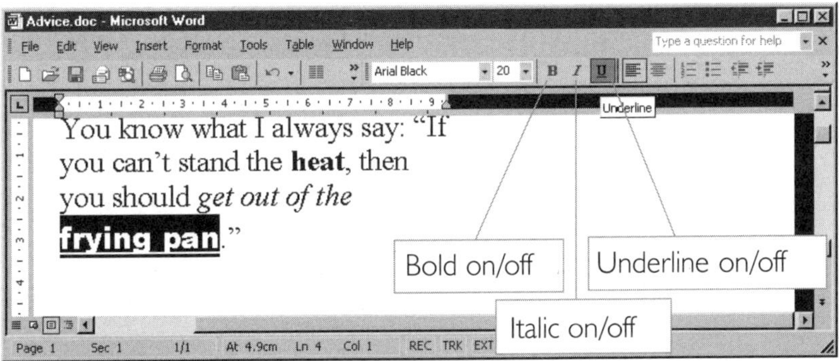

The Font Dialog Box

This controls all aspects of character-level formatting.

1 Select the text to change.

2 Either choose Font from the Format menu, then go to step 4, or click your right mouse button inside the document window.

Right-clicking brings up a menu that contains options which are relevant to the task in hand. Later you will see that it changes depending on your current context.

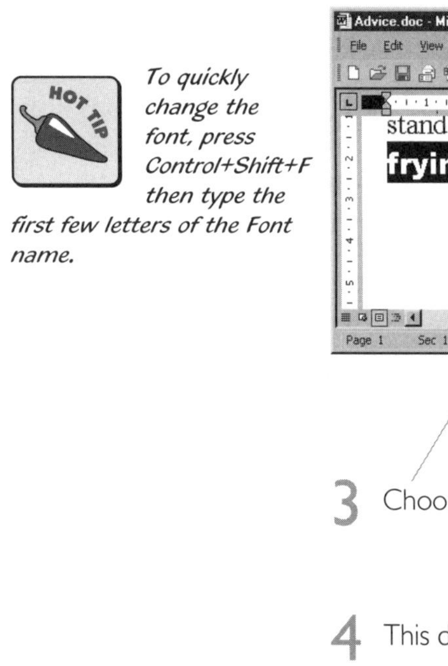

To quickly change the font, press Control+Shift+F then type the first few letters of the Font name.

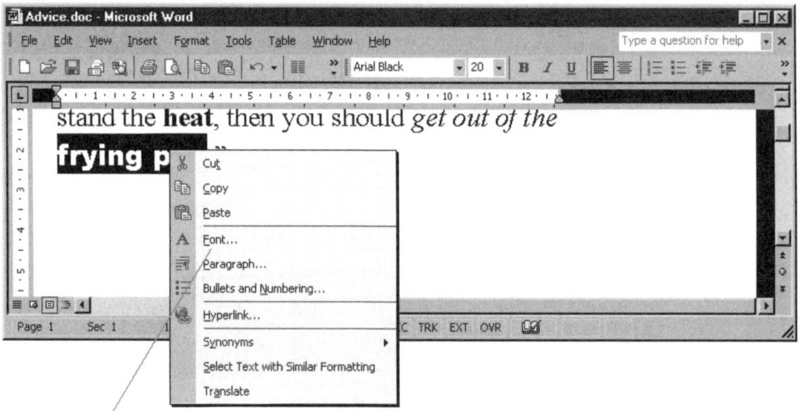

3 Choose Font.

4 This dialog box appears. Experiment with the different options, noting how they affect the Preview image.

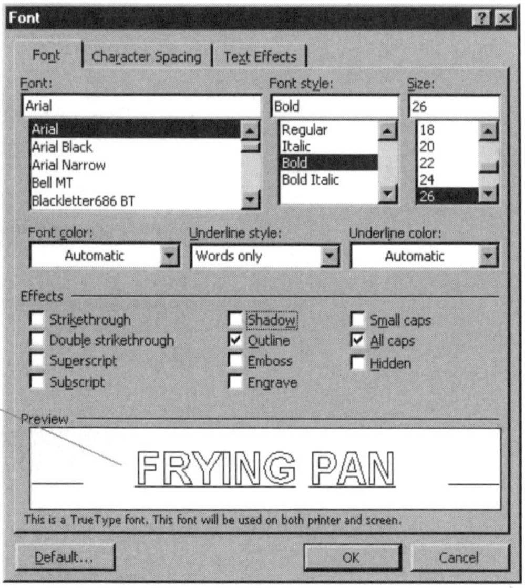

5 Click on the Character Spacing tab.

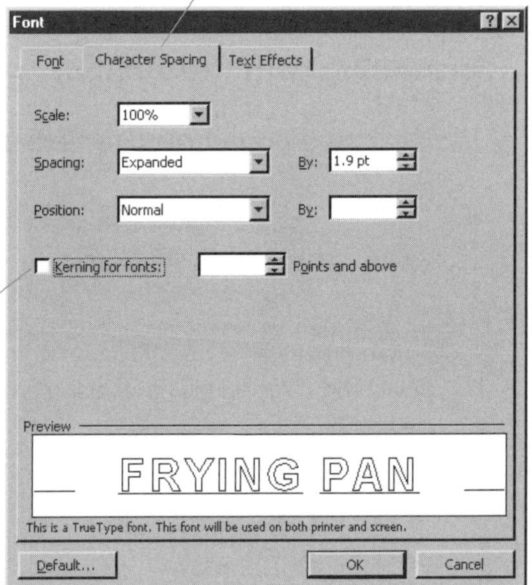

From here you can numerically control the character spacing, the position (for superscript and subscript), and kerning.

HOT TIP

Kerning is a process used to adjust the space between certain combinations of characters. For example, when the letters 'T' and 'o' occur next to each other, normal spacing appears to be too wide. Kerning brings these together to create the illusion of normal spacing.

Since kerning slows down the computer you can either switch it off altogether or activate it only for larger font sizes (where space is more noticeable).

6 Click on the Text Effects tab.

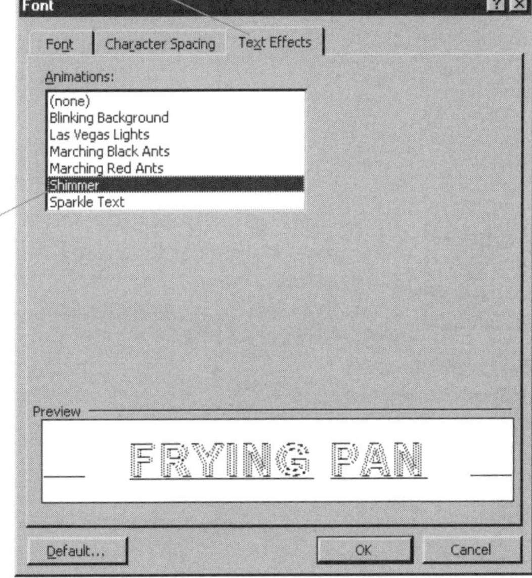

7 This feature allows you to enhance text by adding animated effects to it.

Paragraph-level Formatting

What does 'paragraph-level' mean?

Options like alignment, indents and space above/below refer to whole paragraphs (each has only one set of these attributes).

Formatting with the Toolbar

If you are changing just one paragraph you need only click an insertion point somewhere within it. Any change to a paragraph-level attribute will always affect the entire paragraph surrounding the insertion point.

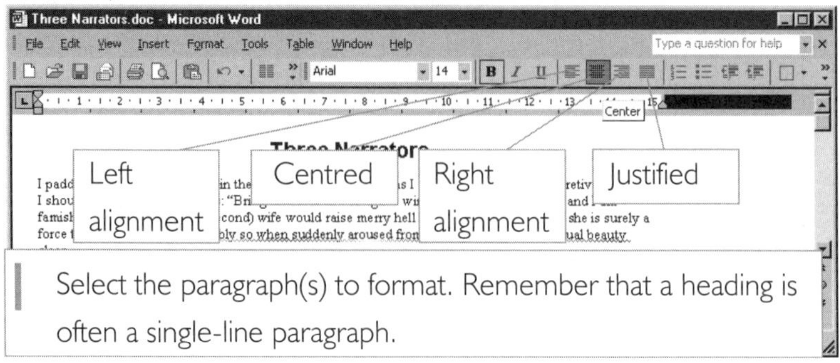

1 Select the paragraph(s) to format. Remember that a heading is often a single-line paragraph.

2 Choose the form of alignment by clicking on the appropriate tool in the formatting toolbar.

Forms of Alignment

Left

Text lines up along its left edge, with a ragged right edge.

Right

The right edge of the text is straight, and the left is ragged.

Centre

Text is centred between the left and right edges.

Justification

Spacing is adjusted so that each line within a paragraph begins and ends in the same position (dictated by the margins and indents), giving a regular appearance. Below is an example of justified text:

The last line of every justified paragraph is only aligned left, allowing the reader to easily distinguish one paragraph from another.

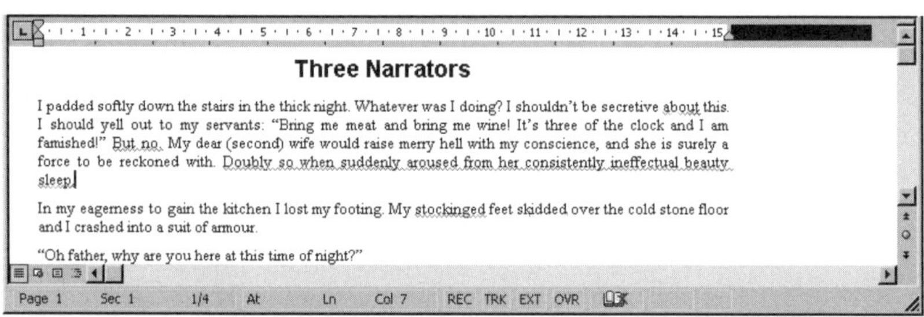

Bulleted Paragraphs

Activating Bullets

1. Select the paragraphs to be bulleted.

2. Click on the Bullet icon in the Formatting toolbar...

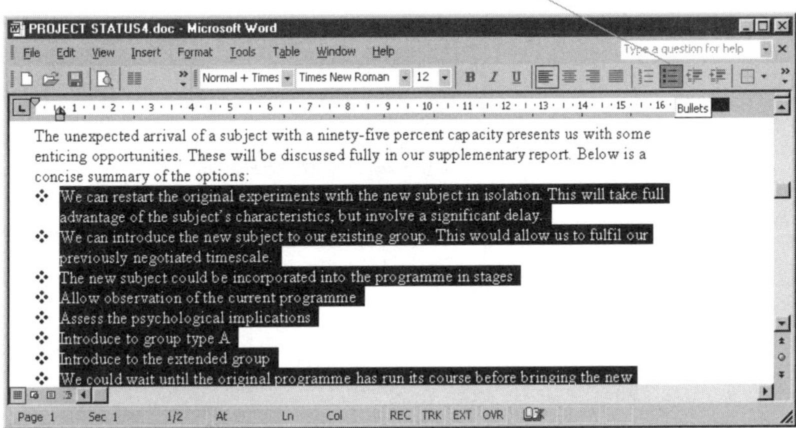

Removing Bullets

1. If necessary, re-select the bulleted paragraphs.

2. Click on the Bullet icon a second time.

Automatic Bullets

This is similar to the automatic numbering feature discussed on page 40. If you begin a paragraph with an asterisk, enter text in the normal way, and then press Return – Word automatically replaces the asterisk with a bullet, and starts the next paragraph with another. When you reach the end of the list that you want bulleted, erase the bullet that has just been created.

Advanced Bulleting

1 Select the text to be bulleted.

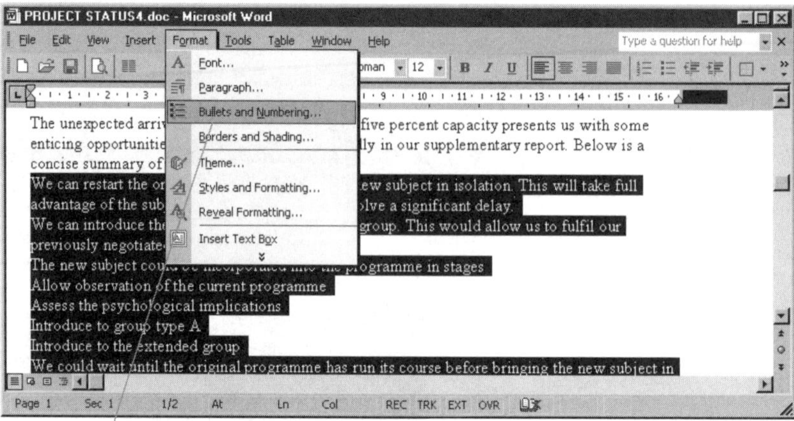

2 Choose Bullets and Numbering from the Format menu.

You can also select Bullets and Numbering from the menu which appears when you click in the document window with the right mouse button.

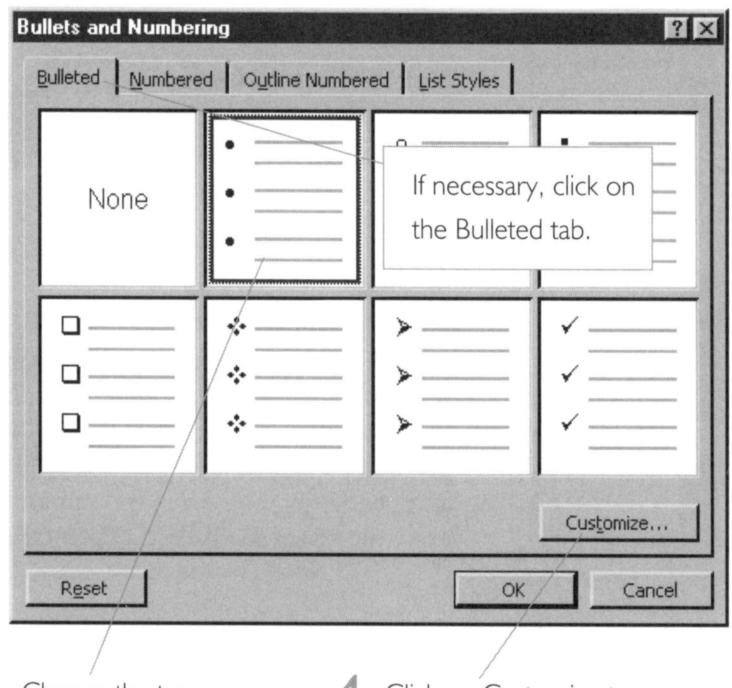

If necessary, click on the Bulleted tab.

3 Choose the type of bullet.

4 Click on Customize to see further options.

If you click on the Picture button in this dialog box you'll be able to select from a range of graphic bullets, or even import a custom graphic from a file.

5 Choose the required settings. Click on the required bullet...

6 ...or click here to select another from the complete range of characters.

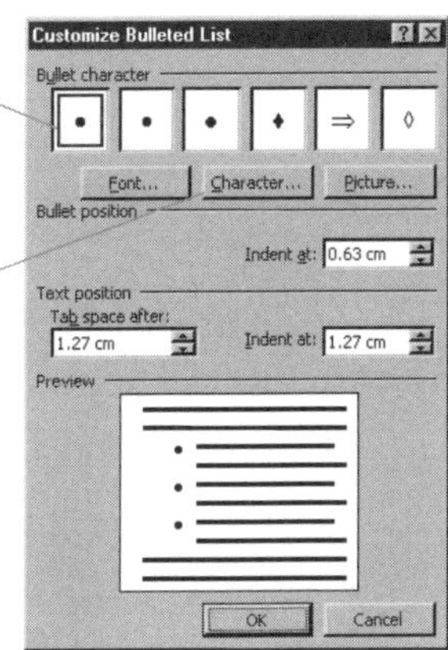

7 Select the font and character.

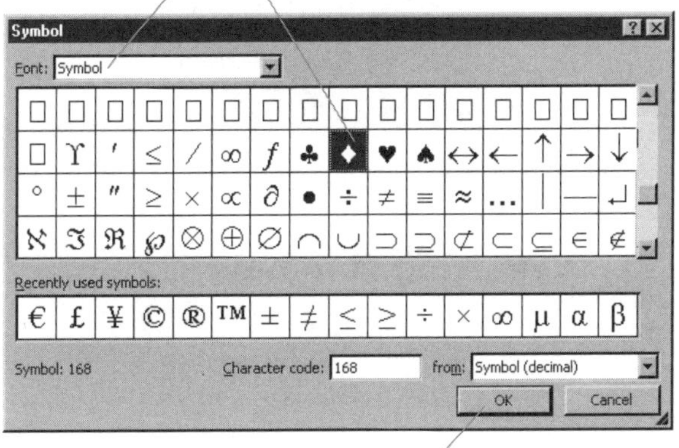

8 Click OK to exit all dialogs.

The selected text is now bulleted:

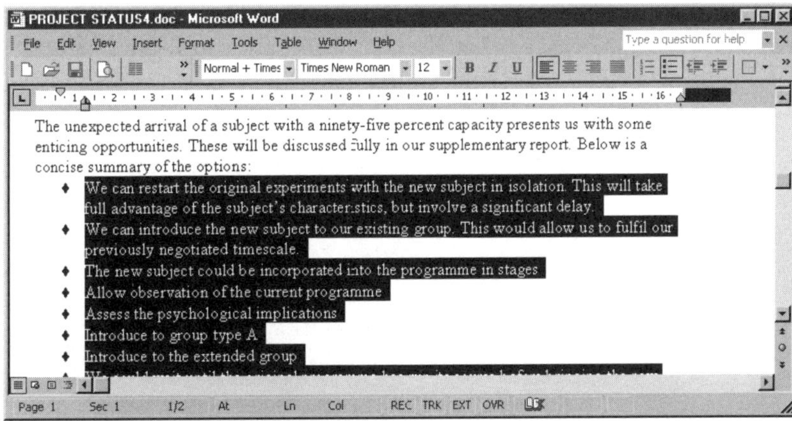

Numbered Paragraphs

1. Select the paragraphs to be numbered.

2. Click on the Numbering icon in the Formatting toolbar:

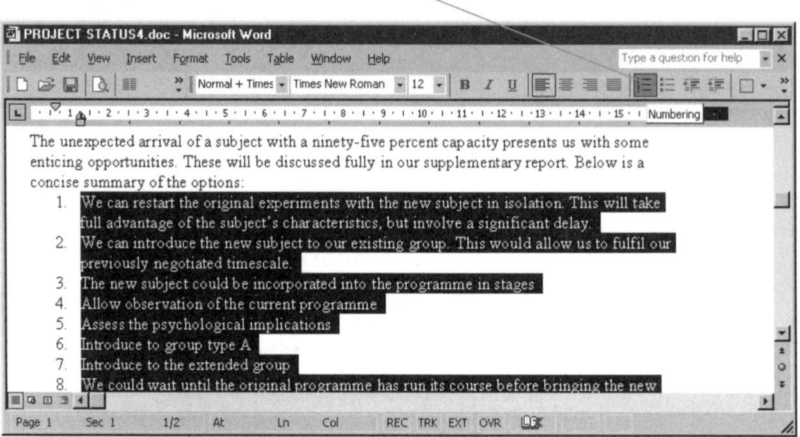

Removing Numbers

1. If necessary, re-select the numbered paragraphs.

2. Click on the Numbering icon a second time.

Automatic Numbering

If you begin a paragraph with a number, enter text in the normal way, and then press Return – Word 2002 automatically starts the next paragraph with the next number. When you reach the end of the list that you want numbered, simply erase the number that has just been created.

Advanced Numbering

1 Select the text to be numbered.

2 Right-click the selected text. Choose Bullets and Numbering from the drop-down menu.

3 Select the Numbered tab.

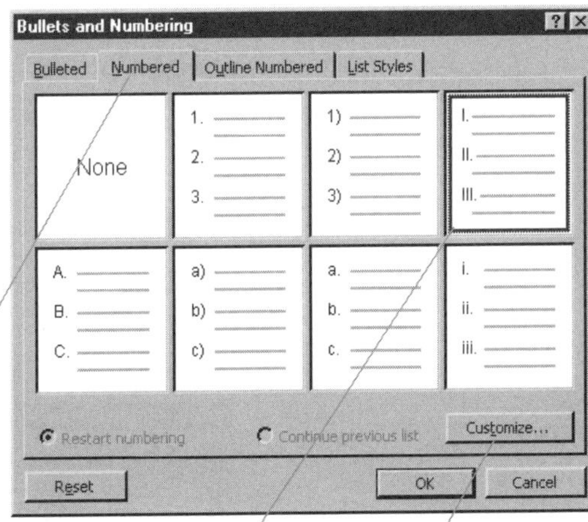

4 Choose a style.

5 Click on Customize.

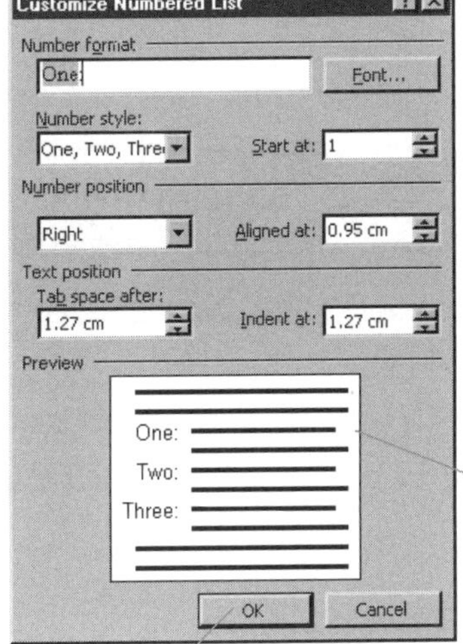

6 Experiment with different settings, referring to the Preview box.

7 Click OK

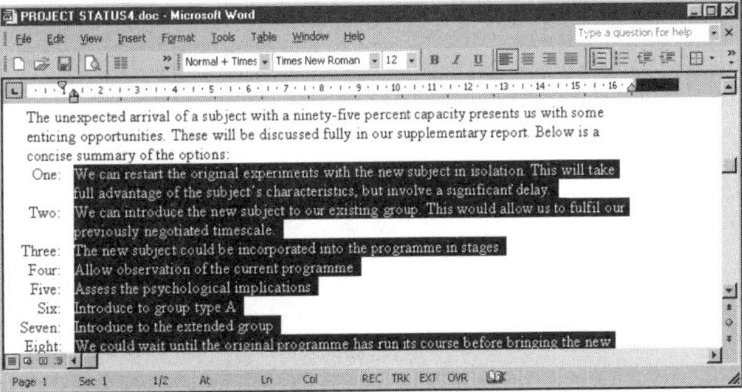

Outline Numbered Lists

Outline numbered lists contain nested sets of headings and subheadings. Because this function helps you to structure your numbered lists, you are likely to use it differently to the normal numbering function (discussed on the previous page).

1. With the cursor positioned at the point where you want to begin your multi-level structured list, select Bullets and Numbering from the Format menu, and choose the Outline Numbered tab.

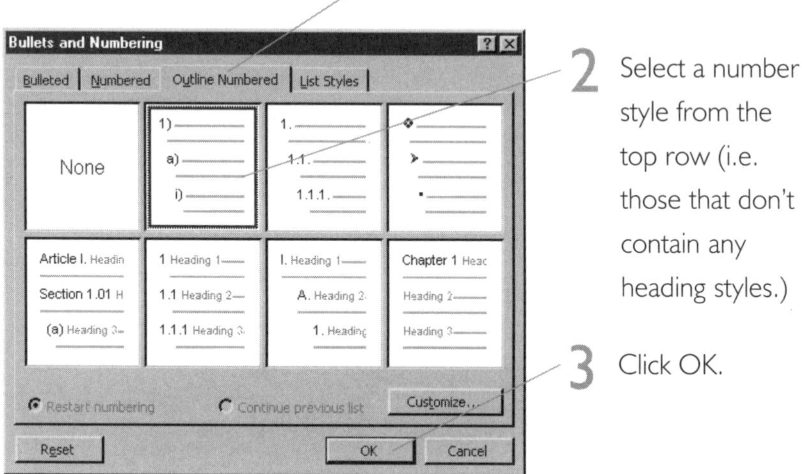

2. Select a number style from the top row (i.e. those that don't contain any heading styles.)

3. Click OK.

4. Back in the Word document enter your list, pressing Return at the end of each element (see the Hot Tip in the margin).

To place a line at a subordinate level to the one above it, right-click anywhere in the line, and select Increase Indent. To move a line to a higher level, select Decrease Indent.

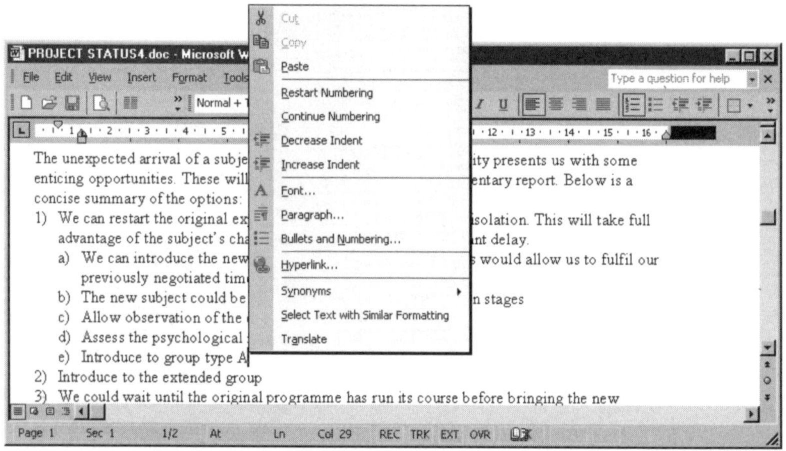

Formatting with the Task Pane

Word 2002's new Task Pane lets you control text formatting without having to open up dialog boxes.

Using the Task Pane means that you can experiment with settings much more interactively, as you'll immediately see the result of any changes.

1 First make sure that the Task Pane can be seen. To switch it on, choose Task Pane from the View Menu.

The Task Pane can be moved, docked and undocked just like any toolbar (see Chapter 1).

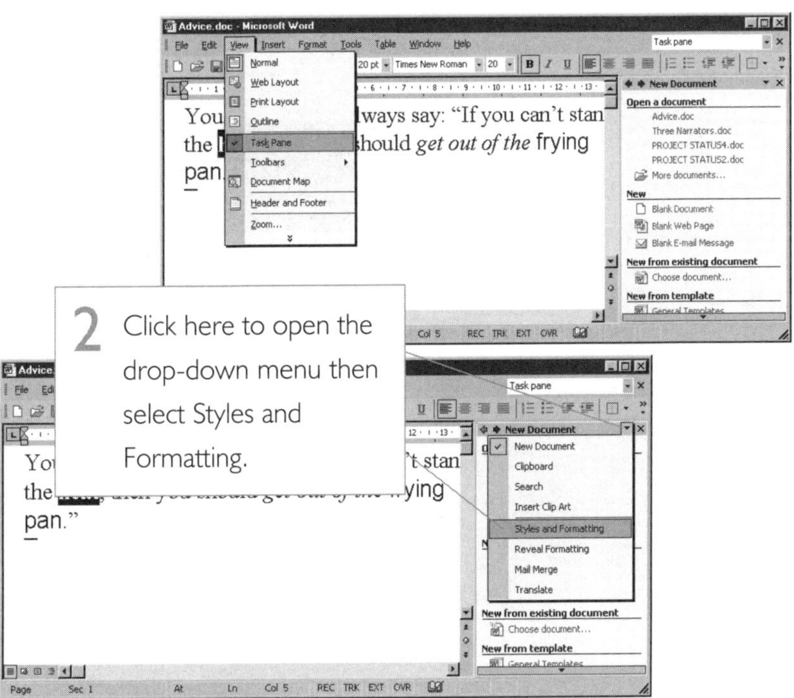

2 Click here to open the drop-down menu then select Styles and Formatting.

3 The Task Pane displays current text settings, which you can modify.

You can also apply and modify Styles using the Task Pane. See Chapter 5 Styles and Themes for more about this.

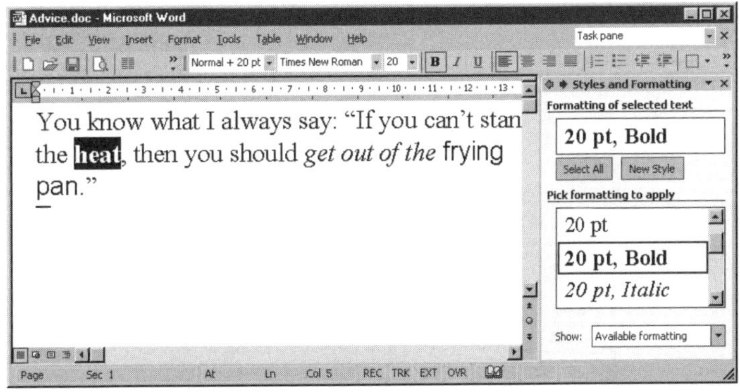

The Paragraph Dialog Box

This controls all aspects of paragraph-level formatting.

1 Select the text to be formatted.

2 Either choose Paragraph from the Format menu, or...

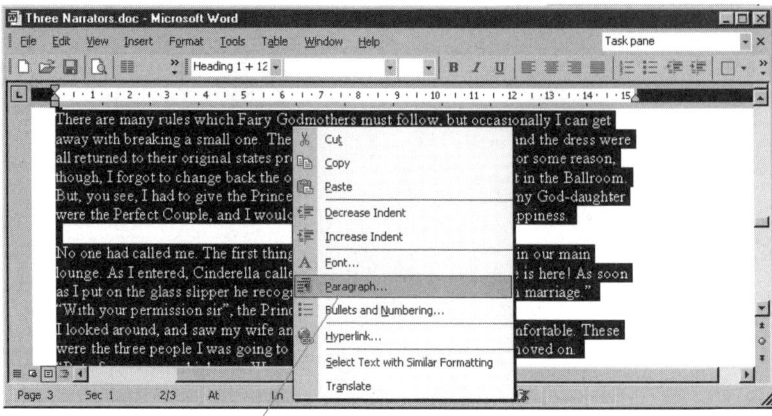

3 ...click your right mouse button somewhere within the document window and select Paragraph from the menu.

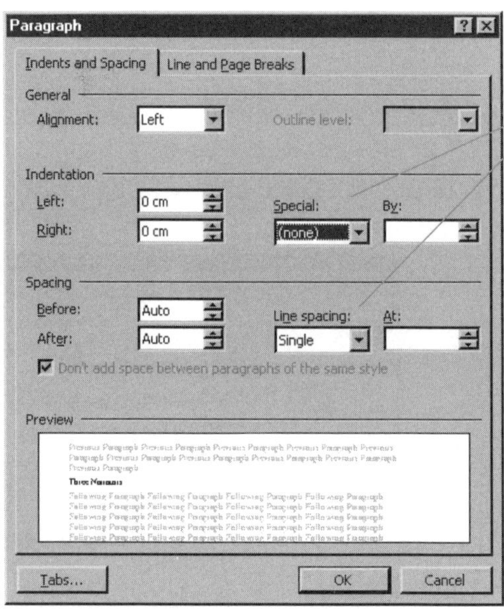

4 Experiment with the different paragraph controls, checking the results in the preview image. You can adjust the left and right indent, the space above and below a paragraph, or the line spacing within a paragraph.

In the example below, a (vertical) space before of 6 points and a special hanging indent of 1.5 cm have been set:

Hanging indents keep the first line of each paragraph exactly at the left margin, while moving all subsequent lines to the right by a fixed distance.

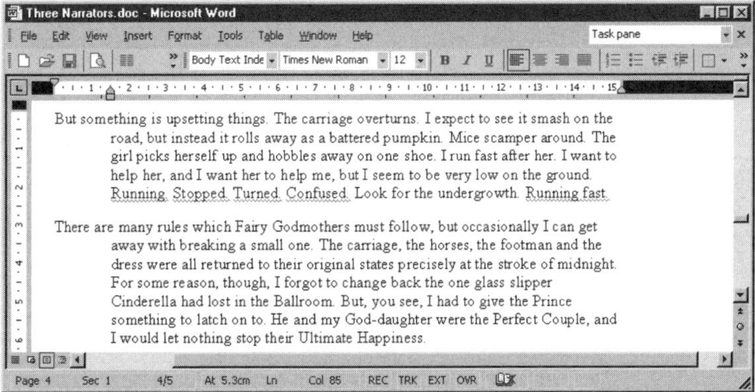

In the following example, line spacing has been changed to exactly 16 points. This means each line in the selected paragraphs will be given exactly 16 points of vertical space regardless of the font size.

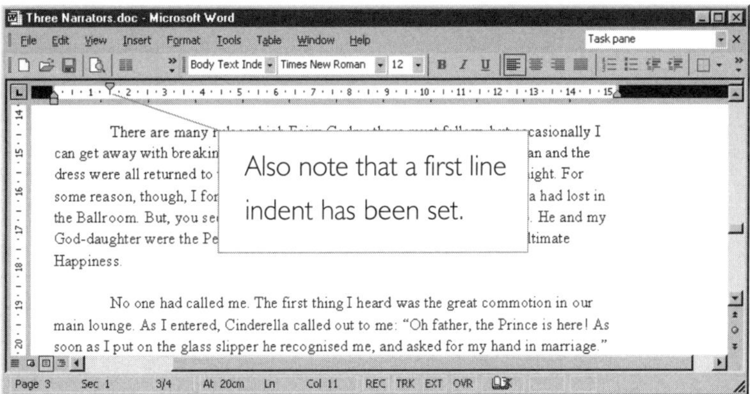

72 points are approximately equal to 1 inch. 12 points are equal to the size of normal typewriter text.

The Points System of Measurement

This system was introduced in the USA in the nineteenth century and then adopted by the UK and some European countries.

It provides a standard way of measuring the size of type, and often refers to the vertical dimension of characters in a given font. For this reason it is often useful to adjust vertical spacing using points, so that the space between paragraphs uses the same measuring system as the paragraphs themselves.

The Line and Page Breaks Tab

1. Activate the Paragraph dialog box (either from the Format menu or by clicking in the document window with the right mouse button).

A widow is a single line of text at the beginning of a paragraph separated from the rest by a page break. An orphan is a similar line at the end of a paragraph. Both widows and orphans look unattractive and should be avoided if possible.

2. Choose the Line and Page Breaks tab.
3. Apply any of these settings – see below

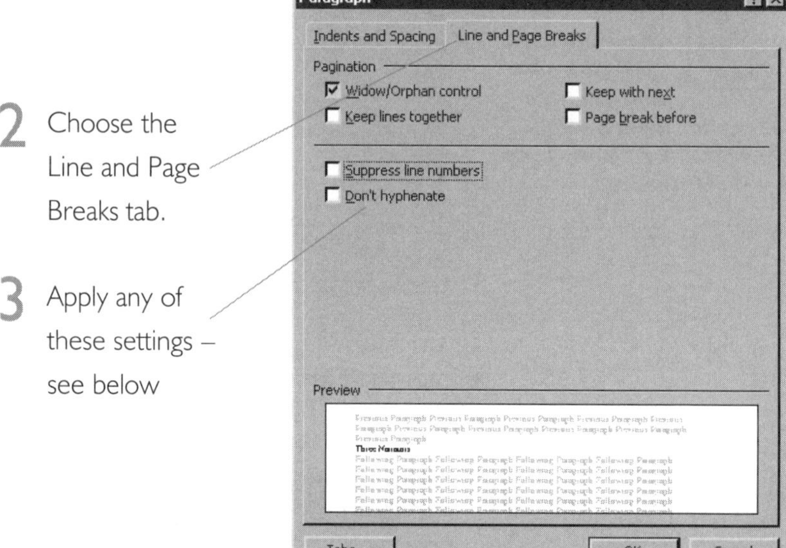

Widow/Orphan Control
This option instructs Word to automatically move text onto the next page if necessary to prevent widows and orphans occurring.

Keep Lines Together
Word will move the text so that the paragraph is not broken over two pages.

Keep With Next
Makes sure that the text is kept with the following paragraph, and not broken over two pages.

Page Break Before
Forces a new page at the start of the paragraph.

Suppress Line Numbers
Switches off numbering for this paragraph if line numbers have been used, renumbering the surrounding paragraphs if necessary.

Don't Hyphenate
Deactivates hyphenation.

Working with a Document

This chapter helps you to find your way around a document, looking at scrolling, selecting different views and zooming in and out of the page. Additionally you'll look at Cut, Copy and Paste, the Format Painter tool and several other helpful document-formatting features.

Covers

Chapter Four

Scrolling

The scroll boxes let you know where you are in a document. For example, when the vertical scroll box is right at the top of the scroll bar, you are looking at the top (the beginning) of the document.

When your text is too large for the document window, you'll need to use one of the following navigation methods:

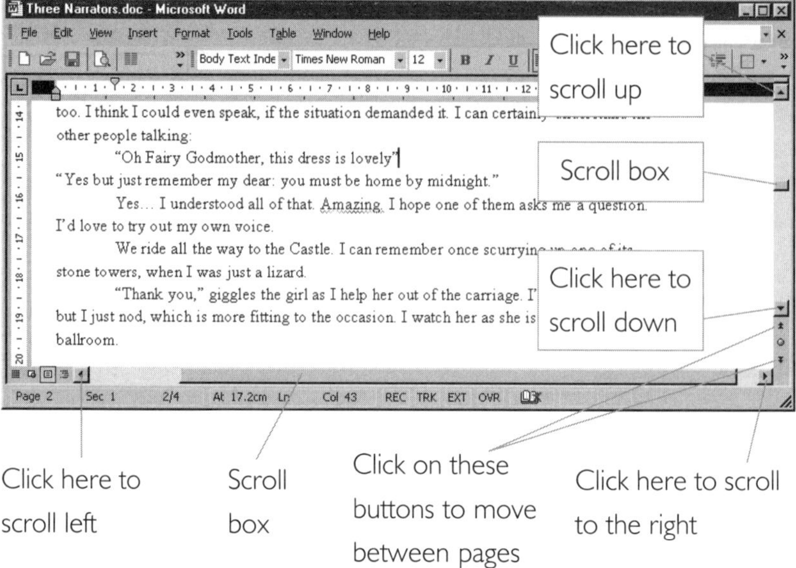

As you scroll down, the scroll box moves down like a lift through a lift shaft. The size of the box indicates how much of the document you are currently viewing. For example, if the box is one third the size of the scroll bar, then you're viewing a third of the document.

Quick Ways to Scroll

- Drag the scroll box directly to a new position.
- Click in the scroll bar to either side of the scroll box. The document will scroll in that direction one screen at a time.
- As you move your insertion point, Word will scroll automatically so that it can always be seen.

The Page Up and Page Down keys will scroll you up and down one screen at a time.

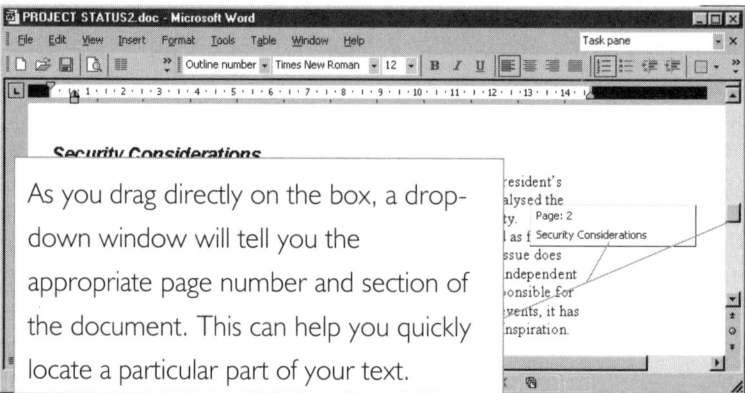

PROJECT STATUS2.doc - Microsoft Word
Page: 2
Security Considerations
As you drag directly on the box, a drop-down window will tell you the appropriate page number and section of the document. This can help you quickly locate a particular part of your text.

Zooming

You can use the Zoom drop-down menu to control the level of magnification used by the document window.

Either choose an option from the drop-down menu or enter a new percentage value between 10 and 500.

If you can afford the space on screen, always maximise both the document window and the Word window itself by clicking on the Maximise button.

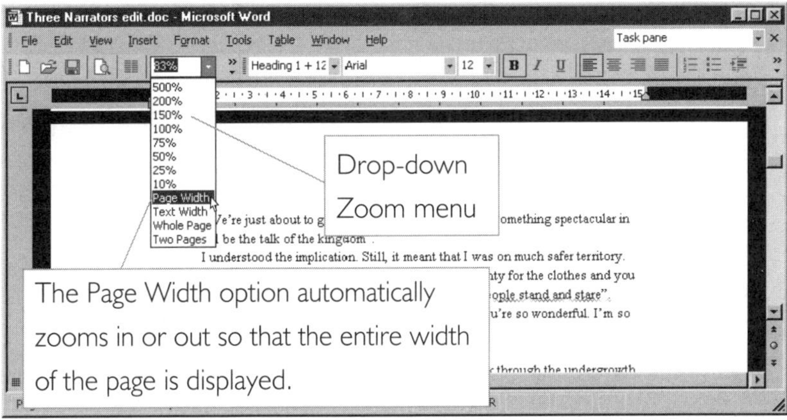
Drop-down
Zoom menu
The Page Width option automatically zooms in or out so that the entire width of the page is displayed.

In Print Layout view there are options to display one or more entire pages at a time.

Remember that the more you magnify the page, the more you'll need to scroll. Always try to view the entire horizontal line of text, since frequent horizontal scrolling can be tedious.

Resizing Windows

If the Restore symbol is visible then this indicates that a window is already maximised. Click on this to restore the window to its normal size.

To allocate the greatest possible amount of space to a window, click on the Maximise button. To restore it to its non-maximised size, click on the Restore button.

Maximise button

Restore button

These are located in a window's top right-hand corner. To adjust the dimensions of a non-maximised window, rest the cursor over one of the window's edges (the cursor changes to a double-headed arrow), then drag the edge to where you want it.

The Ruler

The ruler shows the tabs and indents used for any selected text.

1. If the ruler is not visible, choose Ruler from the View menu.

2. Select paragraphs of text. Try moving the indent markers:

You can also access these controls numerically from the Paragraph dialog box. See Chapter Three.

There is a small square block directly below the left indent marker. Dragging this will move both the left and first line indent markers together.

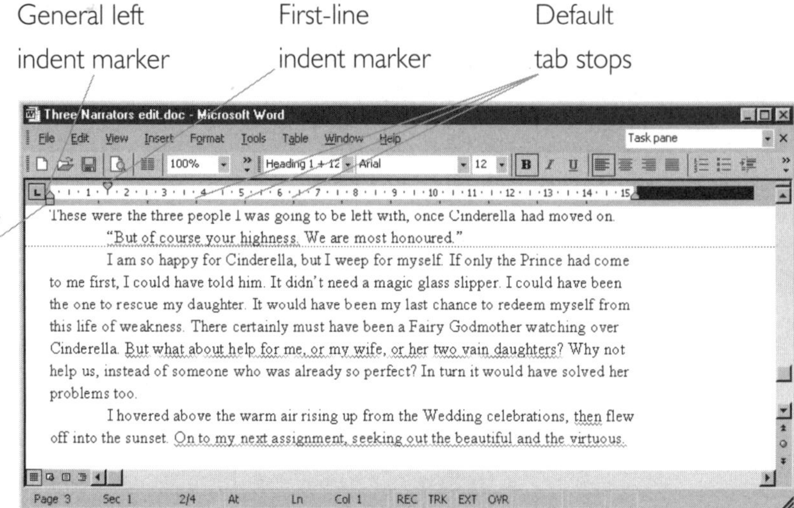

Cut and Paste

1. Select the text to be moved.

2. Right-click on the selected text, then choose Cut.

You can also Cut and Paste using the Edit menu, or the keyboard shortcuts Control+X, Control+V respectively.

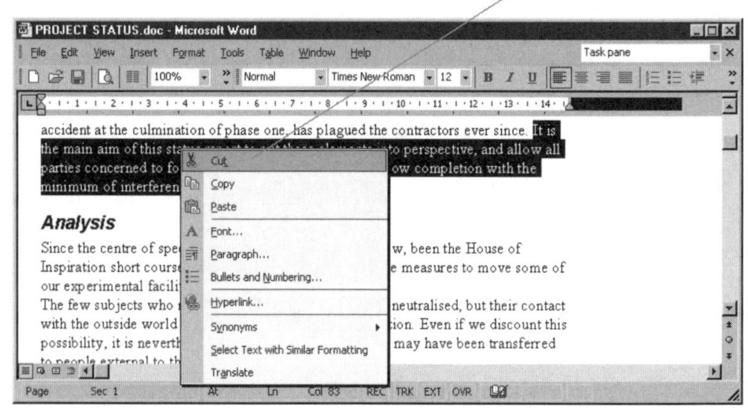

You can also make use of the Cut, Copy and Paste buttons in the Standard Toolbar:

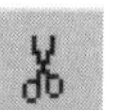 *Cut*

 *Copy*

 *Paste*

The text is removed and put into the Clipboard.

3 Next position the insertion point at the destination. Holding down the right mouse button, choose Paste.

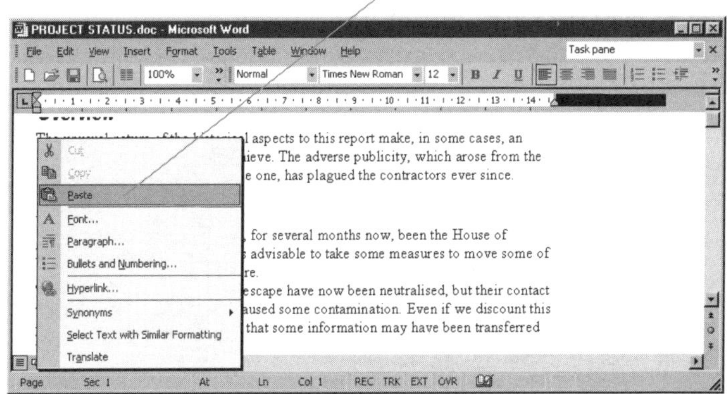

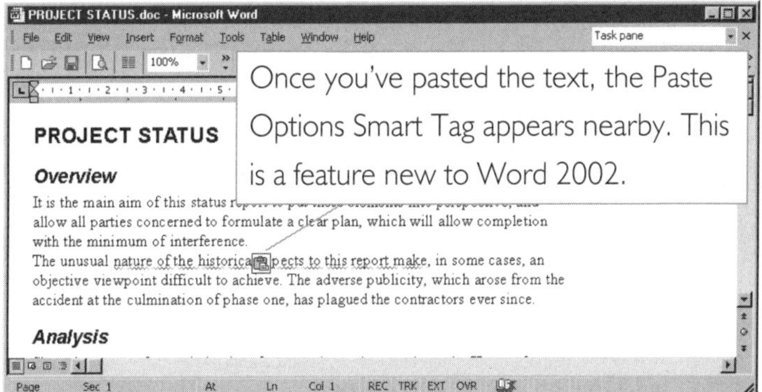

Once you've pasted the text, the Paste Options Smart Tag appears nearby. This is a feature new to Word 2002.

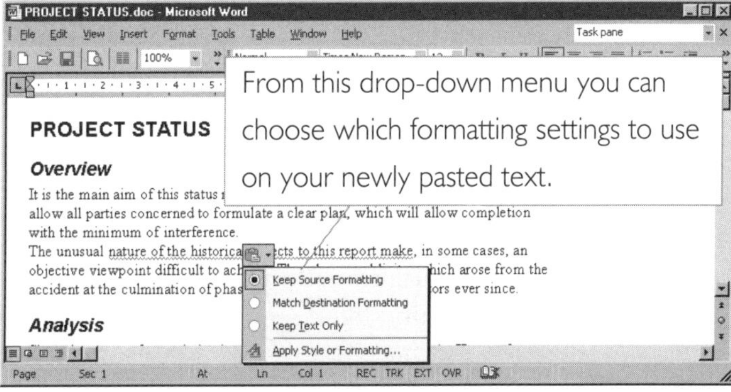

From this drop-down menu you can choose which formatting settings to use on your newly pasted text.

Copy and Paste

You can also Copy and Paste using the Edit menu, or the keyboard shortcuts Control +C, Control+V respectively.

1. Select the text to be copied.

2. Right-click on the selected text, then choose Copy.

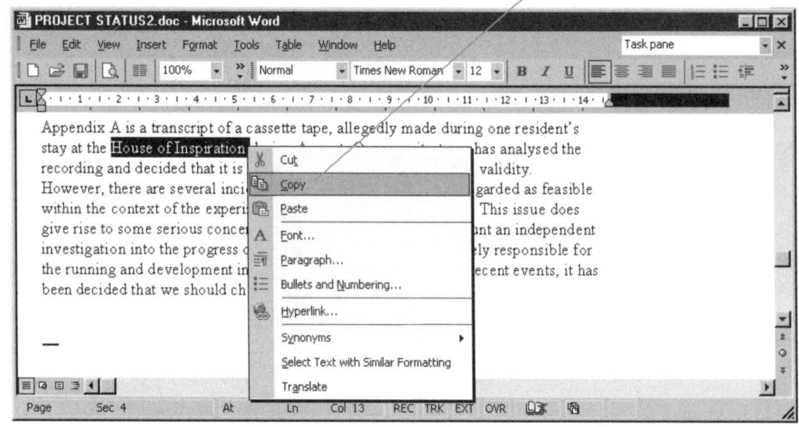

The quickest way to move text is to select it, then drag (from anywhere within the selected area) directly to the new position.

The text is copied into the Clipboard.

3. Position the insertion point at the destination. Click the right mouse button, then choose Paste.

If you drag the selected area with the Control key held down, then the text will be copied to the new position.

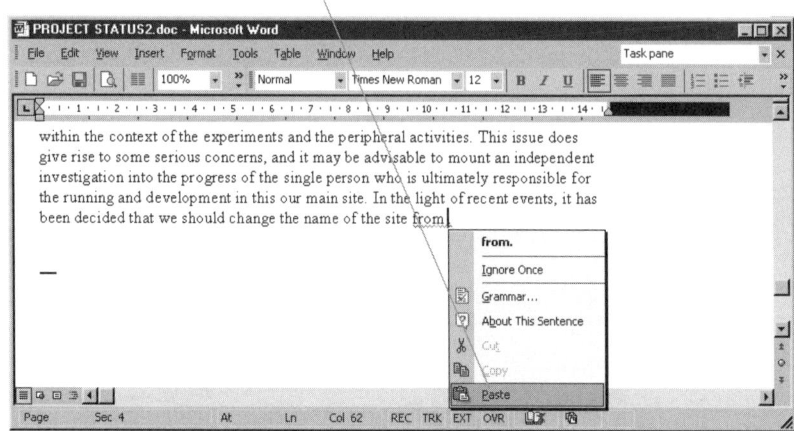

Once something is in the Clipboard, you can paste it as many times as you like.

The Task Pane Clipboard

The Task Pane has a Clipboard section offering additional features.

Versions prior to Word 2002 offered similar functionality using a special Clipboard Toolbar.

1 Make sure the Task Pane is visible (if not then activate it from the View menu), then open its drop-down menu and select Clipboard.

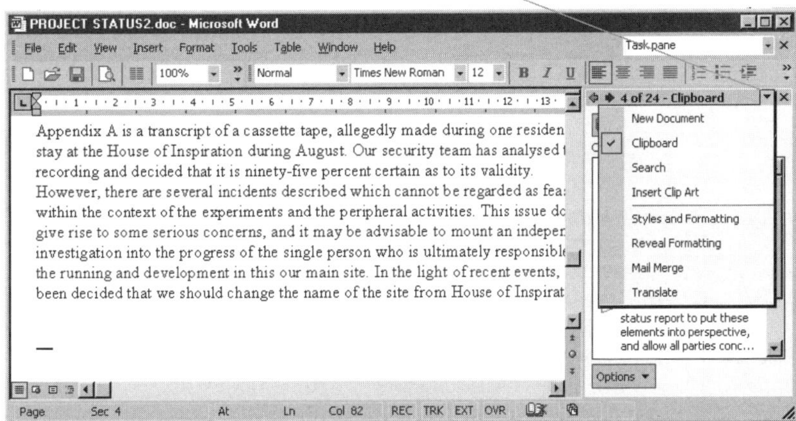

2 Each time you choose Copy, an extra item appears in the Clipboard area. If you click directly on the item in the Clipboard a drop-down menu allows you to delete or paste the item.

Note that buttons near the top of the Clipboard area allow you to Paste All or Clear All items in the Clipboard.

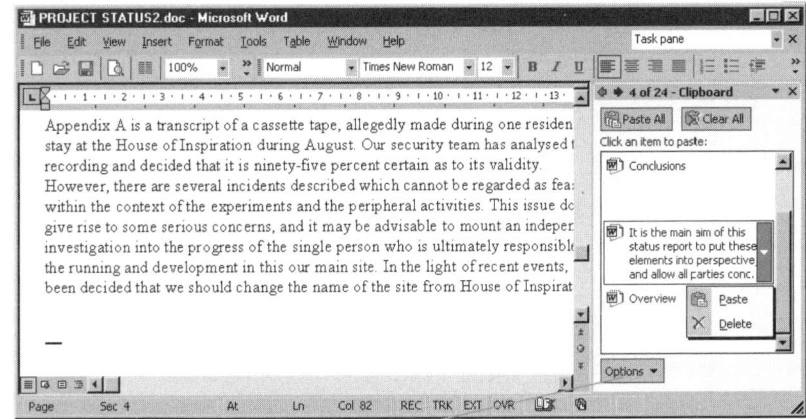

The Options button lets you place an icon for the Clipboard in the Windows System Tray. This may be useful if you are copying and pasting between different Clipboard-compatible applications (e.g. Microsoft Excel or PowerPoint).

Undo and Redo

- Click the Undo button or type Control+Z to undo the last action.
- Alternatively, open the Undo drop-down menu to review and undo more than one action:

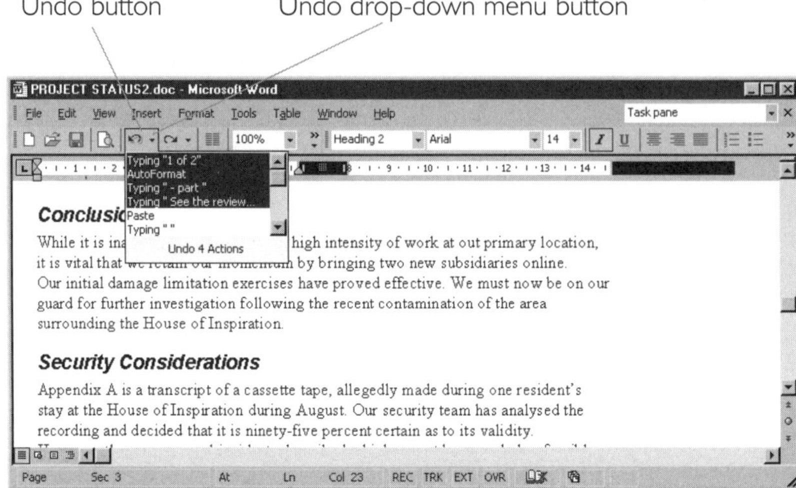

DON'T FORGET

When undoing or redoing actions using the drop-down menus, drag the cursor down until the actions that you want to undo or redo are highlighted, then release the mouse button.

- To redo the undone actions, type Control+Y or use the Redo drop-down menu.

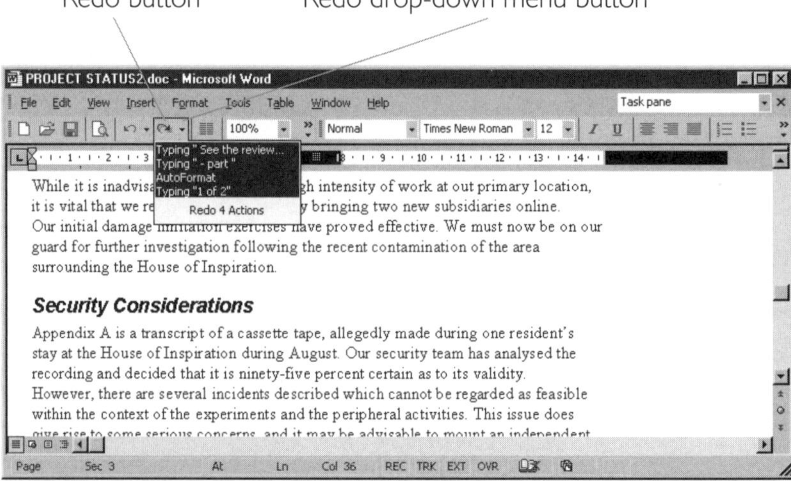

Page Breaks

The keyboard shortcut for page break is Control+ Return (or Enter).

To delete a page break, simply select it by clicking in the left margin area and press Delete.

Word automatically calculates the position of page breaks. These appear in the document window as a dotted horizontal line (a 'soft' page break). However, you can force page breaks, as follows:

1. Choose Break... from the Insert menu.
2. Make sure that Page Break is selected.

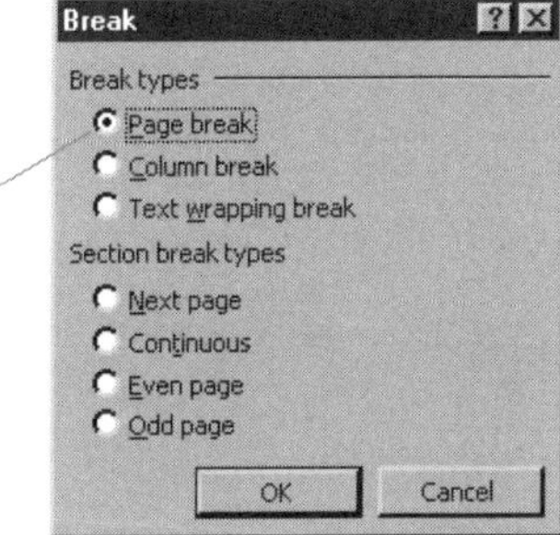

A 'hard' page break is inserted.

Defining Sections

Sections can be used to help organise your document. They also allow you to vary its layout, even within a single page.

1. Click an insertion point part of the way through your document (between paragraphs).

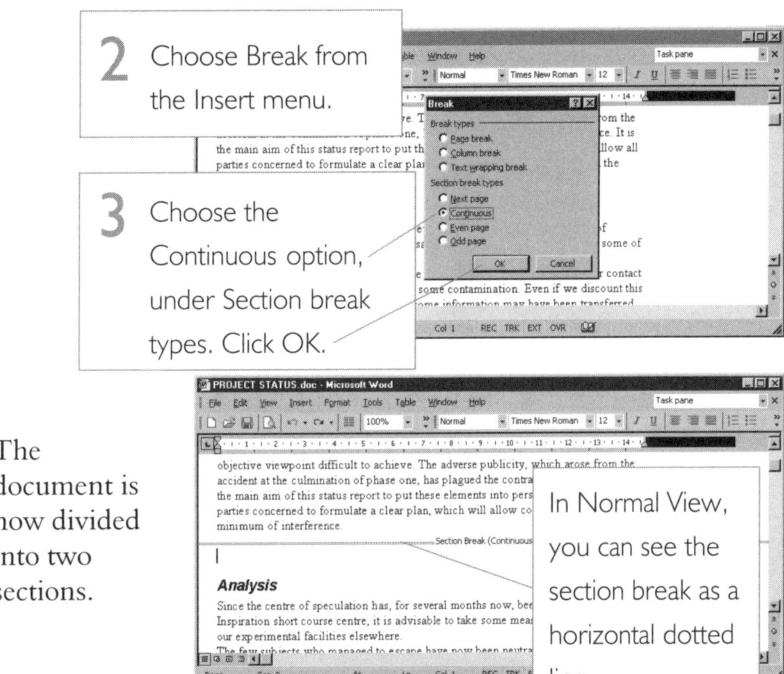

2. Choose Break from the Insert menu.
3. Choose the Continuous option, under Section break types. Click OK.

The document is now divided into two sections.

In Normal View, you can see the section break as a horizontal dotted line.

Using Columns with Sections

1. Make sure you are using a document which has been divided into two or more sections.

2. Click the insertion point somewhere in the second section, then choose Columns from the Format menu:

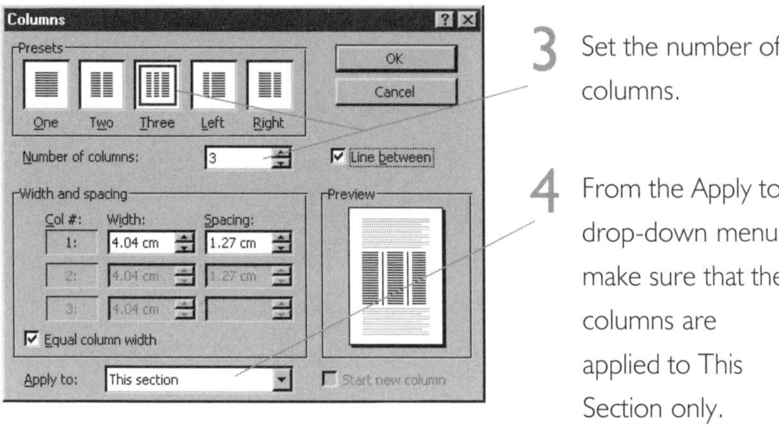

3. Set the number of columns.

4. From the Apply to drop-down menu, make sure that the columns are applied to This Section only.

5. Click OK.

You now have a mixed column layout:

If you drag with the Alt key held down, Word will display the horizontal measurements in the ruler.

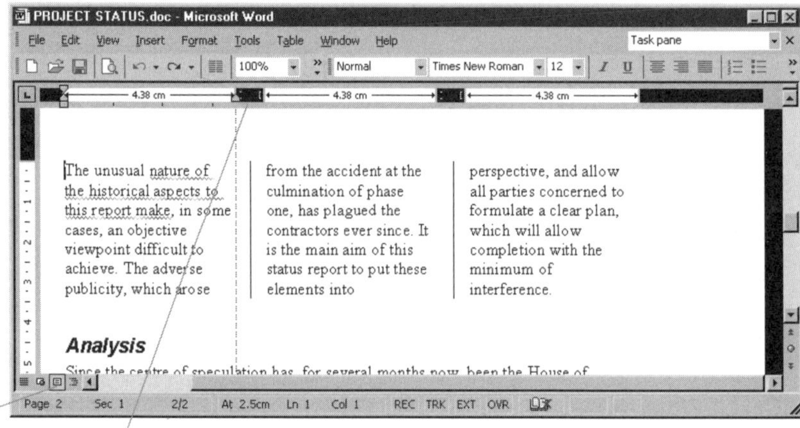

Note that you'll need to select Print Layout view if you want to see your text arranged in columns.

6. You can also adjust the width of columns by dragging the columns' boundary markers in the ruler.

Column Breaks

You can force text to start in a new column by adding a hard break.

1. Place your insertion point and choose Break from the Insert menu.

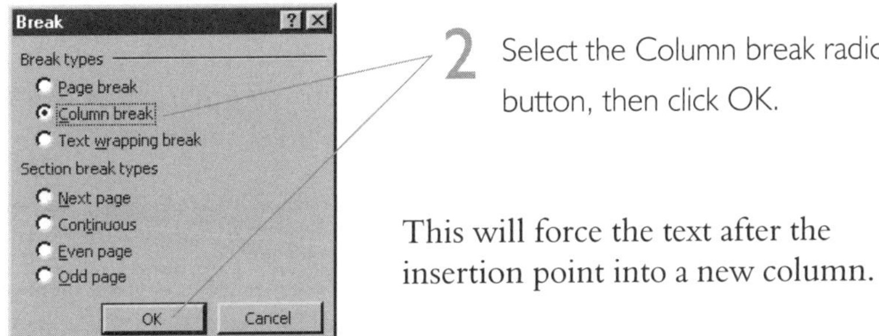

2. Select the Column break radio button, then click OK.

This will force the text after the insertion point into a new column.

Balancing Columns

If there is enough space on the page to accommodate all of your column text, you can balance the columns neatly:

1. Click the insertion point at the end of the last column and choose Break from the Insert menu.
2. Insert a Continuous section break.

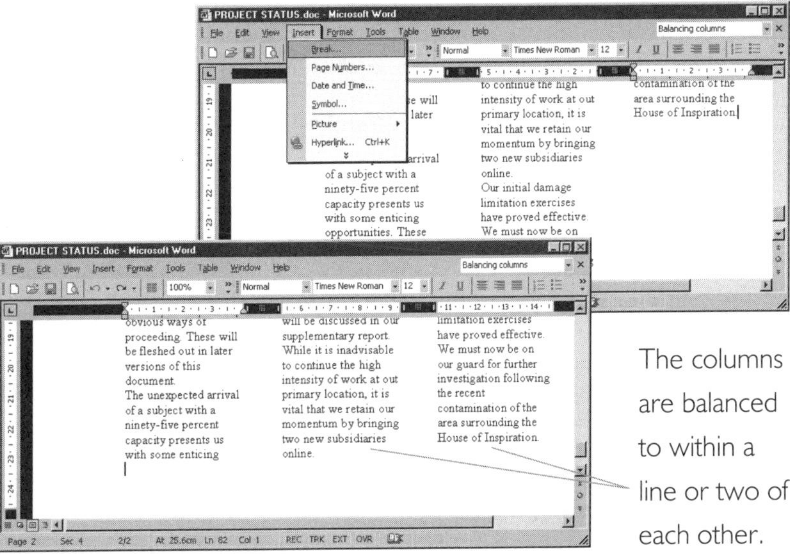

The columns are balanced to within a line or two of each other.

Headers and Footers

Headers normally appear at the top of every page, footers at the bottom (an example being 'Word 2002 in easy steps' on this page).

Creating/Modifying a Header

1 Choose Header and Footer from the View menu.

Word will automatically change to Print Layout View. The main page text will be greyed out to let you concentrate on the header. The Header and Footer toolbar will also appear.

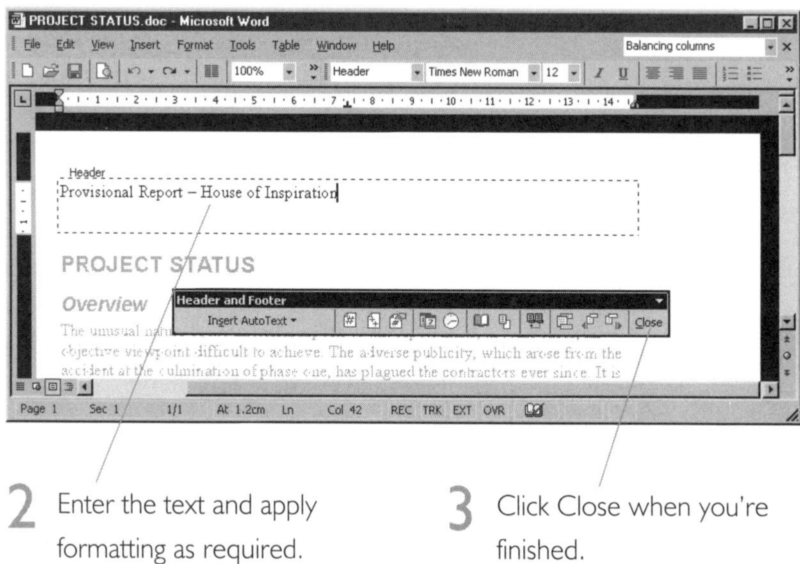

2 Enter the text and apply formatting as required.

3 Click Close when you're finished.

The Header and Footer Toolbar

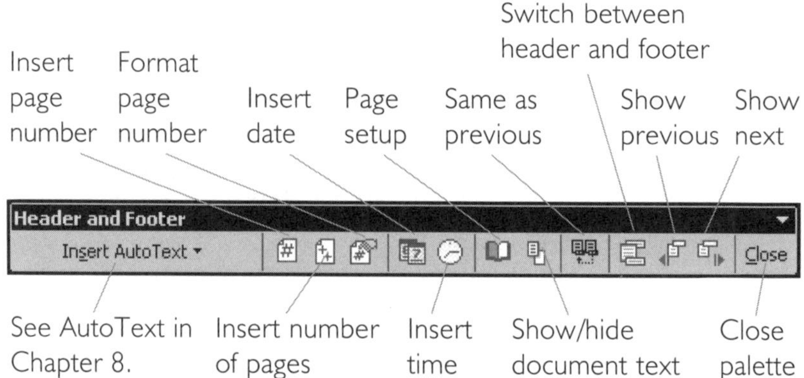

Creating/Modifying a Footer

1. Click on the Switch between header and footer button in the toolbar. This will take you to the footer text.

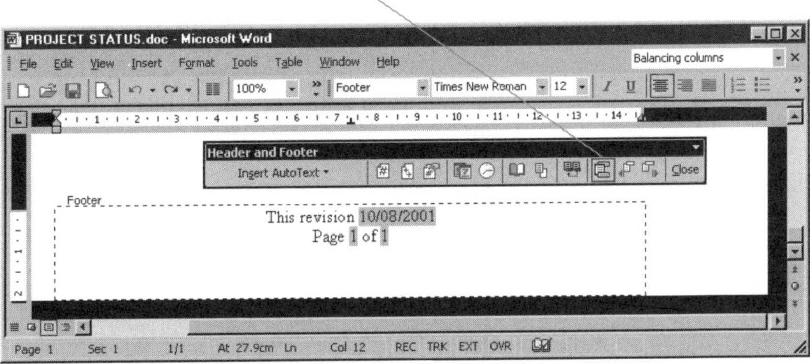

2. Enter the footer text. You can include automatic page numbers, or the current date or time by clicking on the relevant button in the toolbar.

3. Click Close when you've finished.

Now the header and footer text is greyed out, and you can edit the main text again. Note that the picture below shows Print Layout View. In Normal View, headers and footers do not appear at all.

By default, the header and footer on a page will apply to all remaining pages in the document. You can override this by editing the headers/footers for other pages separately.

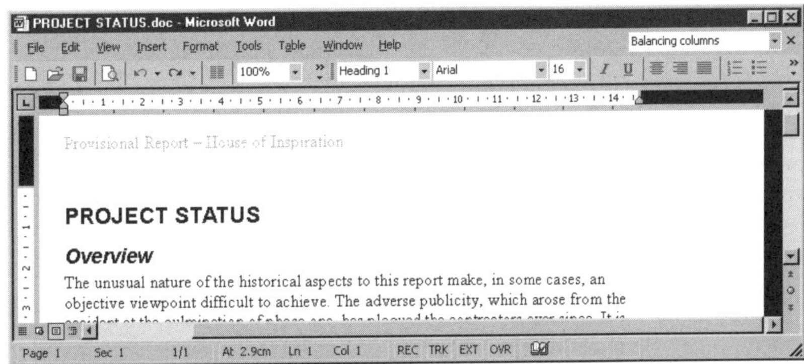

The Format Painter

This allows you to copy the formatting options from one piece of text to another:

1. Select the source text and click on the Format Painter icon.

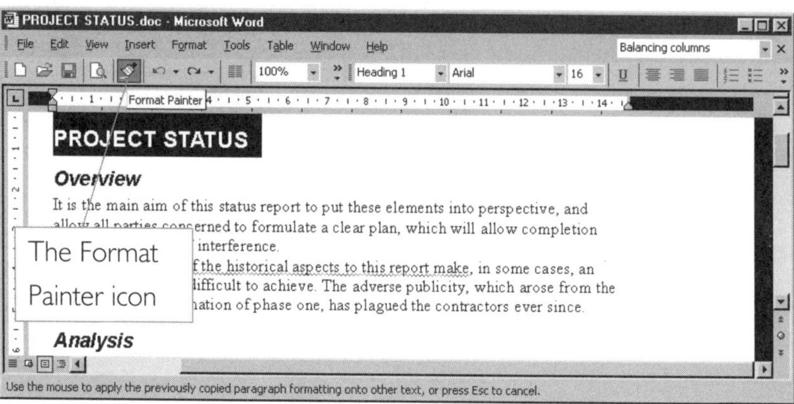

2. Now drag across the destination text. The formatting is applied to the new text.

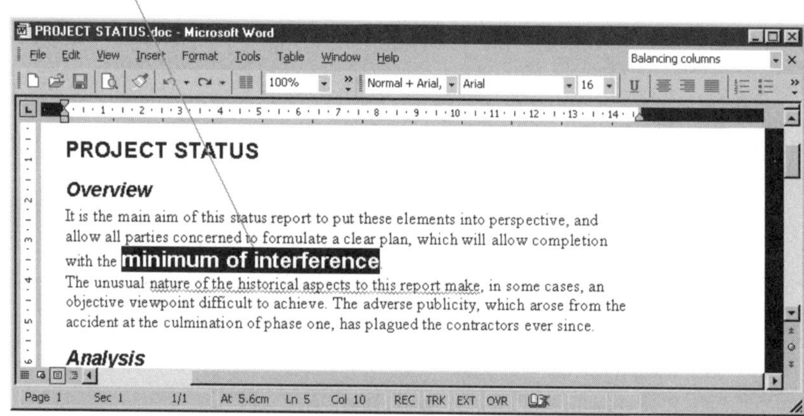

To copy formatting to more than one destination, simply double-click the Format Painter icon. You can then apply the new formatting to as many pieces of text as you wish. When you've finished, either click back on the icon or press the Escape key.

Document Properties

Windows 95 and later versions introduced file names which could be longer (and so more descriptive) than the Spartan eight characters allowed by MS-DOS. Even so, it is useful to record additional information as part of each Word document to help you organise your work, and remember your document's purpose.

1 Go to the File menu and choose Properties.

2 Enter the relevant details. These will be saved along with your document.

3 Click OK when you're done.

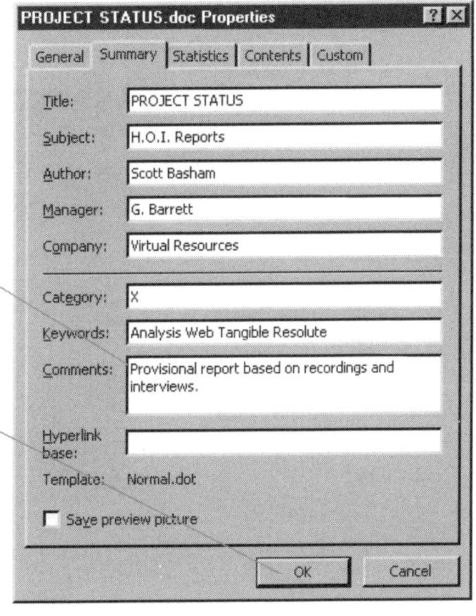

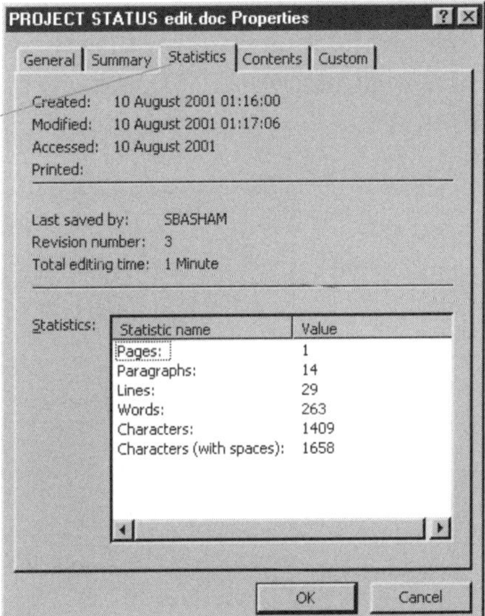

The Statistics tab in the Properties dialog will show you useful information about your document.

4 When you use the Open document dialog, you can click on the Advanced button to tell Word to search on the basis of the information entered in a document's properties.

The Document Map

The Document Map feature will only display useful information if your document already makes use of heading styles. See Chapter 5 'Styles and Themes' to find out how to create and manipulate styles for headings.

The Document Map is a feature which uses the headings in your document to create an outline of the document's structure. It appears in a separate pane to the left of the main editing area, and can be used to navigate easily through the document. To display the Document Map, do the following:

1 Click on the Document Map button.

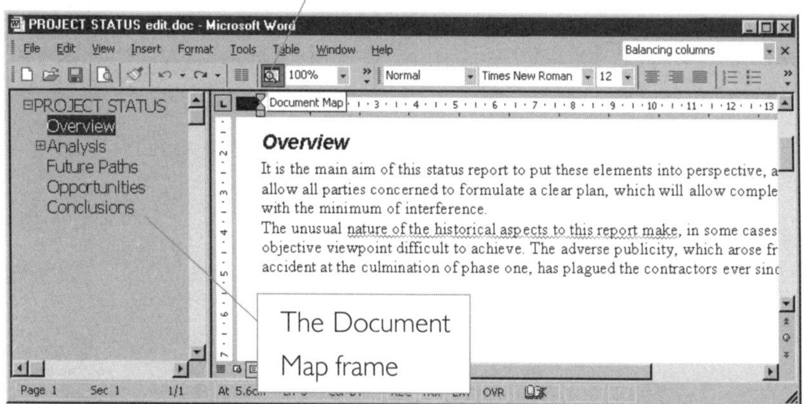

2 To jump to a heading listed in the Document Map, simply click on its entry.

Note that, in the illustration above, the heading Analysis has a small plus-sign next to it. This indicates that there are subheadings beneath it. To display these headings, click on the plus sign:

To collapse the structure to show only the main headings, click on the minus-sign.

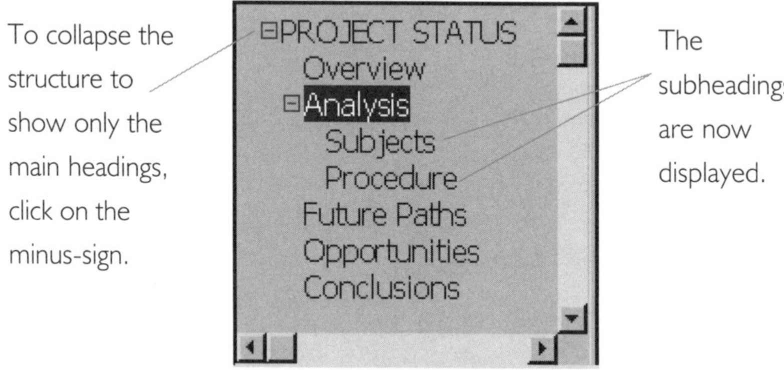

The subheadings are now displayed.

Styles and Themes

Styles help you to easily apply a consistent set of formatting commands to main text, headings and other elements of your document. Once you start using styles, you'll be able to control your document's presentation with the minimum of tedious manual editing.

Themes allow you to give a collection of your documents the same consistent look and feel.

Covers

Chapter Five

Using the Default Styles

A style is a complete collection of type attributes saved under a single name. There are two main benefits to this:

- Your document will have a visual consistency if, for example, all your subheadings look the same.
- You can quickly make drastic but coherent changes to the format of your document by redefining the styles already used by the text.

Applying a Style

1. Select the text.
2. Select a style from the drop-down menu:

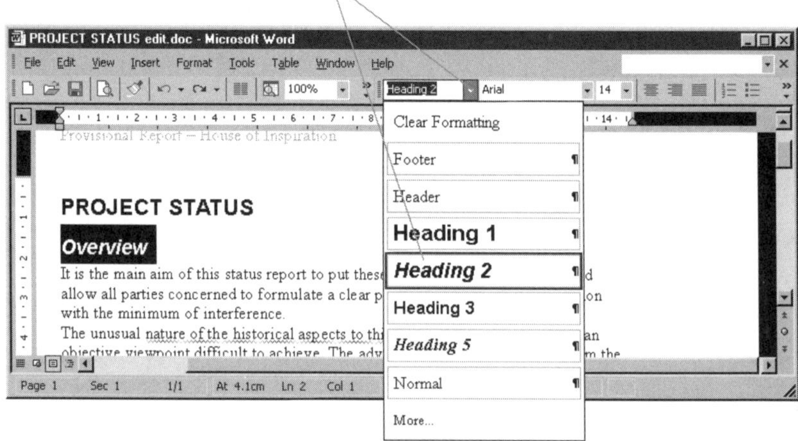

You can also use the keyboard shortcut Control+Shift+S to open the Style drop-down menu. Then type the first few letters of the style, press the down arrow key, and press Return to apply the style.

The text has now been set to this style. Whenever you select text on the page, the drop-down menu will indicate which style is currently being used.

By default all text starts off using the style Normal.

Editing an Existing Style

1 Make sure the Task Pane is visible, if not then activate it using the View menu. Use its drop-down menu to select the Styles and Formatting controls.

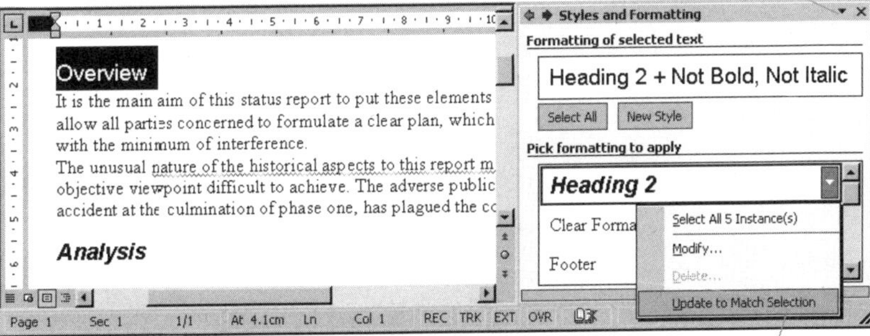

In earlier versions of Word, you could update a style definition by altering the text properties and then reselecting the style name from the Styles drop-down list. Word would then display a dialog box asking if you wanted to update the style or reset the text to the style's definition.

2 Select some text in the document which already uses the style to be changed.

3 Use the toolbar and menus as normal to experiment with changes in formatting (see Chapter Three).

4 Once the text has the desired attributes, click on the style's drop-down menu and choose Update to Match Selection.

All text in the document using this style will now change automatically...

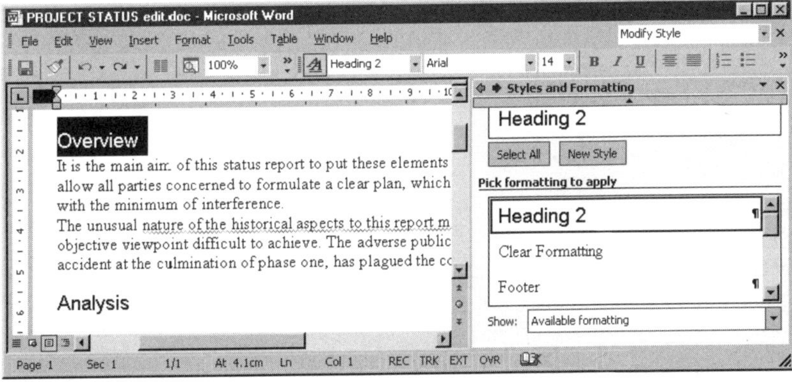

Creating a New Style

You can easily create a new style by altering existing text and then entering a name for the new style, which will take these properties.

1. Make sure the Task Pane is visible and displaying its Styles and Formatting controls.
2. Format the text as normal in the document (see Chapter Three), then select it.

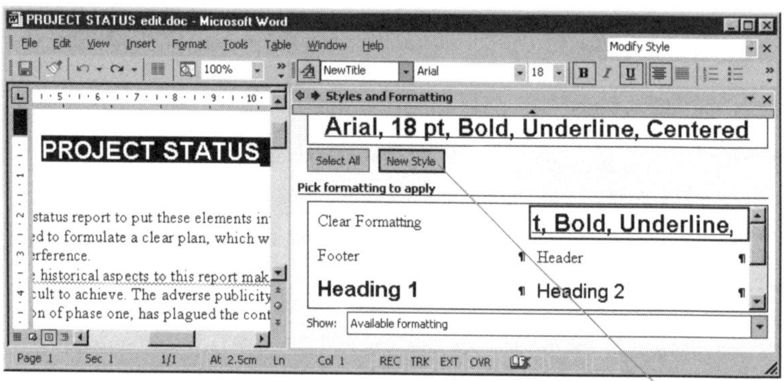

3. When you are happy with its appearance, click on the New Style button in the Task Pane. In the dialog box which appears, enter a name for your style then click OK.

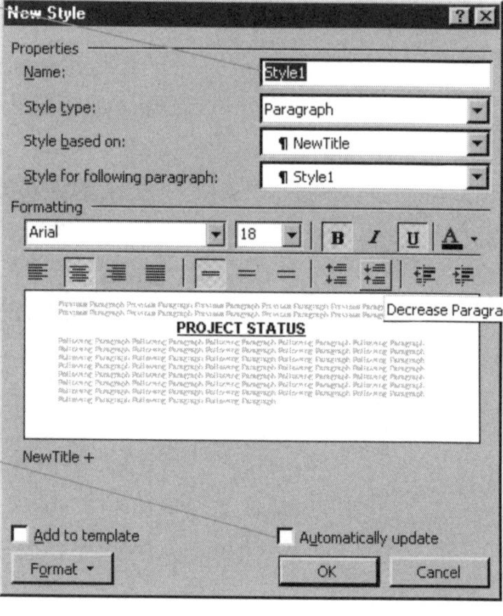

4. The new style is automatically created, and can now be applied to other text.

You can select this option to Automatically update the style. If set, then changing the formatting on any text already using the style will cause the style's definition to update straightaway.

The Style Dialog Box

Word 2002 allows you to make most changes from the Formatting toolbar; but the Style dialog allows you to preview potential style changes on a large portion of text, and then (if you change your mind) to cancel out of the dialog without actually making any of the changes. To open the dialog, do the following:

Remember that you'll need to make sure that the Task Pane is visible and set to display its Styles and Formatting controls.

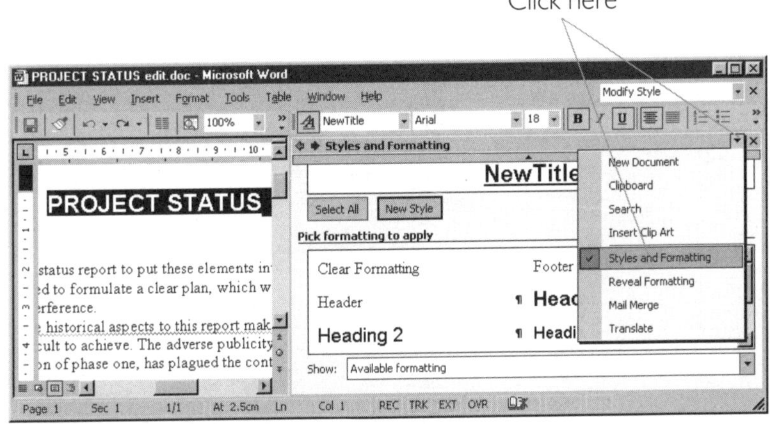

If the Task Pane is not visible then a quick way to get to the Styles settings is to choose Styles and Formatting from the Format menu. This will both open the Task Pane and switch to the Styles and Formatting controls.

Creating a New Style Using the Style Dialog Box

1. Click on the New Style button in the Task Pane.
2. Enter the new style's name.
3. Use the Format button to fully define the style. The following pages explain this process in more detail.

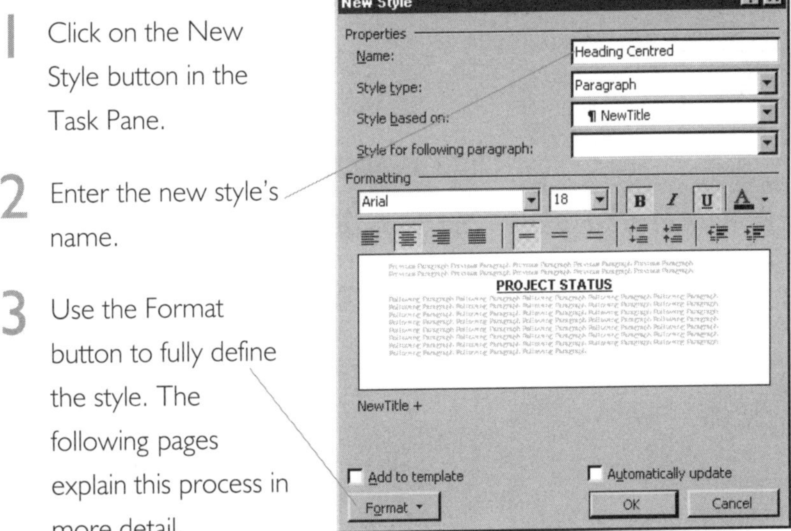

4. When you click OK the new style will be created.

Setting the Format

1 Click on the Format button in the New Style dialog box.

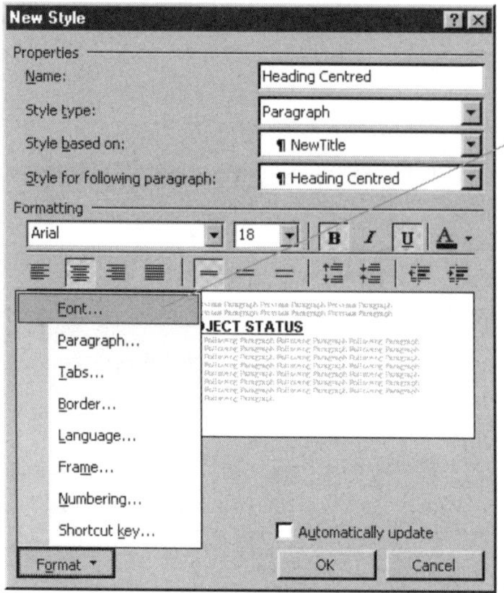

2 This menu appears. Select the dialogs that control the various properties of the style. Make the appropriate changes, referring to the formatting topics in Chapters Two, Three and Four.

3 When you have made your changes, click OK. The new style is added to the list.

Modifying a Style

Step 1 in 'Modifying a Style' takes you to the Modify Style dialog, which functions in the same way as the New Style dialog:

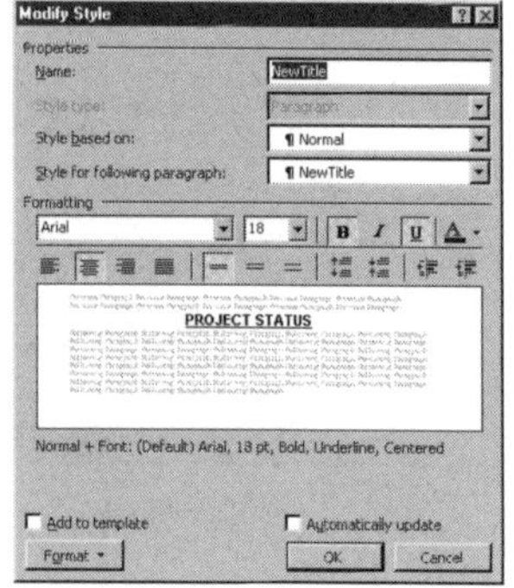

1 Select Modify from the drop-down menu next to the style within the Task Pane.

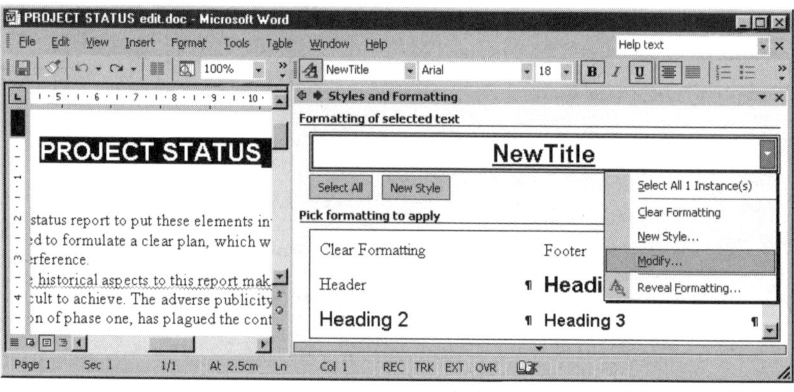

Setting a Keyboard Shortcut for a Style

1 Choose Shortcut Key from the Format drop-down menu in the Modify Style or New Style dialog box.

The Customize Keyboard dialog appears:

Word tells you if your proposed shortcut key is currently being used for something else. If you go ahead, then your style shortcut will override the previous setting.

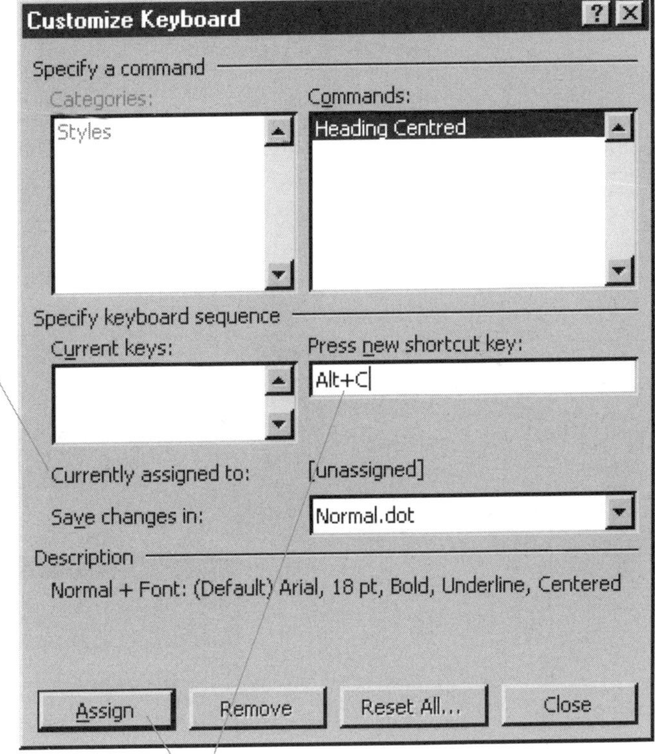

Most single keystrokes will already be assigned a function, so you will probably need to use a combination of keys, using the Ctrl and/or Alt keys. When you enter the shortcut key combination, all you have to do is press the keys that you want to use: you shouldn't type out Ctrl or Alt in full.

2 Enter the shortcut key combination for the style and click the Assign button. You can repeat this process to add more than one keyboard shortcut for the same style.

3 When you have finished, click the Close button to return to the previous dialog box.

Character-level Styles

Normally styles only apply to whole paragraphs.

Creating a Character-level Style

1 Choose New Style from the Task Pane.

2 Enter a name for the new style in the usual way.

3 Select Character from the Style type drop-down menu.

4 Use the Format drop-down to set the character-level attributes.

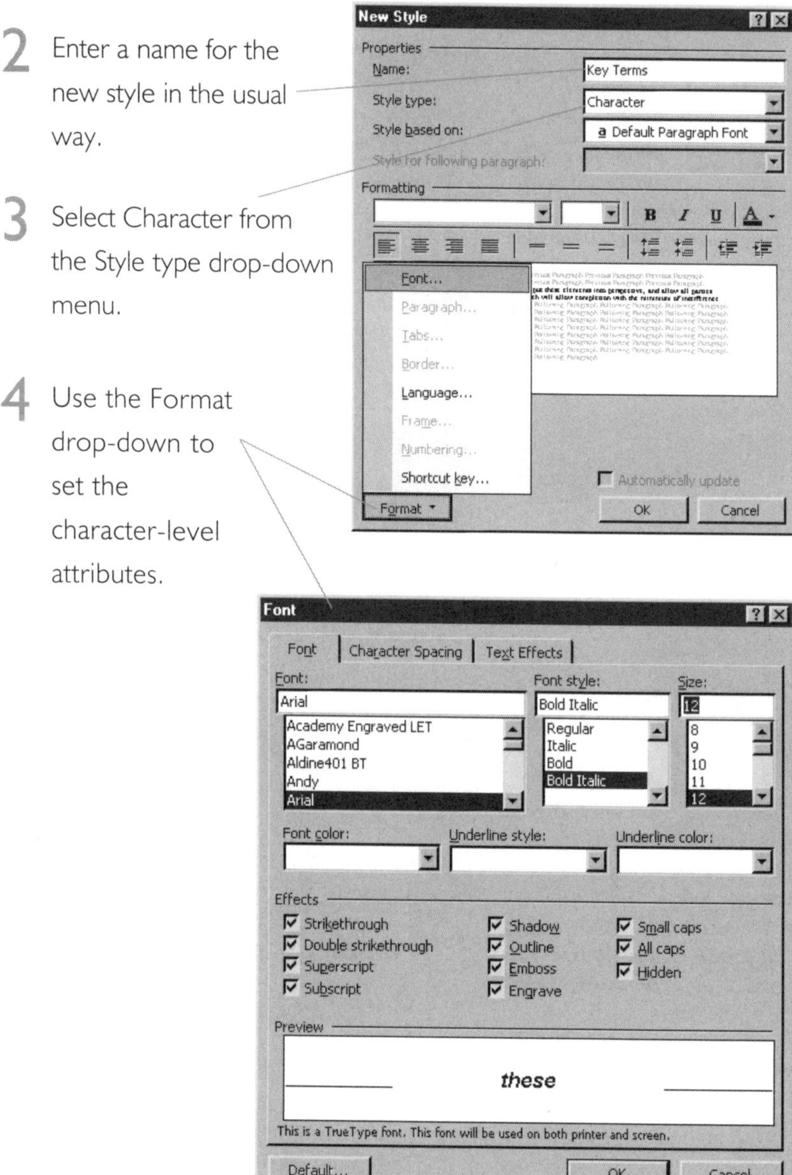

You can now apply your character style to individual words or phrases without affecting the entire surrounding paragraph.

If text already uses a paragraph style, then the character style will override these settings:

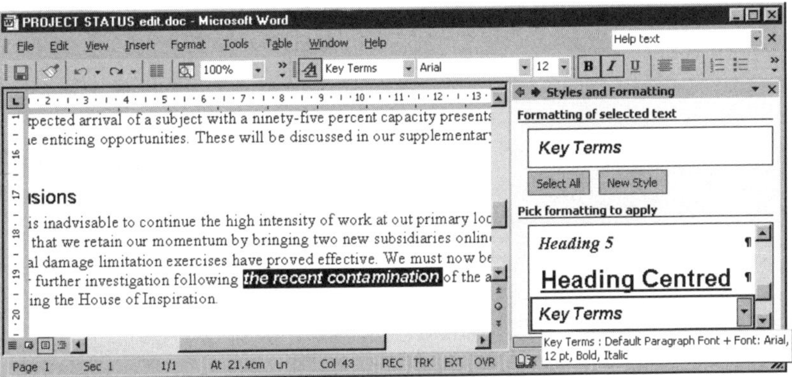

Identifying Character and Paragraph Style Names

Character-level style names are labelled in the drop-down list with **a**. Paragraph styles are labelled with ¶.

Once a style has been created, it cannot be changed from a character to a paragraph style or vice versa. However, you can always create a new copy of the style by choosing Styles from the Format menu, then selecting the style you want to copy and then clicking on New. Since this is a new style you can now select the style type.

AutoFormat

Word uses a feature called AutoFormat to apply suitable styles automatically to the different parts of your document, without you having to select them. For example, it analyses whether a paragraph seems to be functioning as body text, as a heading, or as part of a list. You can control AutoFormat settings from the Tools menu.

1 Choose AutoCorrect Options from the Tools menu, then select the AutoFormat As You Type tab.

2 Select which formatting changes AutoFormat should make automatically as you enter your text.

3 Click OK.

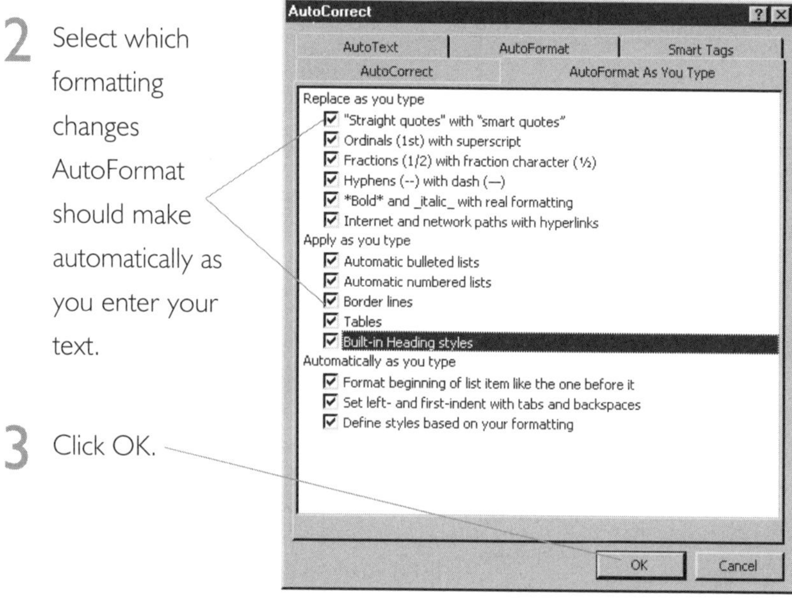

If you click the Options button, you will be presented with the AutoFormat Options tab, which will allow you to control the types of changes that Word will make.

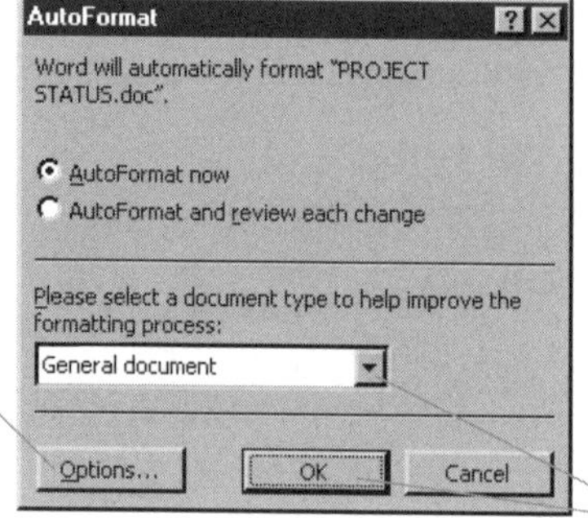

If AutoFormat was deactivated while you typed in a document, and you subsequently want to have the document formatted automatically, do the following:

1 Select AutoFormat from the Format menu.

2 Tell Word what sort of document this is then click OK.

Themes

Themes allow you to provide a unified look/feel to a document. They contain setting for styles, bullets, colour and graphics.

If you have Microsoft FrontPage version 4 or later installed, you can use its themes as well as those supplied with Word.

You can also download additional themes by choosing Office on the Web from the Help menu.

Applying a Theme to a Document

1. Choose Theme from the Format menu. The following dialog box appears:

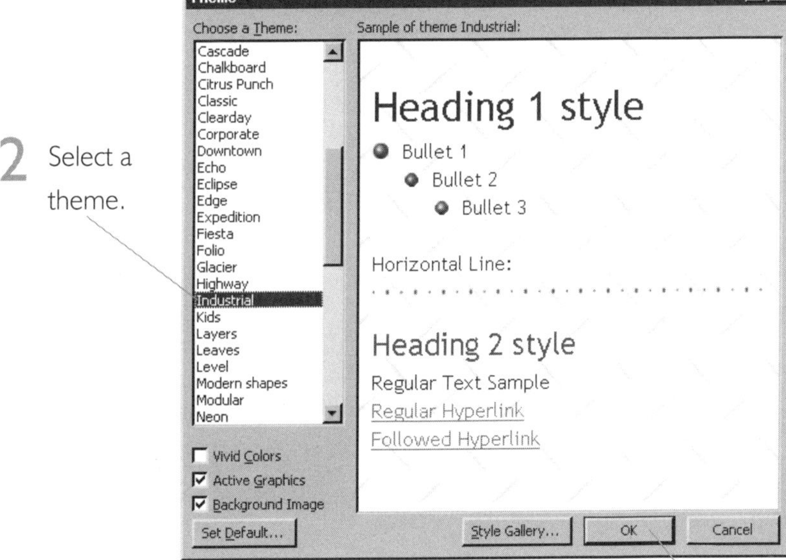

2. Select a theme.

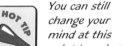

3. Check the theme sample. If you are happy with its look, click OK.

Your document will now reflect the new theme.

You can still change your mind at this point by using the Undo button. Alternatively select a different theme from the Theme dialog box.

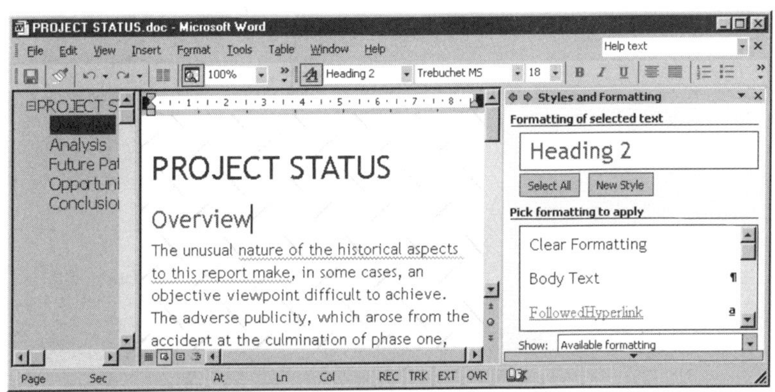

The Style Gallery

When you work on a document, a template is used to tell Word which formatting properties to use for the different character and paragraph styles. You can use the Style Gallery to apply the properties of different templates, to produce an instant overall change to the appearance of your document.

A template differs from a theme in that it only contains style definitions, and no colour schemes or graphics. However, a template will generally contain far more style definitions than a theme.

1. Go to the Format menu, and choose Theme.

2. Click on the Style Gallery button.

3. Choose a template design then a Preview option. Document shows how your document would look with the proposed style definitions. Example gives a document showing the different styles.

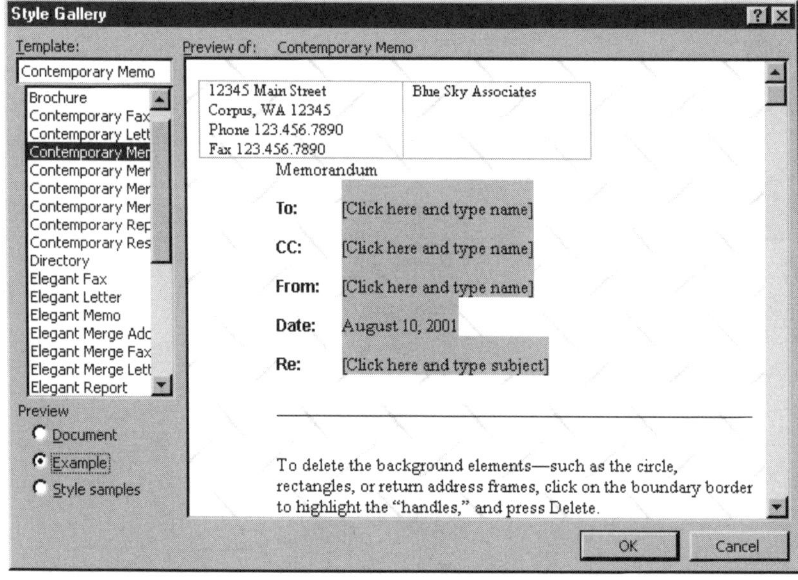

Style samples lists each style name using its own attributes.

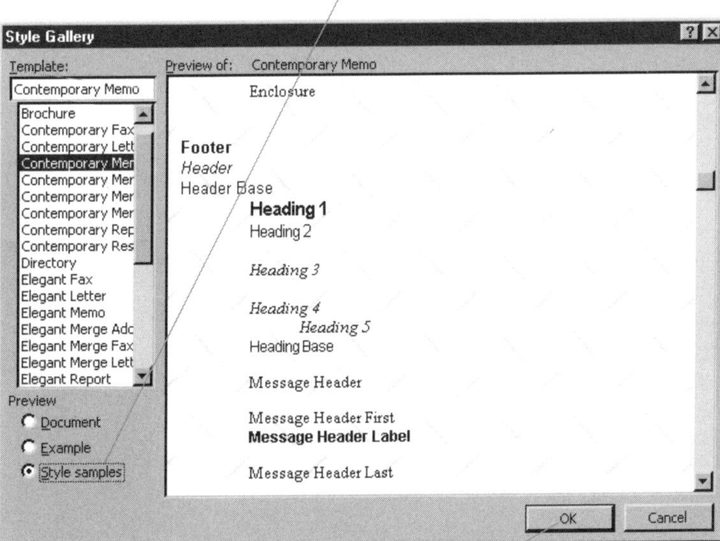

4 Click OK if you want your document to adopt these new style definitions.

Your document will now use the styles from the template.

If your document currently doesn't use any of the style names defined in the template, then applying the template will have no initial visible effect. However you can now use these new styles by applying them manually to your text.

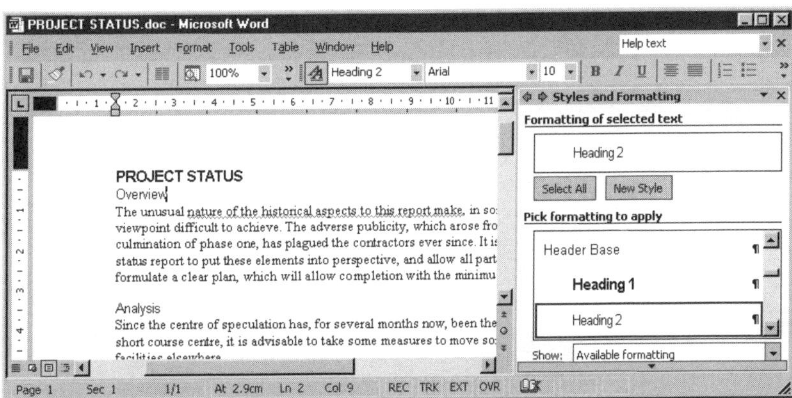

Displaying Style Names

Sometimes it's useful to see instantly which styles are being used by the paragraphs in your document.

1 Make sure that Normal View is active (you can set this using the View menu or the icon at the bottom left of the screen).

2 Choose Options from the Tools menu.

3 Click on the View tab.

4 Set the Style area width to a figure greater than zero.

5 Click OK.

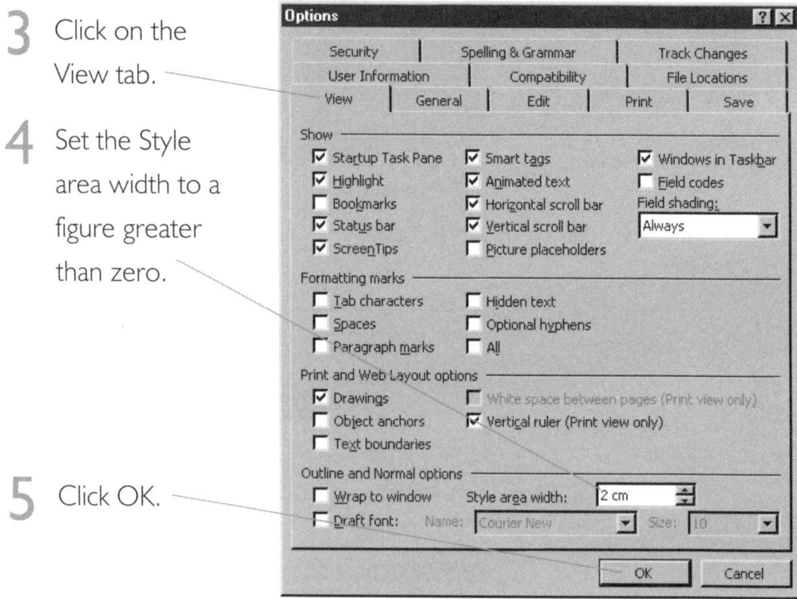

In this example we've used a 2cm margin area in which to list the styles used.

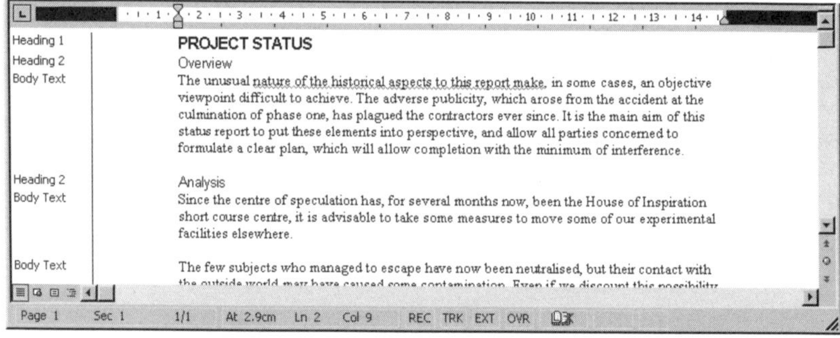

Using Speech Recognition

You can dictate text into Word 2002 and have it turned into on-screen text. When errors occur, you can correct them with the mouse and keyboard (in the usual way) or by dictating the replacement. You can also launch menus, toolbar buttons and dialogs with dedicated voice commands.

Covers

Chapter Six

Preparing to Use Speech Recognition

To use speech recognition, you need the following:

- *a high-quality headset, preferably with USB (Universal Serial Bus) support and gain adjustment*
- *a minimum chip speed of 400 MHz (slower chips make dictation extremely laborious)*
- *a minimum of 128 Mb of RAM*
- *Windows 98 (or NT 4.0) or later*
- *Internet Explorer 5.0 (or later)*

For more information on requirements, visit (no spaces or line breaks):

http://office.microsoft.com/assistance/2002/articles/oSpeechRequirements_aw.htm

The Microphone Wizard only launches the first time you follow step 1 (after this, step 1 activates speech recognition).

Your use of speech recognition will benefit from repeated training. Click the Tools button on the Language Bar and select Training. Complete the wizard which launches.

You can dictate text directly into Word. You can also make selections in menus, toolbars, dialogs and the Task Pane.

Installing/Running Speech Recognition

If you haven't installed speech recognition via a custom install, pull down the Tools menu and click Speech.

Preparing Speech Recognition

Before you can dictate into Word, you have to adjust your microphone and carry out a brief 'training' procedure to acclimatise Word to the sound of your voice:

1. Pull down the Tools menu and click Speech.

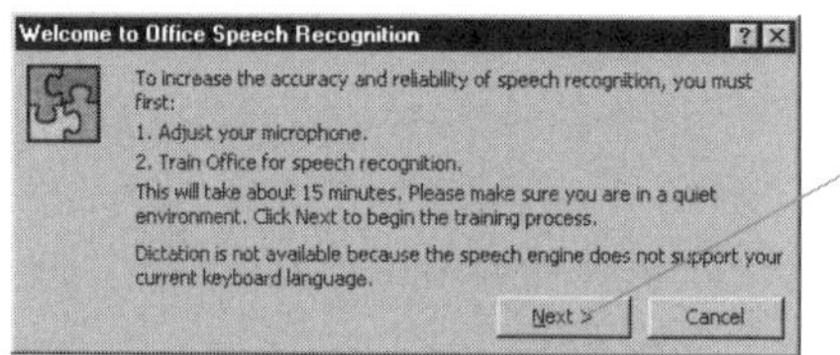

2. Click Next to begin the training process

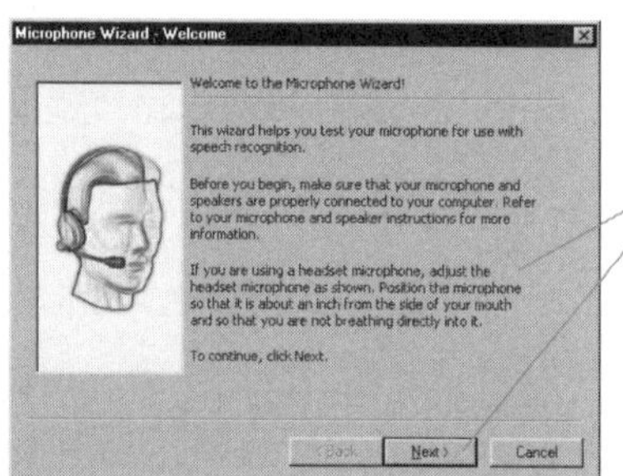

3. Adjust your microphone in line with the instructions then click Next

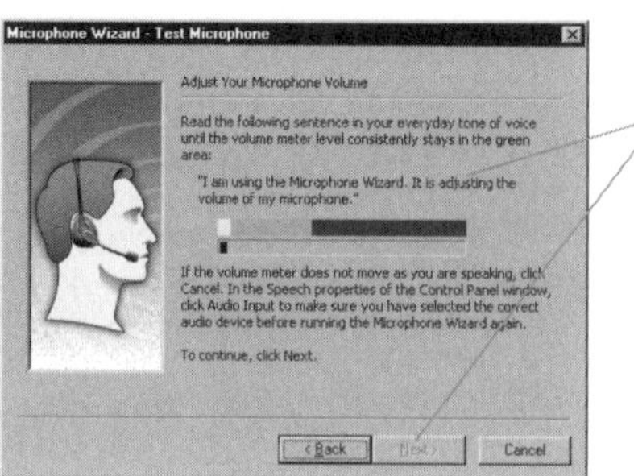

4. Read out the sentence shown then click Next. Complete the rest of the wizard

Dictating Text

If you run speech recognition in less than optimal conditions, the results may well be poor.

1 Follow step 1 on page 78

2 If the microphone isn't already turned on, click here

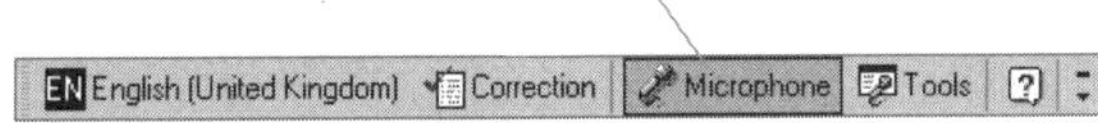

To get the best out of speech recognition, you need to carry out the following:

- *keep your environment as quiet as possible*
- *keep the microphone in the same position relative to your mouth*
- *run the training wizard as often as possible*
- *pronounce words clearly but don't pause between them or between individual letters – only pause at the end of your train of thought*
- *turn off the microphone when not in use (by repeating step 1)*

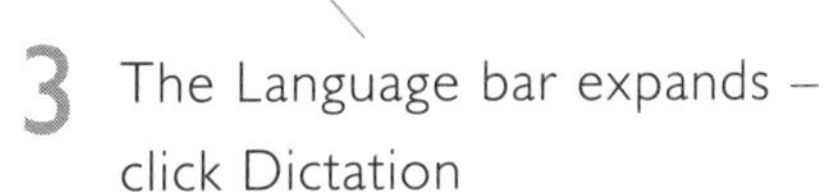

3 The Language bar expands – click Dictation

4 Begin dictating. Initially, Word inserts a blue bar on the screen – the text appears as soon as it's recognised

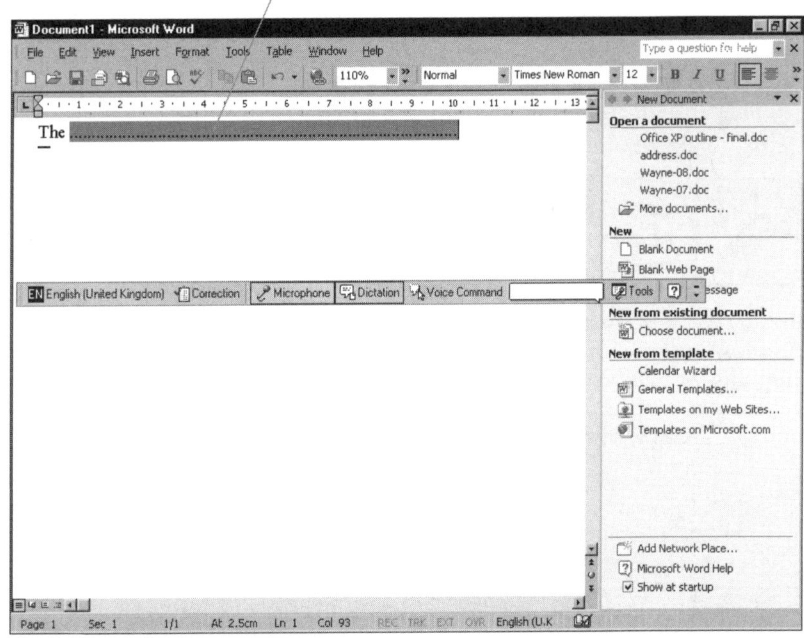

For the best results, use speech recognition in conjunction with mouse and keyboard use.

5 To close speech recognition, repeat step 1

Entering Voice Commands

You can switch to Voice Command by saying 'Voice Command', or dictation by saying 'Dictation'.

Commands you speak appear in the following Language bar field:

Task Pane

For more details of voice commands, see the HELP topic 'Getting started with speech recognition'.

1 Follow step 1 on page 78

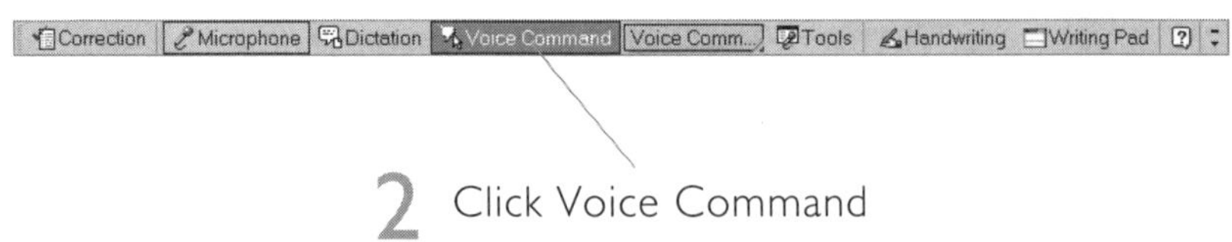

2 Click Voice Command

3 Issue the appropriate command e.g.:

- to launch the File menu say 'file' or 'file menu' (to select a menu entry say the name)
- to open the Font dialog say 'font' (to select a typeface, say the name)
- to close a dialog say 'OK'
- to select a toolbar button, say the name
- to launch the Task Pane, say 'Task Pane'

Correcting Errors

If the Language Bar isn't visible or minimised on the Taskbar, go to Control Panel. Double-click Text Services. In the dialog, click Language Bar. Select Show the Language bar on the desktop. Click OK twice.

1 Replace wrong text with corrections in the usual way

2 Or right-click the error. Choose a replacement in the menu or click More and select it from the list:

1 Force
2 cause
3 close
4 place
5 price
6 course
7 trust command
8 post command
9 forest command

3 Or select the error with your mouse. In Dictation mode, say 'spelling mode'. Now spell out the substitution e.g. n-o-w

4 Or select the error with your mouse. In Dictation mode, say the corrected version

Re step 4 – it's best to correct phrases rather than individual words.

Tabulation

Text which is laid out with correct and accurate horizontal alignment greatly helps to give a document a professional look.

Effective use of white space, including tabulation, is one of the most important considerations when formatting documents. This chapter deals with a range of tabulation features and examples.

Covers

Chapter Seven

Default Tabulation

Do not feel tempted to space out text by pressing the Spacebar lots of times. This will not produce consistent results – use tabulation instead.

The default tab stops are set every half inch. When you press the Tab key, Word automatically moves across the page, stopping when it reaches the next tab stop position.

To see how this works:

1. Make sure that the ¶ button is active.
2. Enter items of text separated by a single tab character.

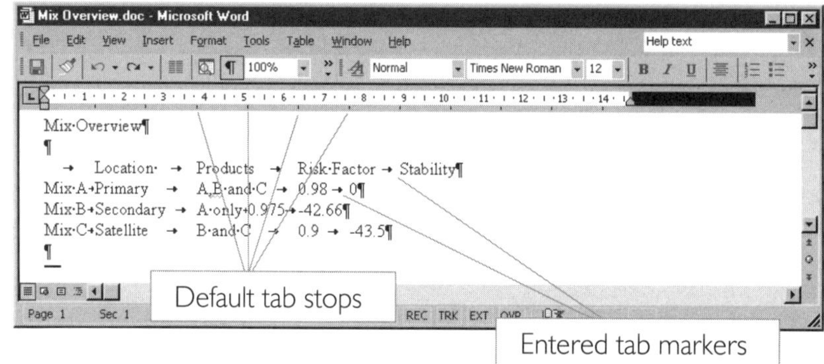

Creating Your Own Tabulation

1. Select the text.
2. Click in the lower half of the ruler (or the grey bar beneath it) to create a new tab (shaped like an 'L') and drag to adjust its position.

To make the ruler display the distances between tab stops when dragging a new tab, hold down the Alt key.

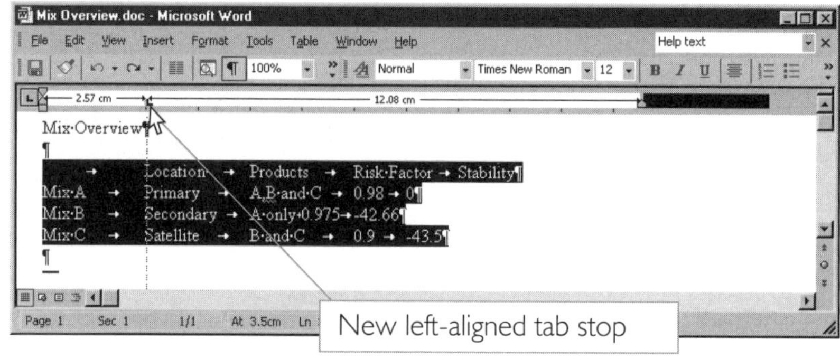

3 Repeat this process to create more tab stops.

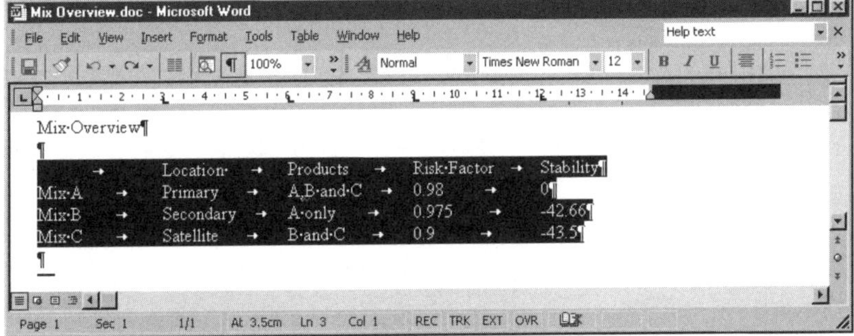

Any new tab stops you create will automatically override the default tabs.

Deleting Tabs

You can delete your tab stops simply by dragging them downwards out of the ruler.

Different Types of Tab

So far you've created left-aligned tabs, which cause text to align along its left edge under the tab stop.

1 Click the Tab Alignment button once to change to centre tabs.

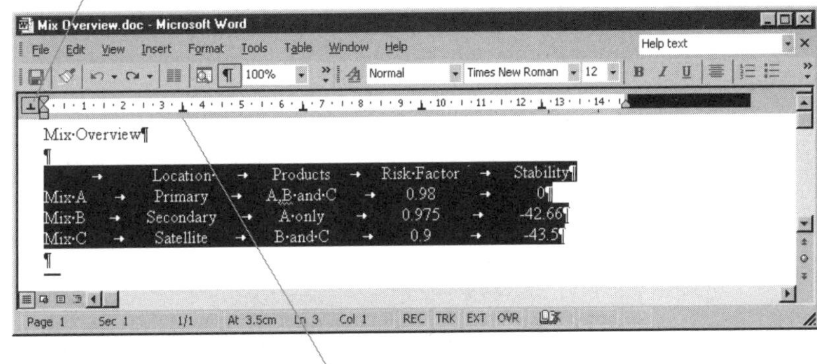

BEWARE

You can move your own tab stops at any time by dragging them within the ruler – but be sure to select the main text first.

2 You can now create centred tabs by clicking in the ruler.

As you click on the Tab Alignment button, it cycles between Left, Center, Right and Decimal alignment.

Here is an example of right-aligned tabs:

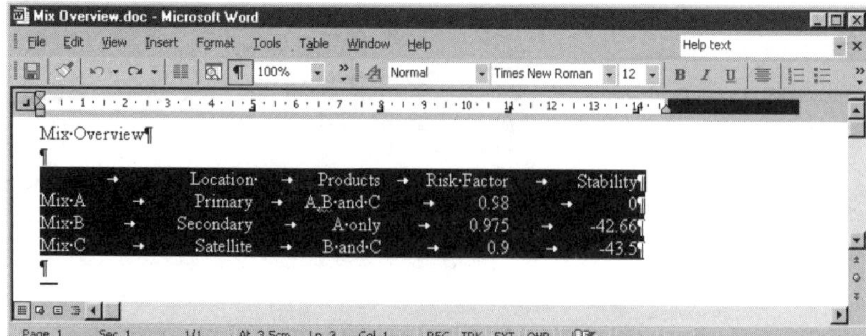

Tabulation is a paragraph-level attribute. Each paragraph can have its own tab stops if necessary.

Decimal tabs are used to line up numbers along the decimal point:

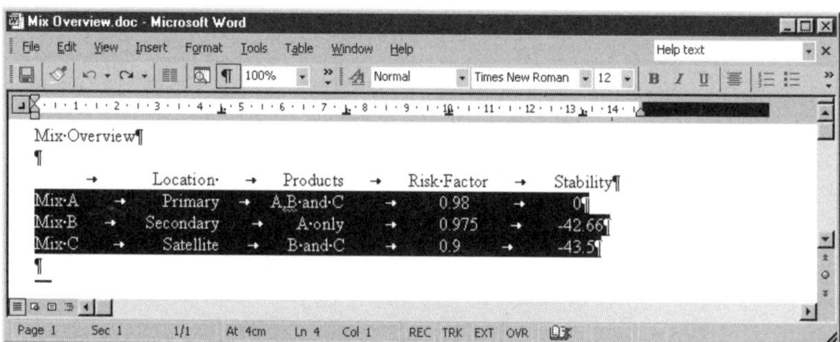

Usually a mixture of different tabs is required:

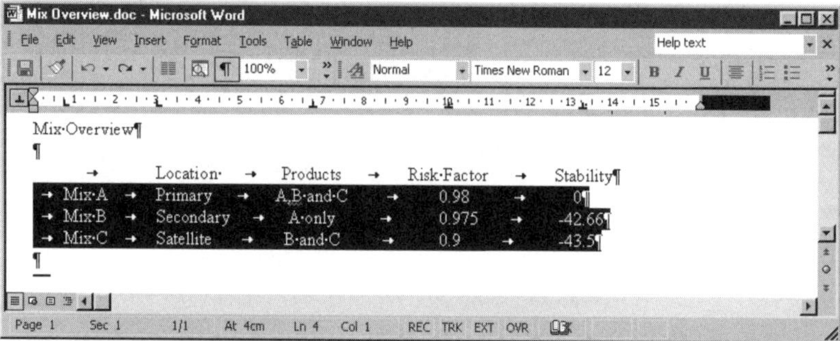

The Tabs Dialog Box

You can also access the Tabs dialog box by double-clicking directly on a Tab marker in the Ruler.

More options can be found in the Tabs dialog box.

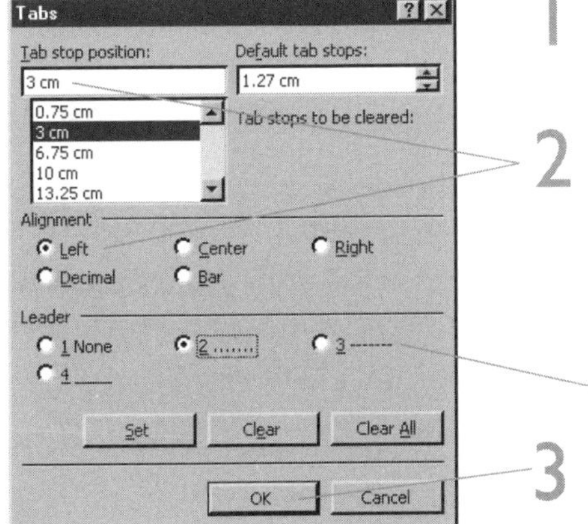

1. Choose Tabs from the Format menu.
2. Set the position and alignment of the tab. You can also fill the tab space with lines or dots using the Leader setting.
3. Click OK.

This example also uses a leader consisting of a row of dots.

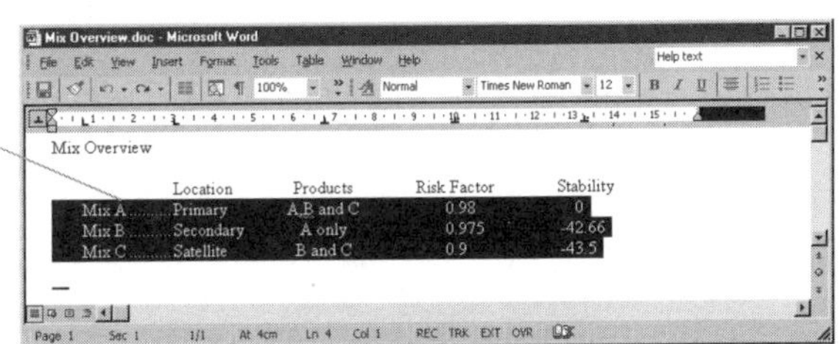

Bar Tabs

These can only be accessed from the Tabs dialog box, as shown above. Setting a bar tab causes a vertical line to appear in the text at the specified position.

You can also access the Tabs dialog via the Paragraph dialog.

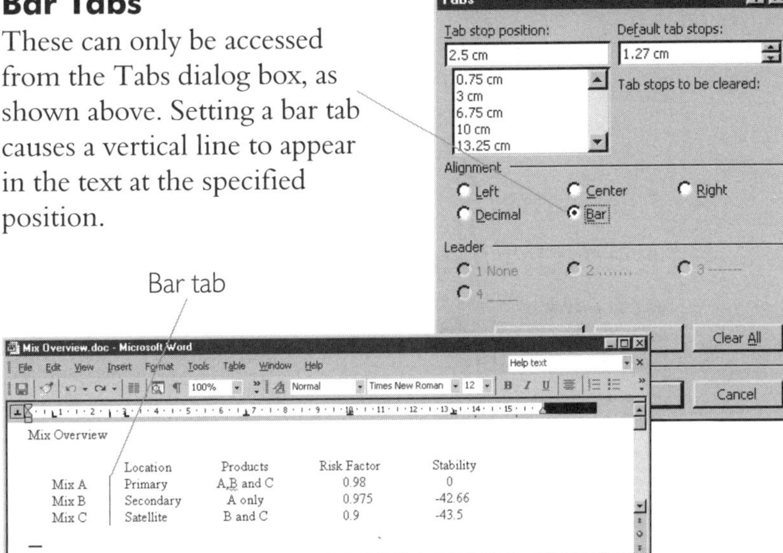

Using Tabs to Create Tables

The examples used on the preceding pages have demonstrated the properties of tabs by using them to create a simple table. However, although this table presents a small amount of information clearly, it contains none of the additional effects that are often used to enhance the presentation of tables: borders, shaded cells etc.

Word does allow you to create tables with these effects, using a very simple click-and-drag method (see Chapter 11), but if you have already entered your table data as we have in this chapter, you won't want to type it in again. Fortunately, you can convert such data into true tables very easily.

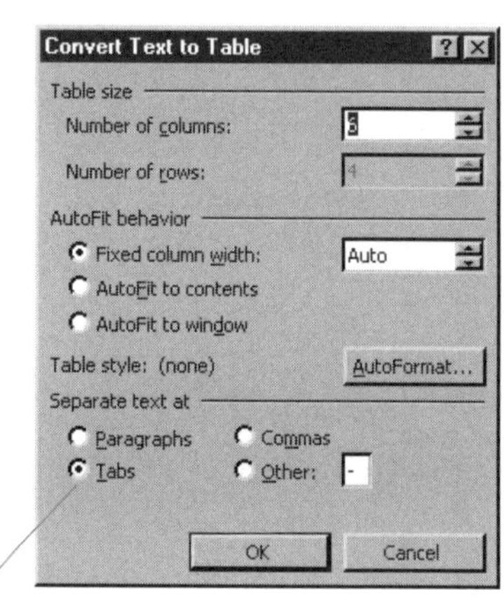

1. Highlight the data you want to convert.

2. Go to the Table menu, open the Convert submenu and choose Text to Table.

3. If you have separated your columns using tabs, make sure this option is selected.

4. Click OK. The table is created automatically:

If the width of a column needs adjusting, rest your cursor over the table column icon to its right, then click and drag it to where you want it.

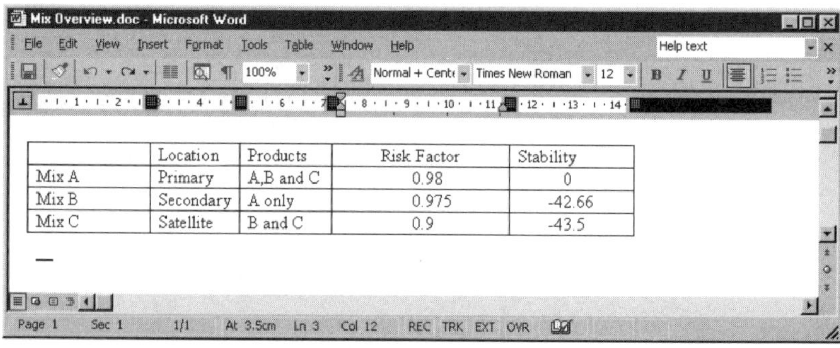

	Location	Products	Risk Factor	Stability
Mix A	Primary	A,B and C	0.98	0
Mix B	Secondary	A only	0.975	-42.66
Mix C	Satellite	B and C	0.9	-43.5

Automatic Features

Word has many automatic features which will operate on selected text or a complete document. This chapter looks at many of these, including search and replace tools and facilities for correction of spelling and grammar.

Covers

Chapter Eight

Find and Replace

Finding Text

Word can be instructed to search through your document for particular words, groups of characters, or formatting attributes.

1 Choose Find from the Edit menu, or type Control+F.

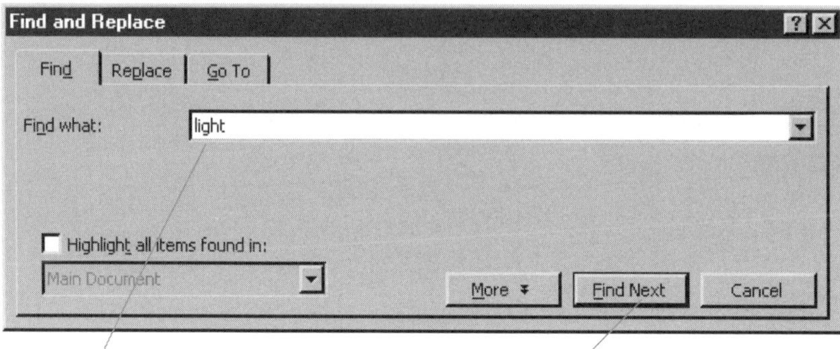

2 Enter your search text here.

3 Click on the Find Next button.

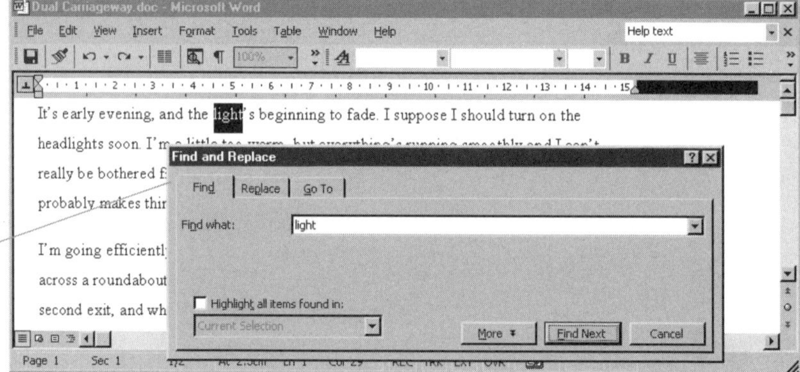

Word keeps this dialog box open in case you want to search on to the next occurrence of your text.

Word will highlight the next instance of the search text within your document. Word will let you know if the end of the document was reached without it finding any occurrences.

Even if you close the dialog, you can still continue your search by using the two blue buttons in the vertical scrollbar.

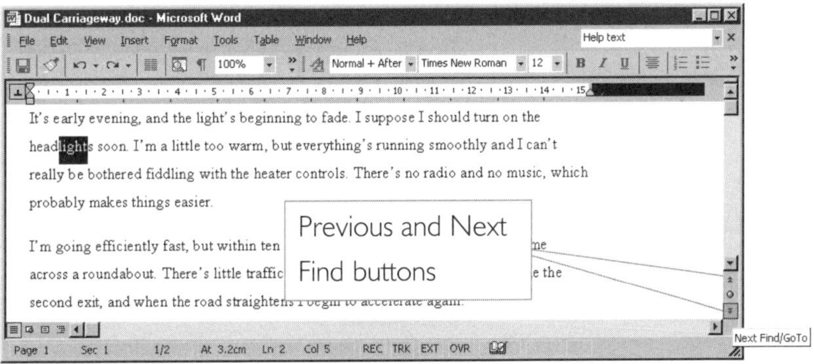

More or Less

1. If the Find and Replace dialog is not currently being displayed, then choose Find from the Edit menu, or type Control+F.

2. Click the More button to display more options, or the Less button to see the abbreviated version of this dialog box.

Using the checkboxes in the lower left area of the dialog, you can set Word to look for text in a particular case, for whole words (rather than groups of letters), to use wildcard searching, or phonetic matching.

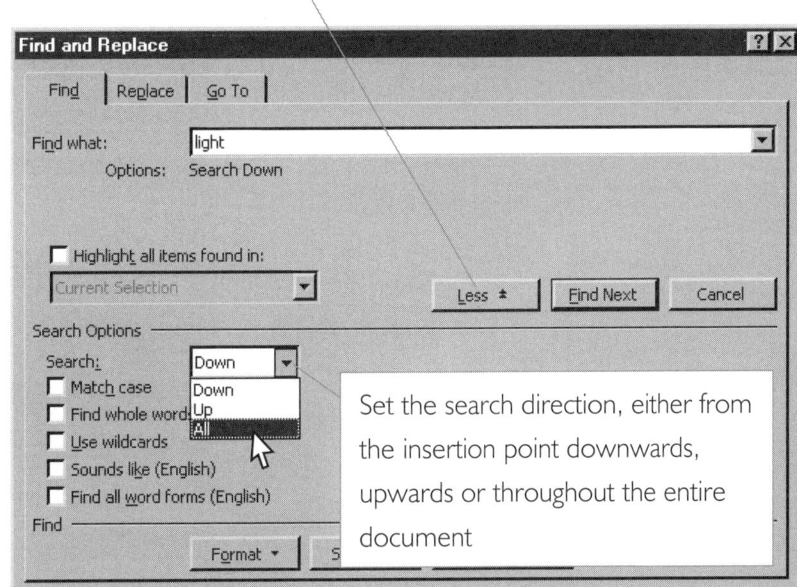

Searches Based on Attributes

Your search can be based on attributes as well as specific text. You can even search for particular text and attributes simultaneously.

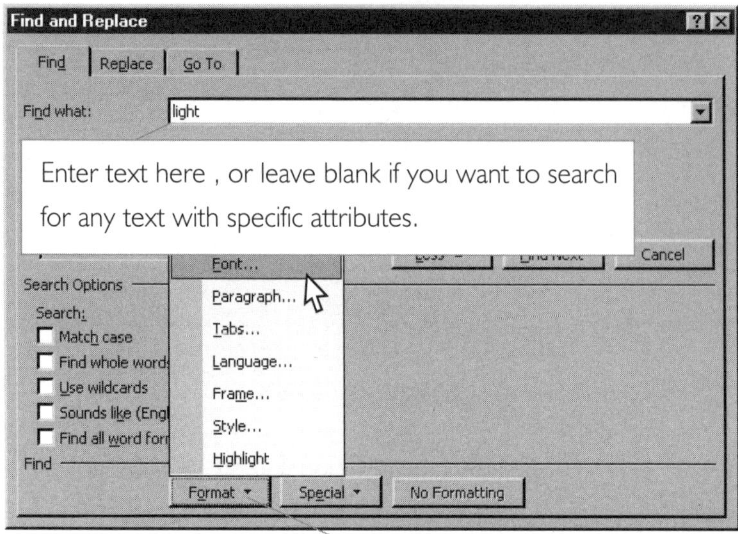

1. In the Find and Replace dialog box, open the Format drop-down menu and choose the relevant option(s).

In this example we're searching for 'Times New Roman Italic 12 point' text.

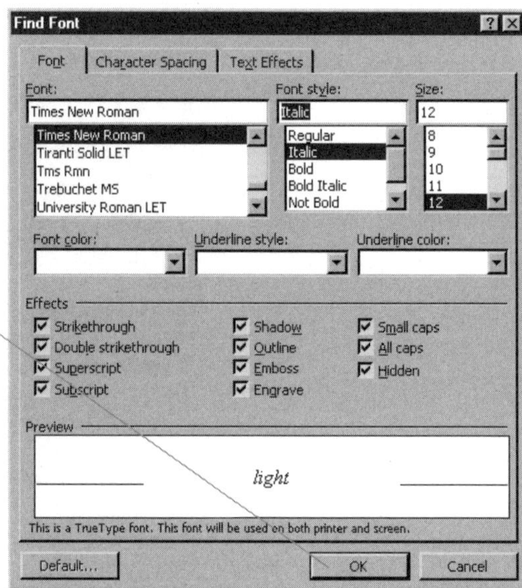

2. Click OK to return to the Find dialog, then click on the Find button to start the search.

Word will now look through your document to find any text which matches *both* what you typed for Find what *and* the attributes you specified:

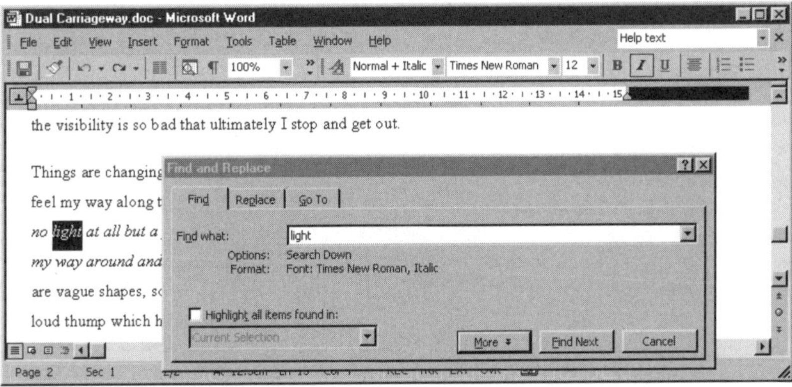

Cancelling Attribute Searches

If you have previously specified attributes for your search, then you can clear these quickly by clicking on the No Formatting button.

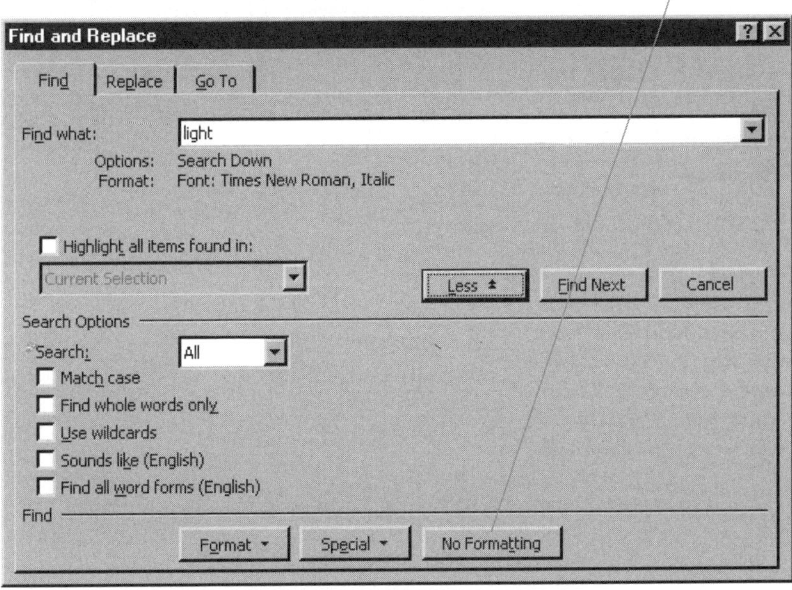

Replacing Text

Once you have found an instance of the text you are searching for, you can choose to replace it with some different text.

Before clicking on the Format button, be sure to click in either the Find what or Replace with parts of the dialog. This determines whether you want to specify a Format to search for, or to replace with.

1. Click on the Replace tab.
2. Enter the Replace with text.

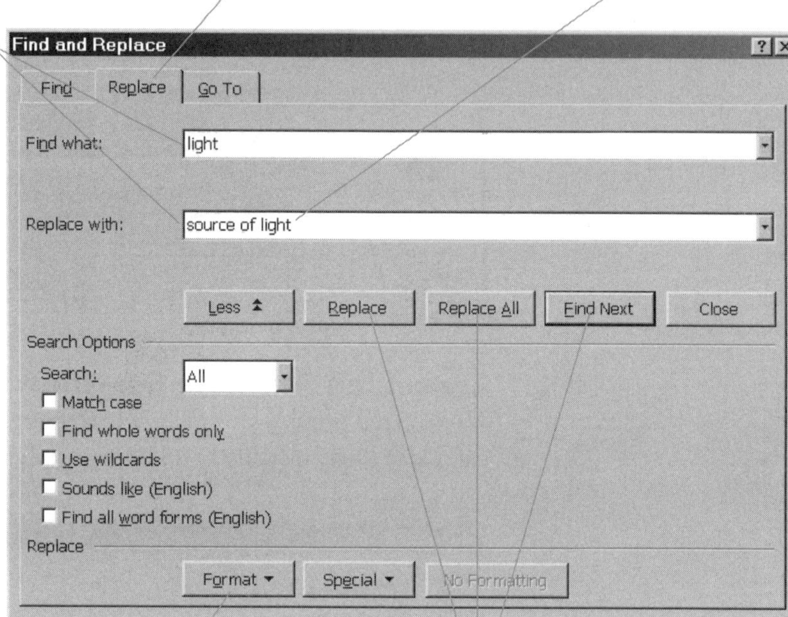

To open the Find and Replace dialog with the Replace tab active, you can choose Replace from the Edit menu, or type Control+H. You can then enter the Find what text here before continuing with step 2. However, if you want to search for text with a particular format, you'll have to use the Find tab.

3. If you wish to replace the search text with text that has different format attributes, click here and choose the relevant options.
4. Click Replace to change just this instance of the target text, Replace All to change every instance in the document, or Find Next to skip to the next instance.
5. When you're done, click Close.

Special Characters

You can use the Special drop-down menu in the Find and Replace tabs to easily insert the keyboard codes for special characters.

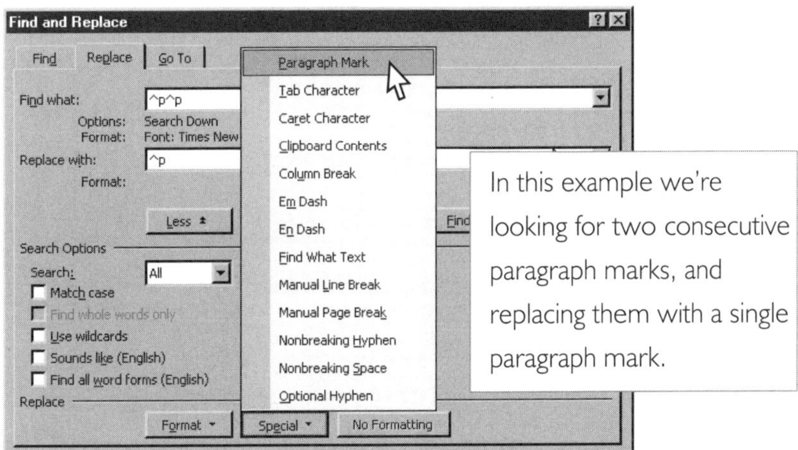

In this example we're looking for two consecutive paragraph marks, and replacing them with a single paragraph mark.

Wildcards

If you want to search not for a specific piece of text, but for text that follows a certain pattern, select the Use wildcards checkbox before clicking the Special button. You will then find that Special drop-down menu contains some extra entries. For example, to search for words that follow the pattern 'g?ve' (where '?' represents any single character), you would do the following:

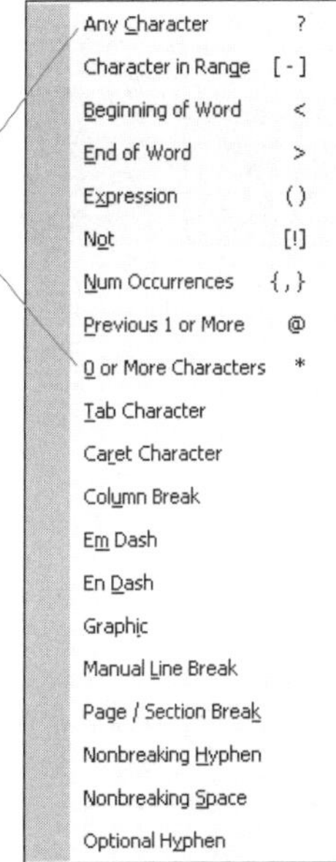

1. Enter the letter 'g' in the Find what box.
2. Click the Special button and select Any Character from the menu.
3. Enter the letters 've'.

This search will highlight all words like 'give', 'gave', and (if you don't have the Find whole words only checkbox selected) words like 'given', too.

Another very useful wildcard feature available from the Special menu is the Character in Range function. This allows you to search for numbers or letters in any range you specify. For example, to search for references to years between 1961 and 1967, make sure that the Use wildcards checkbox is selected, then do the following:

1. In the Find what box, enter '196'
2. Click on the Special button and select Character in Range from the menu. The text '[-]' will be inserted.
3. Edit the contents of the Find what box so it now reads '196[1-7]'.

Spelling and Grammar Checking

Word lets you check your spelling and grammar in two ways: from a special dialog or on-the-fly. The dialog is used as follows:

The shortcut key for Spelling and Grammar Checking is F7.

1. If you don't want to spell check your entire document, then select only the text you require.
2. Choose Spelling and Grammar from the Tools menu, or click on the corresponding icon:

Spelling errors are highlighted in red, grammatical ones in green.

Click on Ignore to skip the current instance of the word, or Ignore All to skip all other instances, too.

Similarly, Change All will apply the current suggestion to all other instances as well.

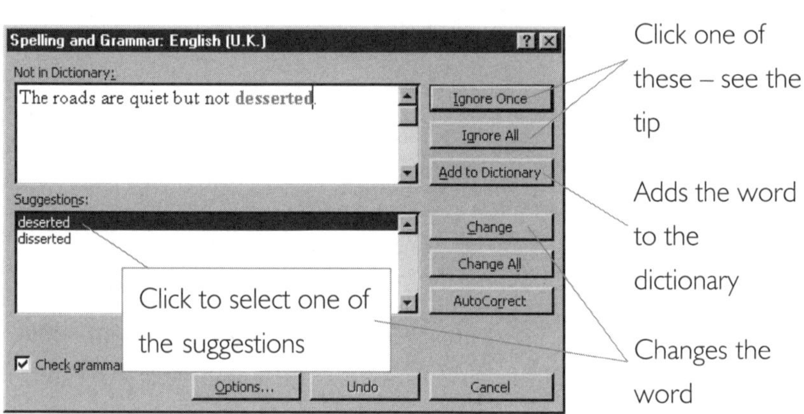

Here's an example of Word questioning some grammar:

If you disagree with Word's grammar advice, then either click Ignore to skip the current phrase or Ignore Rule to stop Word applying the rule altogether.

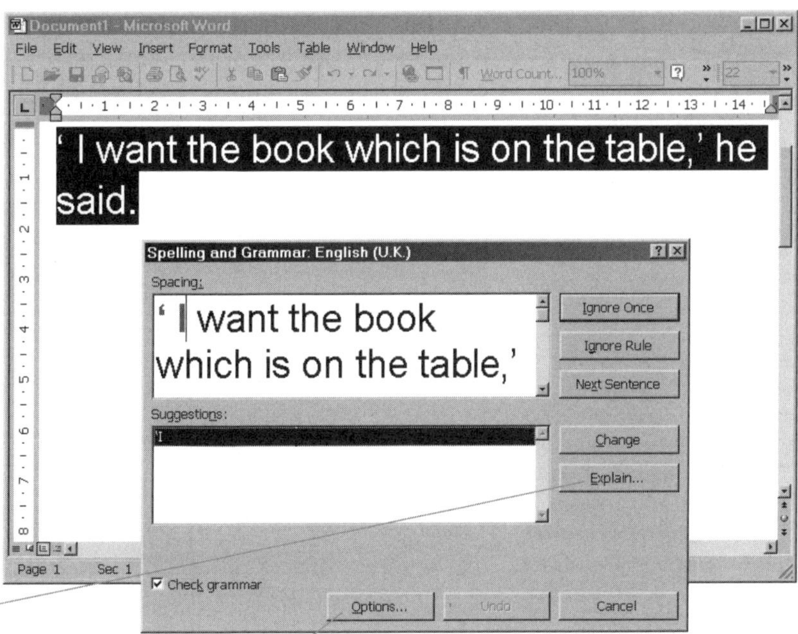

For an explanation of the grammatical point Word is making, click the Explain button. Word launches the Office Assistant with helpful advice.

3 Clicking the Options button takes you to the Spelling & Grammar options dialog box:

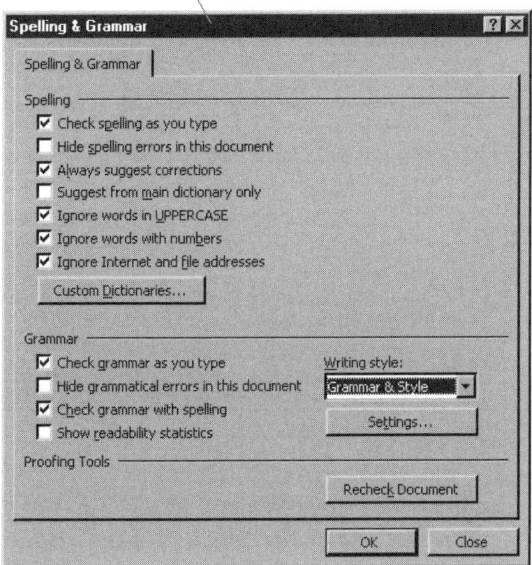

Both the Spelling and the Grammar drop-down menus offer a quick route to the full Spelling and Grammar dialog box: simply select the Spelling entry, marked with:

You can display readability statistics after performing a Spelling and Grammar check.

Select Options from the Tools menu and choose the Spelling and Grammar tab. Make sure that Show readability statistics is checked, then click OK.

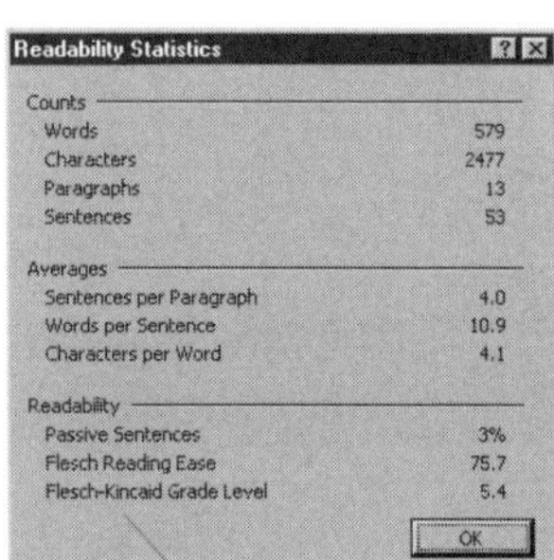

The Flesch Reading Ease value is in the range 0...100, increasing with ease of reading. Standard text rates between 60–70. The Grade Level values indicate the school grade appropriate for your text.

Checking on-the-fly

While the dialog-box method of checking your spelling and grammar offers you the greatest amount of control over exactly how the checking is done, Word 2002 can check your grammar and spelling automatically as you type, highlighting any problems it finds on the page. Consider the following example:

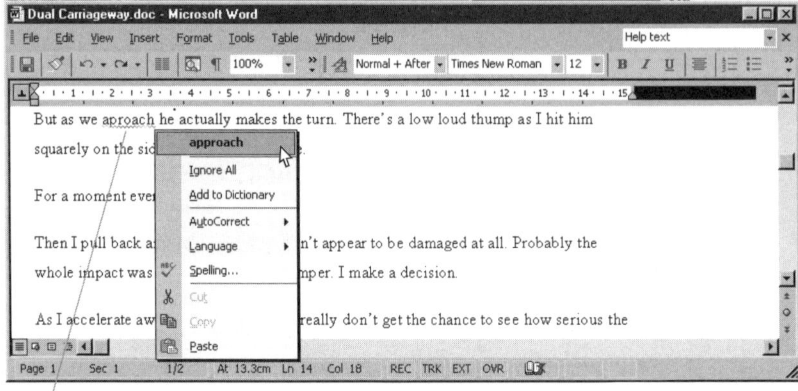

This spelling mistake is underlined in red. To correct, right-click on it then select the correct suggested word from the drop-down menu. If the suggestion is not suitable, attempt to correct it yourself, then see if it is still flagged.

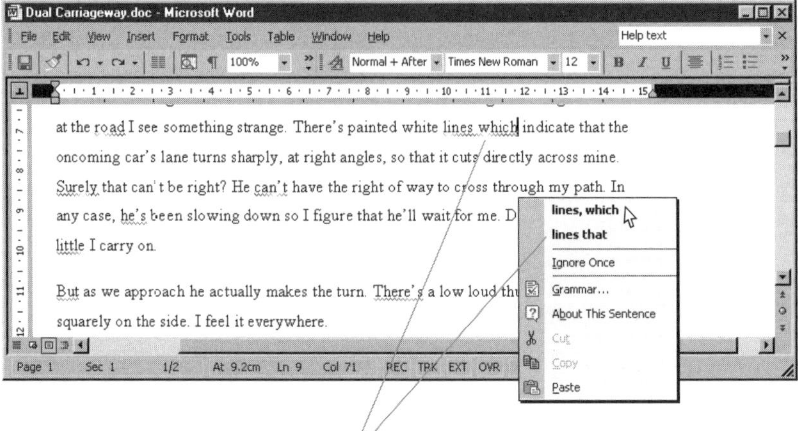

This grammar mistake is underlined in green. Right-click on it, then select the correct suggestion from the menu.

Searching for Synonyms

Word 2002 lets you search for synonyms while you're editing the active document. You do this by calling up Word's resident Thesaurus. The Thesaurus categorises words into meanings; each meaning is allocated various synonyms from which you can choose.

As a bonus, the Thesaurus also supplies antonyms. For example, if you look up 'good' in the Thesaurus (as below), Word lists 'poor' as an antonym.

Using the Thesaurus

First, select the word for which you require a synonym or antonym (or simply position the insertion point within it). Pull down the Tools menu and click Language, Thesaurus. Now do the following:

To count the number of words in the active document, choose Word Count from the Tools menu. (Pre-select text if you want the count restricted to this text.)

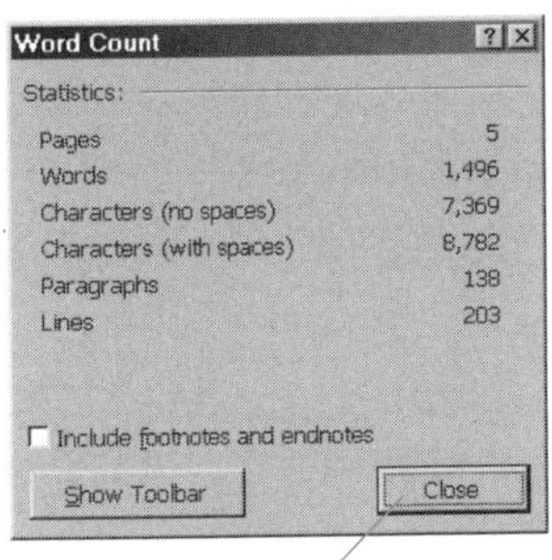

Click Close when you've finished

The selected word appears here

2 Click a replacement synonym or antonym

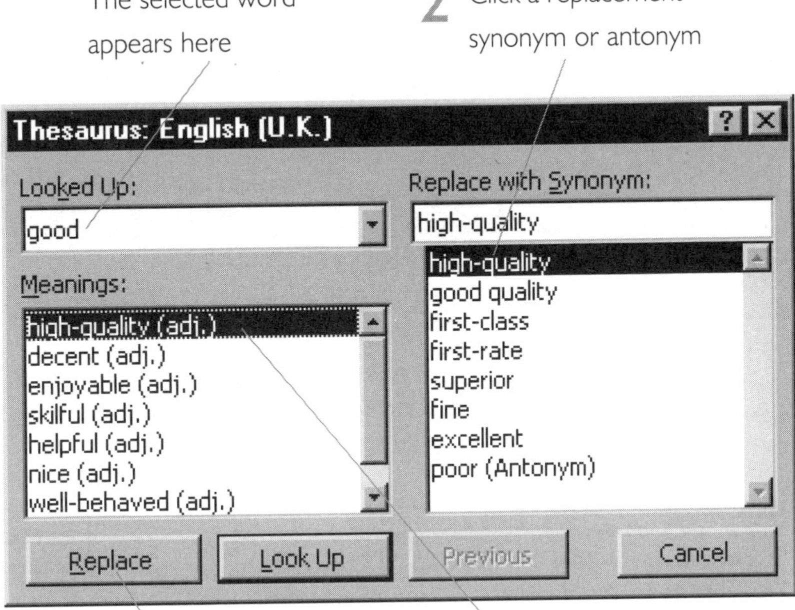

3 Click here to substitute the synonym or antonym for the selected word

1 Click the appropriate meaning

AutoCorrect

You don't have to enter all the AutoCorrect data yourself: Word 2002 contains a large number of corrections, including common mistakes for 'necessary', 'occasion', and transposition errors such as 'knwo' instead of 'know'. You can browse through these from the AutoCorrect dialog.

In effect, Word provides another way to view a document: you can 'summarise' it. When you summarise a document, Word 2002:

- *analyses it and allocates a 'score' to each sentence*
- *allocates a higher score for sentences which contain repeated words*

After this, you specify what percentage of the higher-scoring sentences you want to display.

To summarise the active document, pull down the Tools menu and click AutoSummarize. Word 2002 carries out the initial analysis. When it's completed, select a summary option (e.g. Create a new document...). Enter a percentage and click OK.

Often, the same spelling or typing mistakes are made again and again. You can instruct Word to substitute the correction automatically.

1 Choose AutoCorrect Options from the Tools menu, and make sure that this tab is selected.

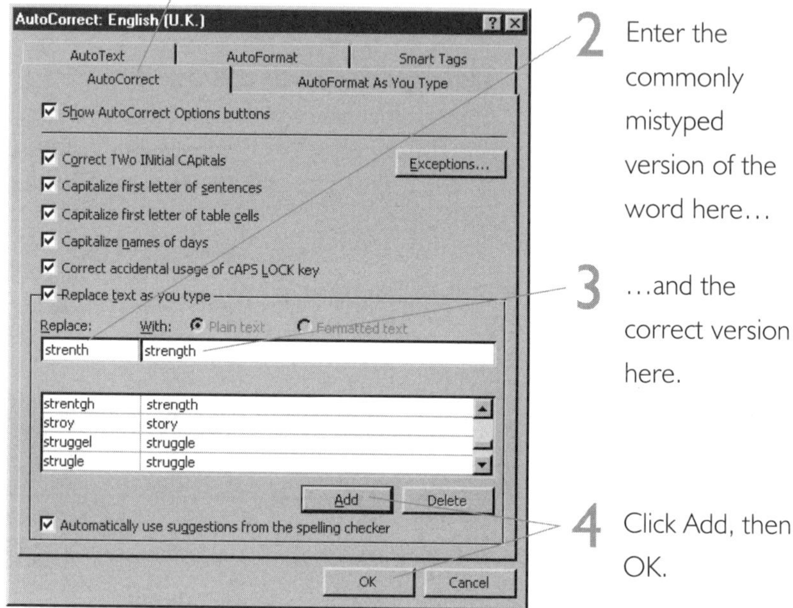

2 Enter the commonly mistyped version of the word here...

3 ...and the correct version here.

4 Click Add, then OK.

If you type the error now, Word spots it and substitutes the correct word automatically, instead of merely flagging it as a possible spelling mistake:

Original text typed *Corrected by Word*

You can now continue through the rest of your life completely unaware that you are consistently failing to spell correctly.

AutoText

This is a less automatic version of AutoCorrect, and is useful for setting up your own abbreviations.

If you find that you often need to type the same text, then it would be worth setting up an AutoText entry.

Creating an AutoText Entry

1 Type the text and select it.

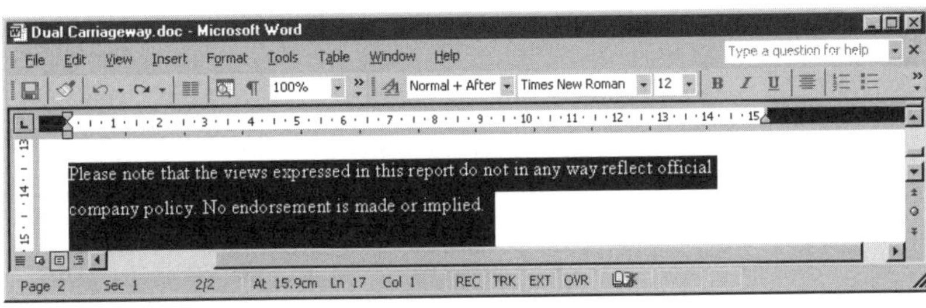

Note that you can also use the AutoText toolbar button:

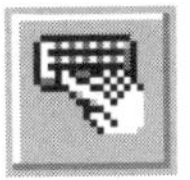

If it isn't visible, you can display it by checking the AutoText entry in the View>Toolbars menu.

2 Choose AutoCorrect Options from the Tools menu and select the AutoText tab.

3 Edit the entry in this box to the abbreviation you require.

4 Click OK.

The selected text is automatically inserted into this area of the AutoText dialog box.

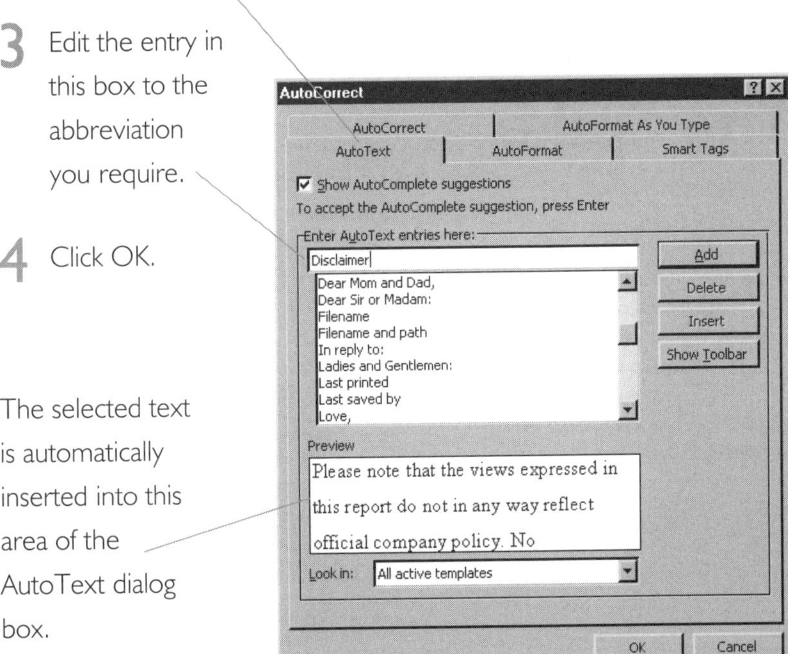

Using AutoText

You can also insert AutoText by selecting it from the AutoText tab of the Tools>AutoCorrect dialog box.

1 Simply type the abbreviation:

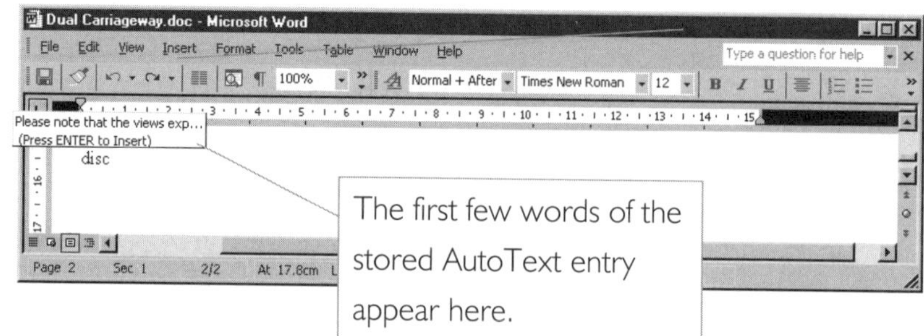

2 Press Enter or F3 to replace the abbreviation with the full text.

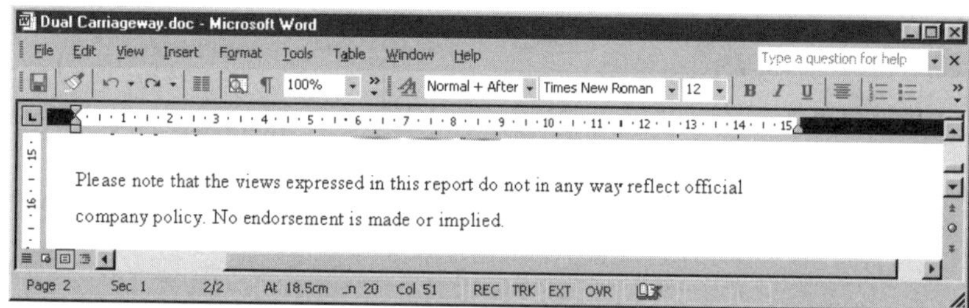

The Spike

The Spike is a temporary piece of AutoText which can be added to with a single key command.

Creating a Spike

You can repeat this more times if necessary. Each time you press Control+F3 any selected text is added to the Spike.

1 Select some text and type Control+F3. The text disappears. It has been impaled on the Spike.

2 Repeat the process with a second piece of text.

3 Finally, place the insertion point at the destination for the text and press Control+Shift+F3. The text is pulled off the Spike and placed back into the document.

AutoComplete

AutoComplete is somewhat akin to AutoText, in that it offers suggestions for the completion of words or phrases that you only need to begin typing. However, while AutoText uses a list of commonly used phrases which have first to be recorded, AutoComplete offers to fill in other sorts of text which can be worked out from the context. For example, AutoComplete can enter:

- the current date
- your name
- your company's name
- any day of the week
- any month

1. Begin to type in one of the words or phrases listed above (here we're entering today's date).

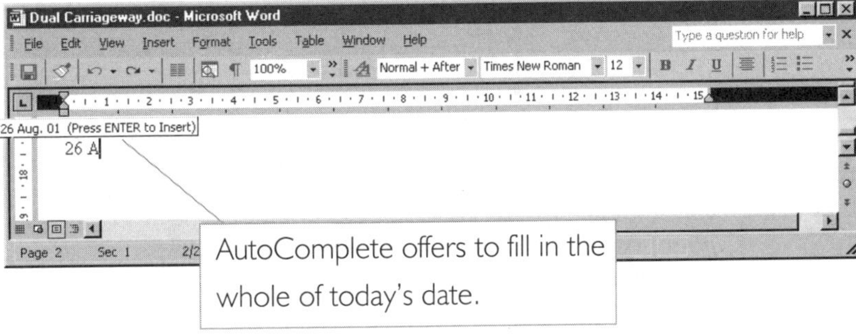

AutoComplete offers to fill in the whole of today's date.

If AutoComplete doesn't appear to be functioning, choose AutoCorrect from the Tools menu, select the AutoText tab, and make sure there is a tick in the checkbox labelled Show AutoComplete tip for AutoText and dates.

2. To fill in the whole date, simply press Enter or F3.

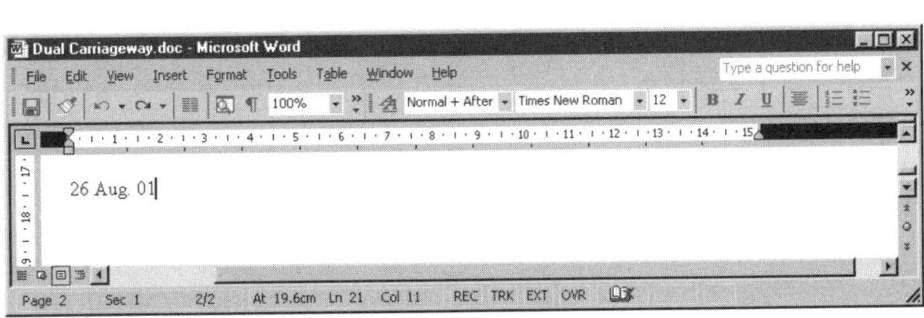

Hyphenation

1 You can change the hyphenation options for your document by choosing Tools>Language>Hyphenation:

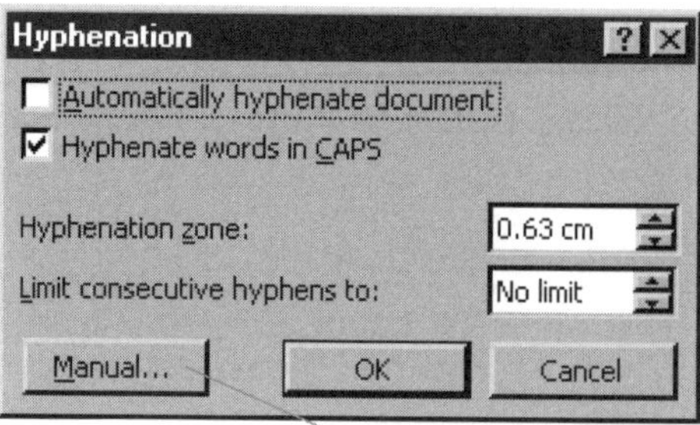

2 If you click on the Manual button you can review hyphenation manually throughout your document...

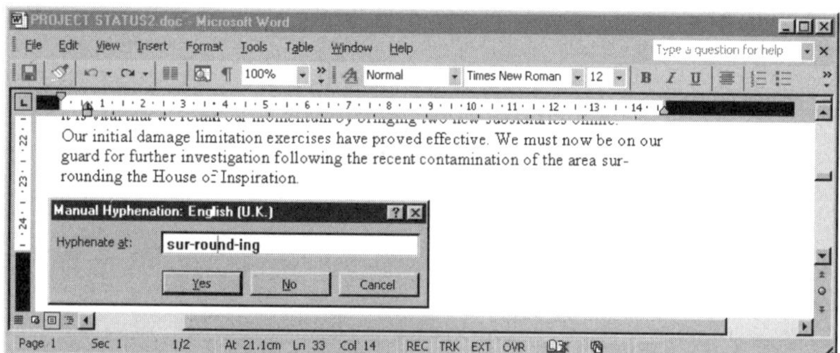

To take even greater control of hyphenation in your text, you may want to use the following keyboard shortcuts:

- *Control + Hyphen will insert an optional hyphen in a word as you type*
- *Control + Shift + Hyphen will insert a non-breaking hyphen into your text (this is a hyphen where Word is not allowed to break the text over successive lines).*

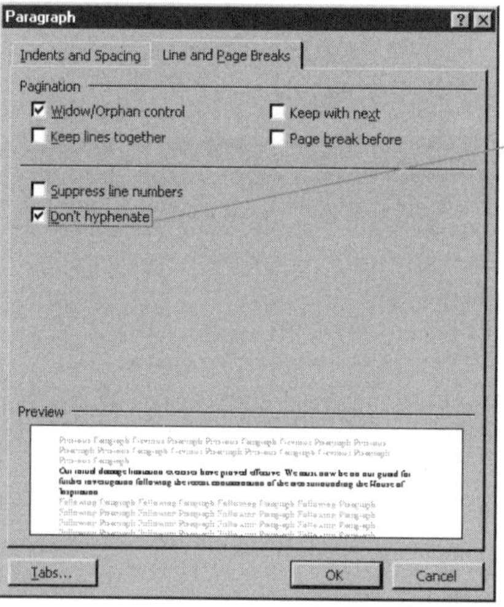

You can also override hyphenation for individual paragraphs by selecting the Don't hyphenate checkbox in the Line and Page Breaks tab of the Paragraph dialog box (choose Paragraph from the Format menu).

Templates and Wizards

Templates act as blueprints for standard types of document which you would need to use again and again. Examples may be standard memos, reports, letters or faxes. A Wizard is a 'live' document which guides you through its own design.

This chapter shows you how to use templates and Wizards, customise a template for your own purposes, or create a new template.

Covers

Chapter Nine

Using Templates

A template contains a range of settings to be used as a starting point for a new document.

If you select the New icon instead of the File menu:

Word uses the Blank Document or Normal template.

The Normal and General Templates

1 Choose New from the File menu:

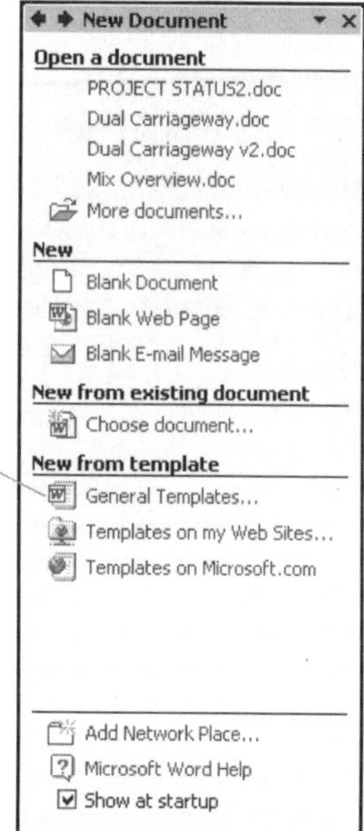

Word makes the Task Pane visible, displaying its New Document controls.

2 Choose General Templates from the New from template section in the Task Pane.

Word lists the templates available. Often you'll use the simple Blank Document template (listed in the General tab).

3 Click on the other tabs to see more available templates.

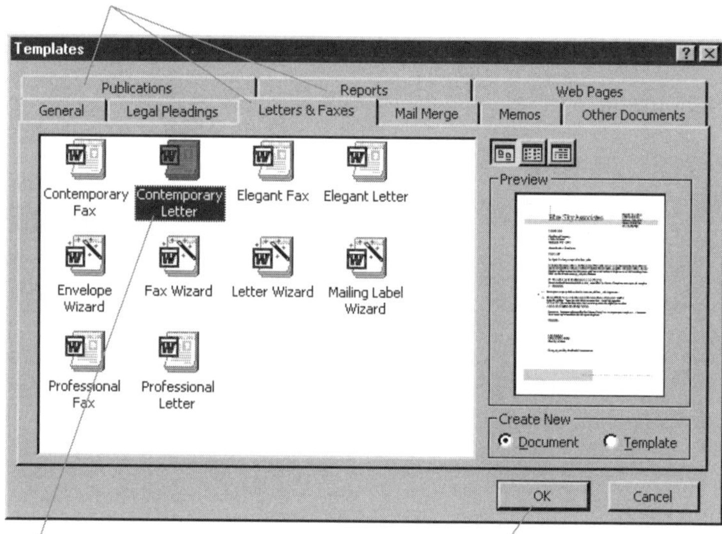

4 Select the template you want to use and click OK.

Template Defaults

Defaults are settings which are used initially when you create a new document or add new text. To change the defaults for a template, do the following with a template open:

1 Open the Font dialog box from the Format menu.

2 Choose your required settings and then click on the Default button.

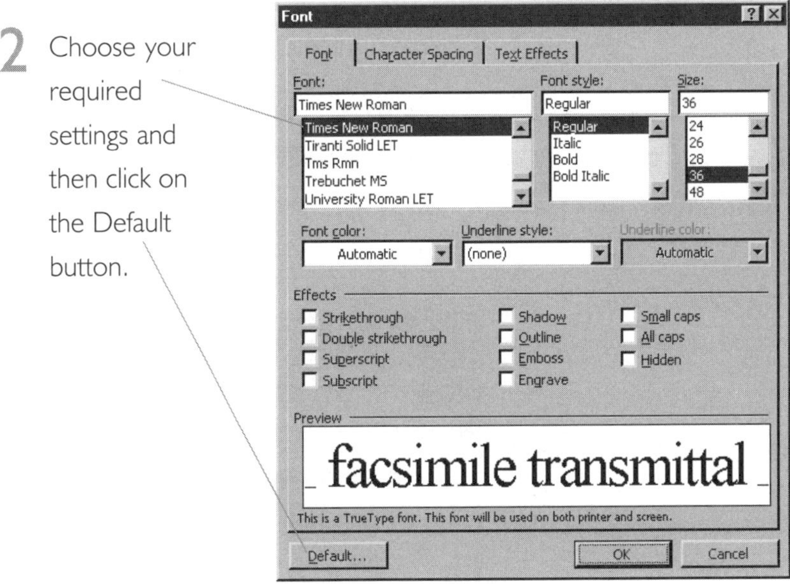

A dialog box will ask you whether you're certain that you want to change the template itself.

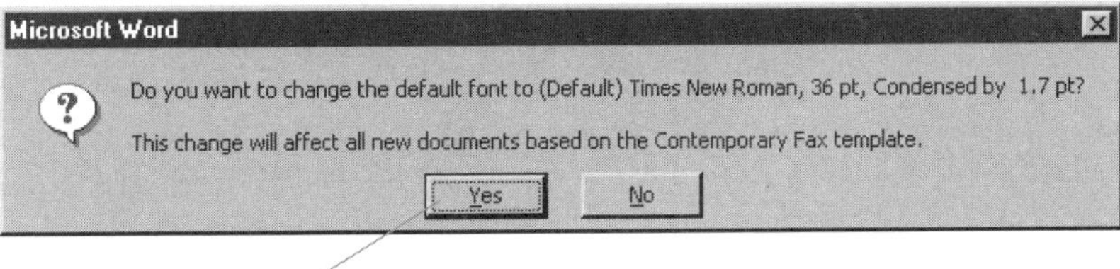

3 If you click Yes, the font information will be saved into the currently used template document.

Form Templates

By designing a Form Template, you can create a document which is very easy to use, even for people who have minimal experience of Word 2002.

You simply create a document in the normal way, apart from adding some special 'form fields'. These can be text containers, checkboxes or drop-down selection fields.

Creating Text Form Fields

1. Make sure the Forms palette is active (if necessary go to the View menu and choose Toolbars, Forms).
2. Place your insertion point where you'd like the field, then click on the Text Form Field button in the Forms palette.

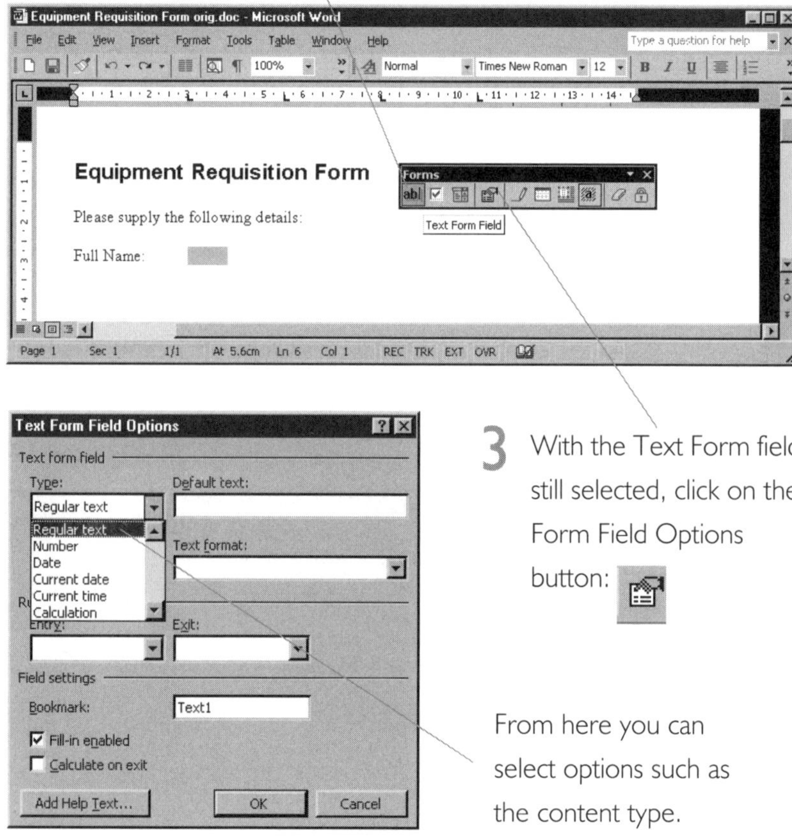

3. With the Text Form field still selected, click on the Form Field Options button:

From here you can select options such as the content type.

Creating Drop-Down Form Fields

Drop-down lists allow users to select from a restricted list of options. This way they can fill out values within a form without typing anything.

1. Decide where you want the field and position your insertion point accordingly.

2. Click on the Drop-Down Form Field icon in the Forms palette.

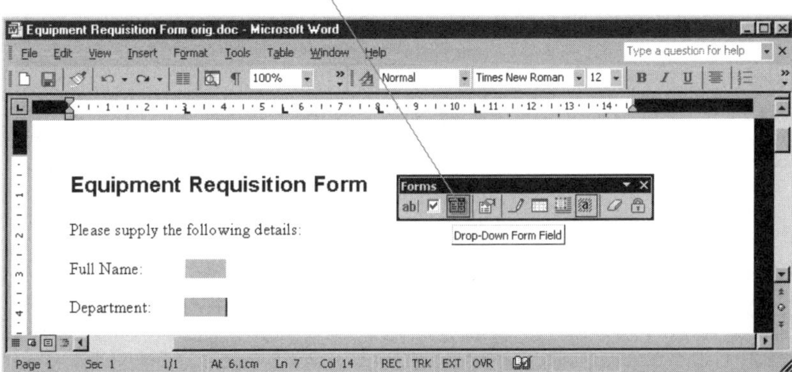

3. With the field still selected, click on the Form Field Options button:

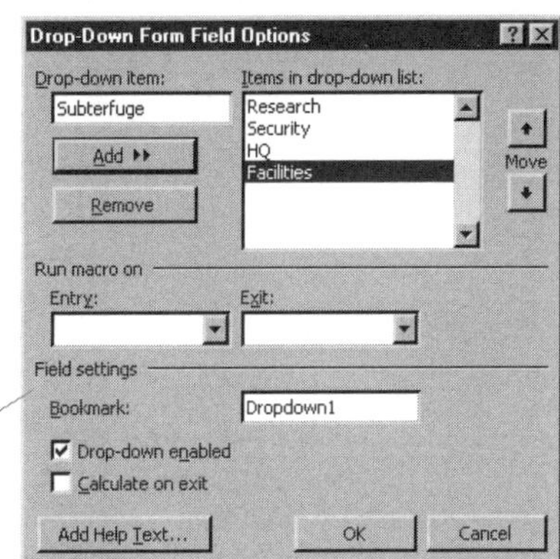

From here you can build the list of values for the drop-down list. Simply enter an item and click the Add button. You can also use the move buttons to reorder the items or remove items altogether.

4. When the list is complete, click OK.

Check Box Form Fields

These act as simple on/off switches for your user. A single-click will toggle a checkmark on and off within the box.

1 Decide where you want the field and position your insertion point accordingly.

2 Click the Check Box Form Field icon in the Forms palette.

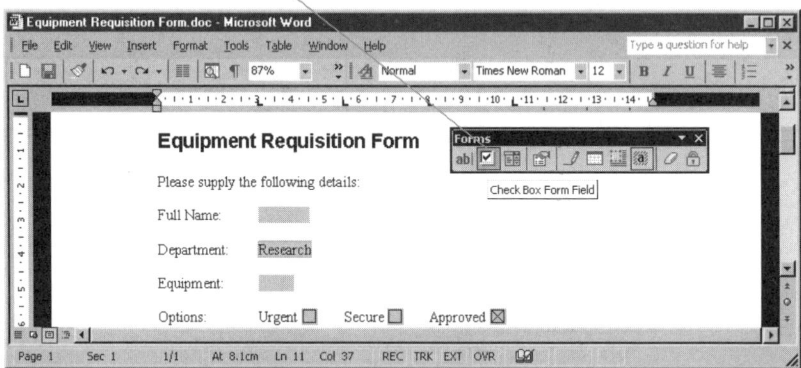

Protecting the Form

1 Click on the Protect Form icon to stop users from editing your document. From now onwards the only items which can be edited are the Form Fields themselves.

Close down the Forms Toolbar when you've completed your form. This will discourage users from attempting to edit the document itself.

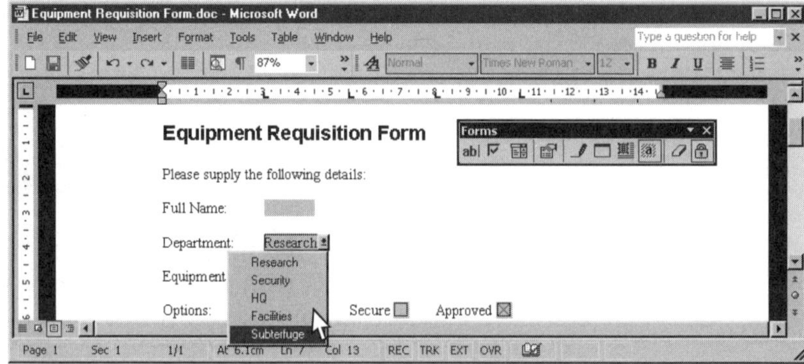

Setting Up a New Template

You can also switch protection on and off using the Forms Toolbar. However, from the dialog box, you can additionally set a password. This would prevent others from unprotecting your document.

Any document can be saved as a template, but in this example we'll use the form we've created. With the document open, do the following:

1. If the document is not already protected, select Protect Document from the Tools menu.

2. Set the Protect document for option to Forms.

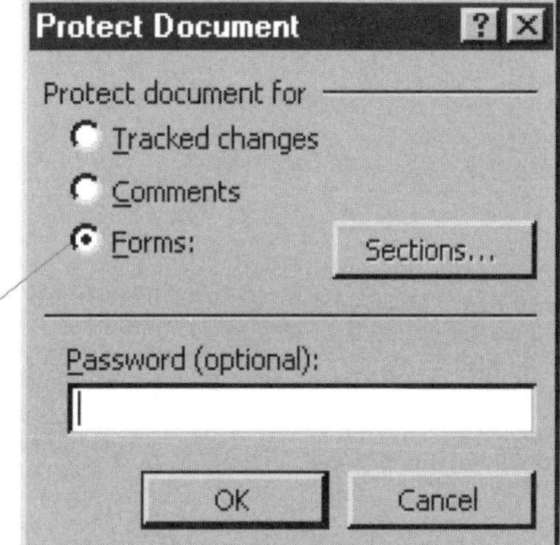

You only need to do this if the template is to be used as a form.

3. Choose Save As from the File menu:

If you're using a normal document, rather than a form, you need only follow steps 3 and 4.

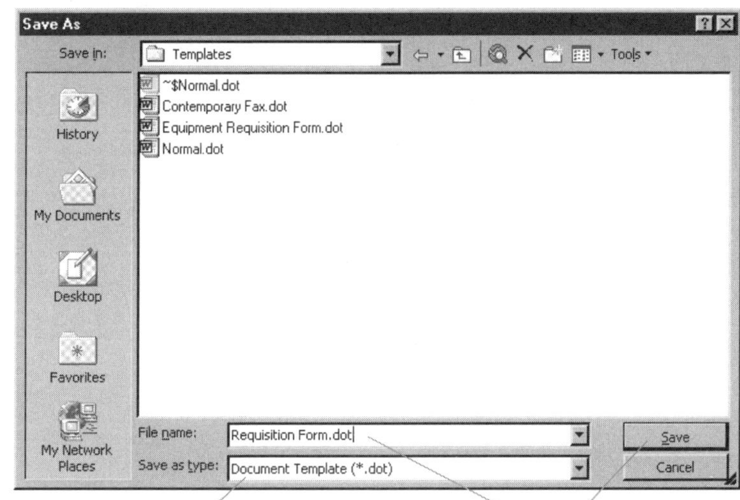

4. Choose Document Template as the file type.

5. Enter a suitable name for the file and click on Save.

The document will automatically be saved with a .DOT extension within Word's Templates folder.

Changing Styles in a Template

When you open a document, Word uses the styles built into the template selected.

As shown earlier, you can alter these styles for individual documents using the Style dialog:

1. Make sure you can see the Styles and Formatting section of the Task Pane (if necessary select Styles and Formatting from the Format menu).

2. Choose a style then select Modify from its drop-down menu in the Task Pane to display the following dialog:

If you record a style change to the Blank Document or Normal template, this will affect most new documents.

3. To copy a style change back into the template itself, make sure the Add to template box is checked.

4. Make any relevant changes using the dialogs that can be selected from the Format button drop-down menu.

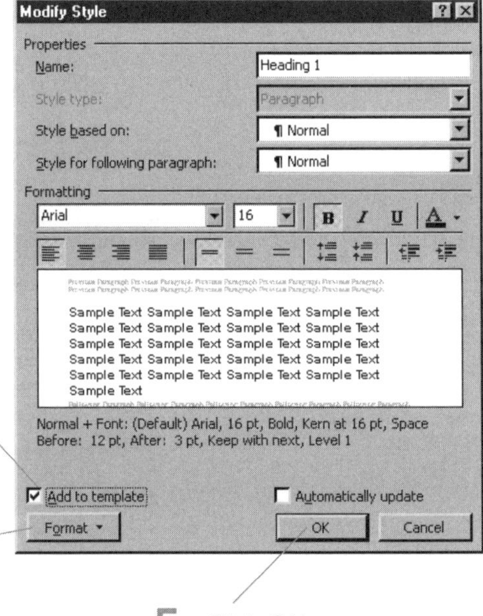

5. Click OK.

The Templates and Add-Ins Dialog

Word always keeps track of the template used to create a document. It is possible to change this even after you've started work.

1 If necessary, unprotect your document (Tools menu).

2 Choose Templates and Add-Ins from the Tools menu.

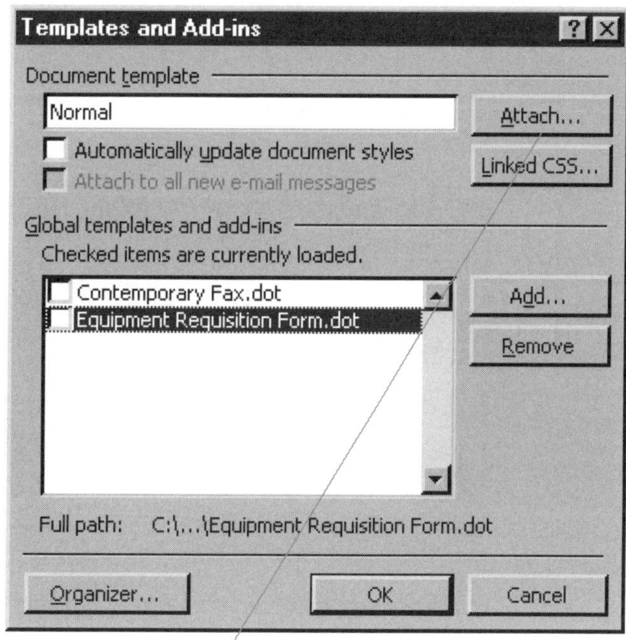

You can use the Add button to make available styles stored in other templates.

Any templates listed in the Global box are always available.

3 Use the Attach button to attach a new template. If you select Automatically Update Document Styles then the styles from the new template will be reapplied to the document text.

4 Click OK when you're done.

Wizards

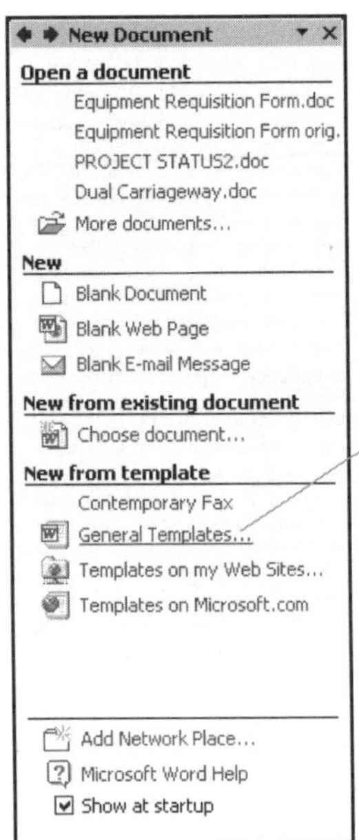

A Wizard is a kind of 'intelligent' template: it helps you design and build a document by asking you a series of questions. You answer these either by selecting from a choice of radio buttons, or by entering text in a box.

An Example

1. If you can't see the New Document controls in the Task Pane then choose New from the File menu.
2. Select General Templates from the Task Pane.
3. Select the Other Documents tab in the Templates dialog box. Click on the Calendar Wizard icon, then click OK.

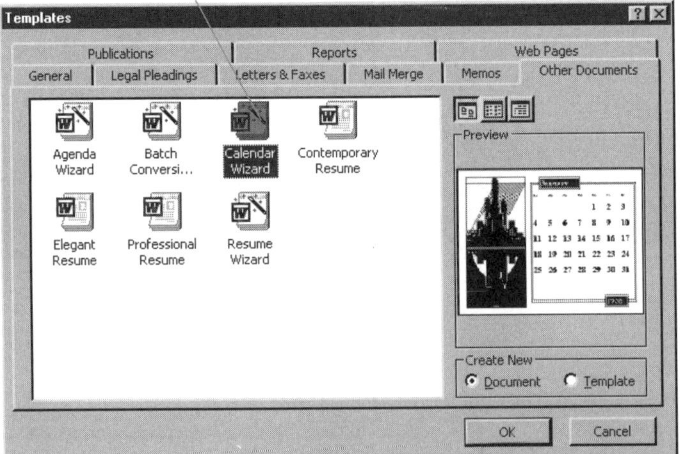

4. Start working through the Wizard by clicking the Next button

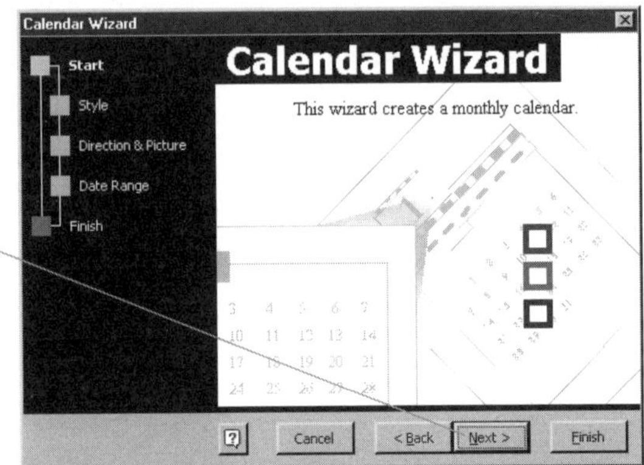

Another useful example is the Fax Wizard. Word is actually capable of sending out faxes directly, provided you have a fax-capable modem properly installed in your system. If you are not set up for this, however, you can still get the Wizard to create a document which you would firstly print, then send manually using a Fax machine.

5 Each page of the Wizard will ask you questions. As you work through these, the flowchart on the left will show your progress.

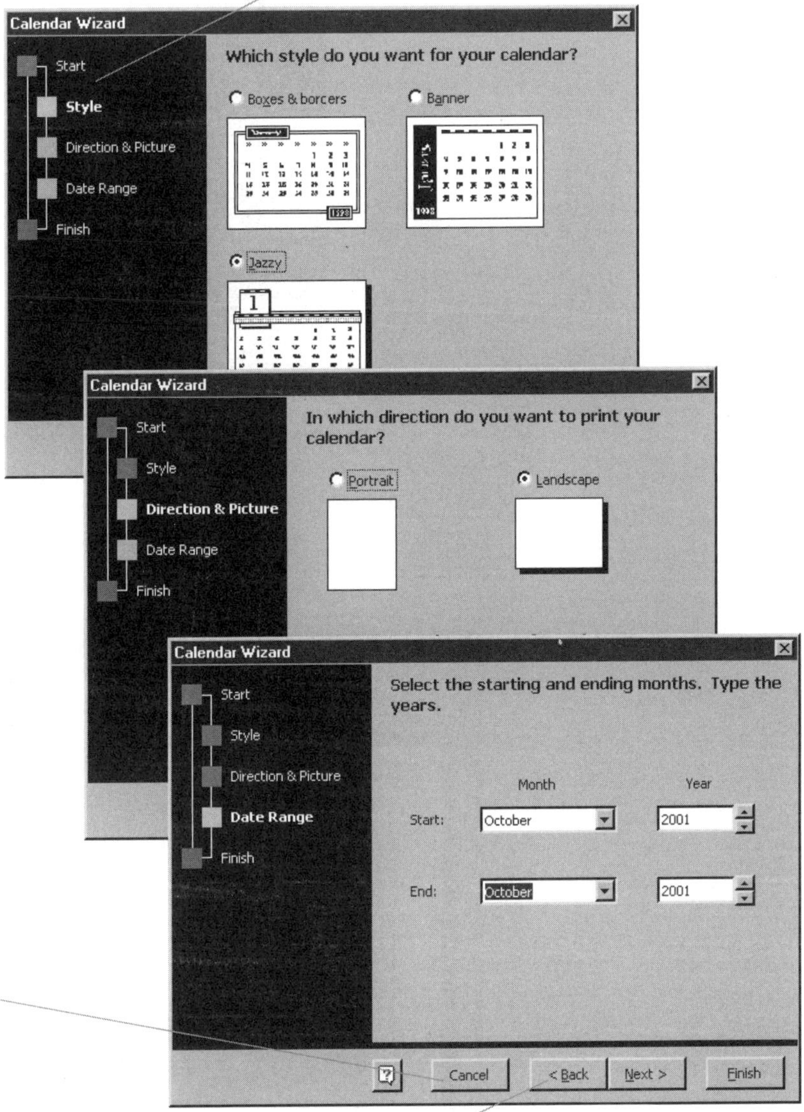

If you decide that this isn't the Wizard for you after all, then click on the Cancel button:

6 At any point you can go back to a previous page simply by clicking the Back button. This way you can fill out the settings in any order you choose.

7 When you've finished making the settings, click Finish.

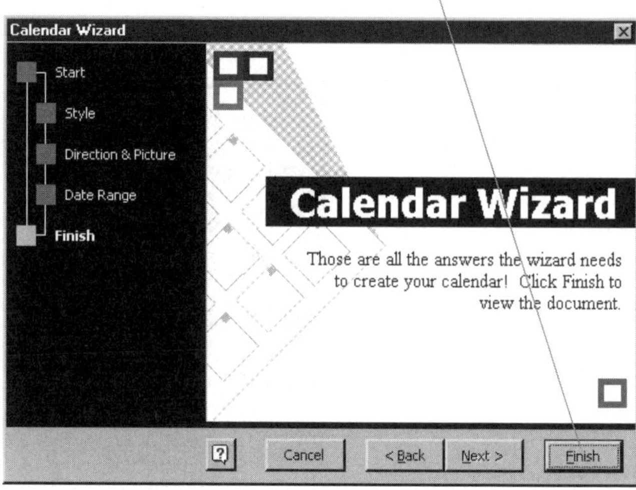

The document is now automatically generated using the settings supplied. You can continue to edit this manually, if appropriate, then save or print in the normal way.

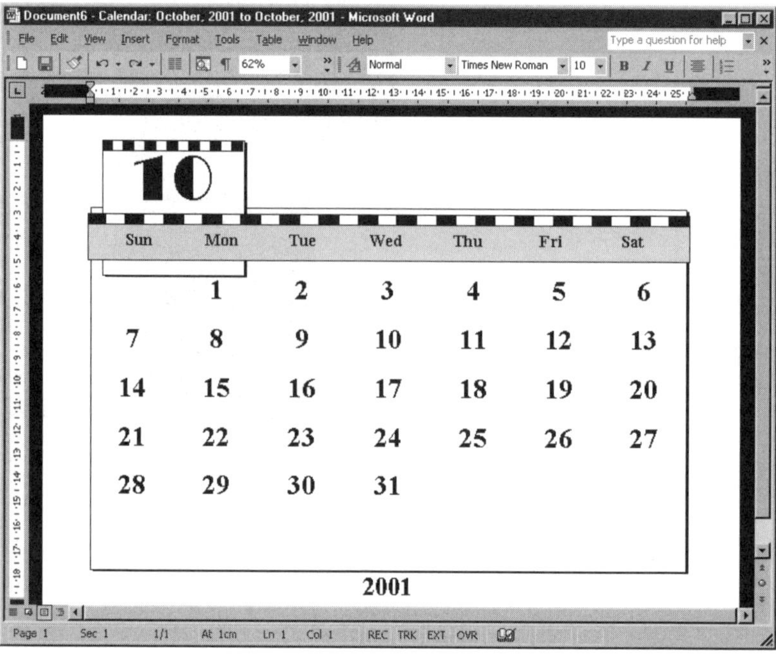

Graphical Features

Although not a full-blown graphics package, Word contains a comprehensive collection of clip art as well as a respectable range of graphical editing features. This chapter takes you through the processes involved with incorporating pictures and illustrations into your document.

Covers

Chapter Ten

Inserting Pictures from Disk

By default Word will embed a copy of the graphic in your file. This will allow you to make changes to the graphic within Word, but tends to make your files larger.

If you choose the Link to File option (by clicking on the downward-pointing arrow at the right hand side of the Insert button), then Word doesn't store its own local copy. This keeps your Word files smaller, but make sure that you keep the original graphic file where Word can find it.

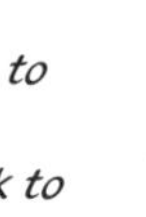

Word can import many types of graphic file format. WMF, CGM, WPG, DRW, EPS and PCT files normally contain draw-type objects which can be scaled up or down with no loss in quality, because they are stored as vectors (mathematical objects).

On the other hand BMP, PCX, TIF, JPG and GIF files are bitmapped: the image is stored as a structure of tiny dots or blocks. Be careful not to enlarge these pictures too much, or the dots will become very noticeable, causing a marked deterioration in quality.

Word 2002 has its own supply of clip art illustrations (see the facing page), but you can also import from a wide range of graphic file formats.

1. Click the insertion point at the destination for the graphic.

2. Go to the Insert menu, choose Picture and From File.

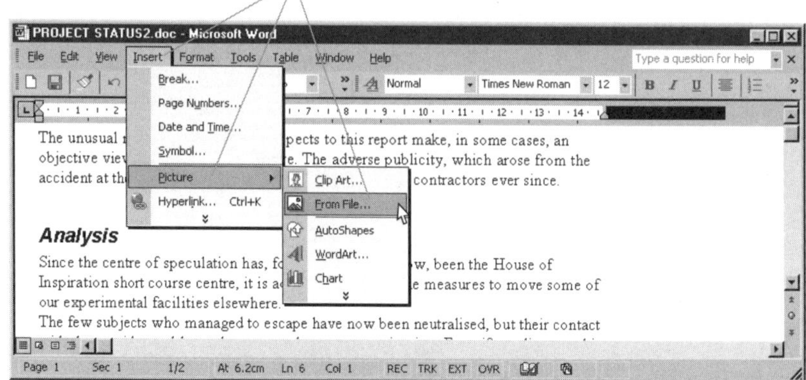

3. Locate the file you require and click Insert.

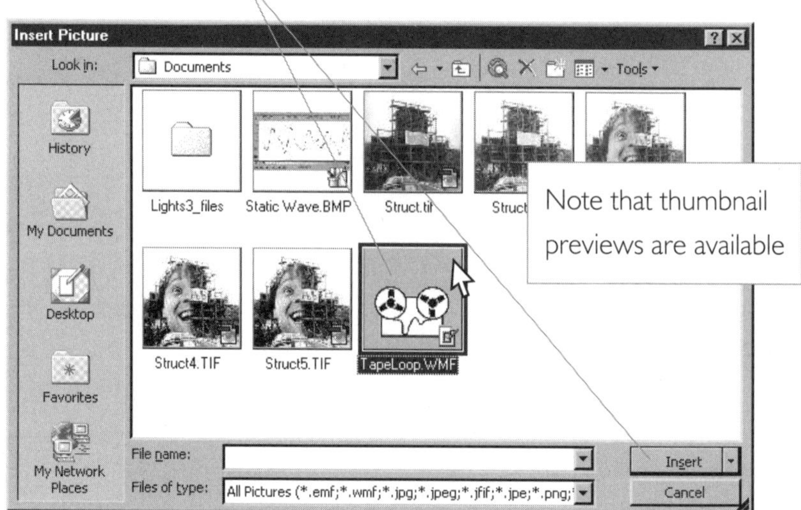

4. Once inserted, pictures (and clip art) can be moved or resized in the normal way

Inserting Clip Art

You can use Click and Type to insert pictures in blank page areas.

Clips have associated keywords. You can use these to locate clips.

You can add new clips to collections (or add new keywords to existing clips) in the Clip Organizer. Click here to launch it:

Using the Insert Clip Art Task Pane

First, position the insertion point at the location within the active document where you want to insert the picture. Pull down the Insert menu and click Picture, Clip Art. Do the following:

1 Enter one or more keywords.

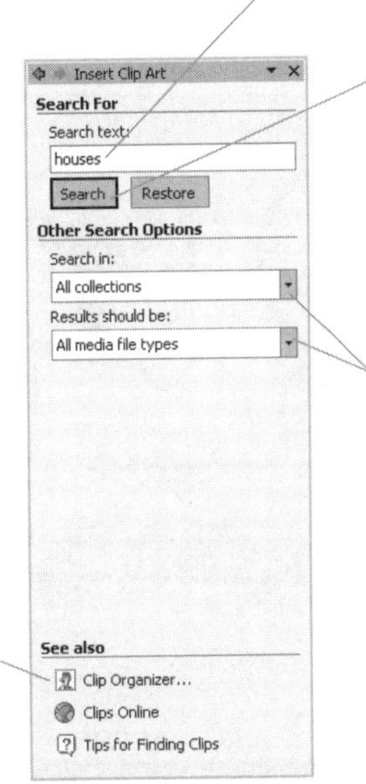

3 Click Search.

2 Optional – click here and make the appropriate choices.

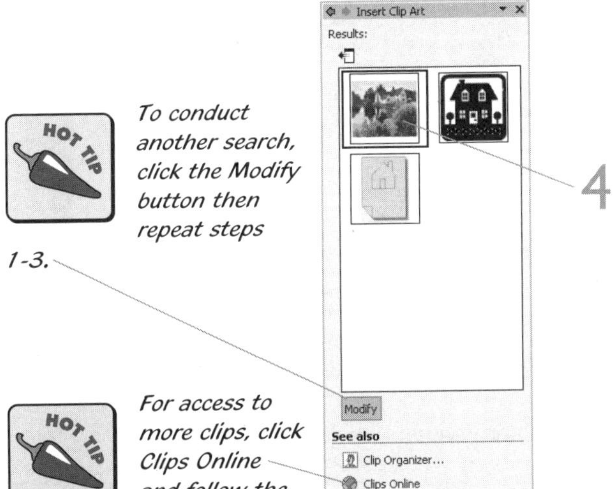

To conduct another search, click the Modify button then repeat steps 1-3.

4 Click an icon to insert the clip.

For access to more clips, click Clips Online and follow the on-screen instructions.

Manipulating Graphics

If you have a scanner or a digital camera connected to your system then you can scan directly into Word. Choose Insert then Picture and From Scanner or Camera.

Word 2002 now automatically creates a 'Drawing Canvas' on which graphic elements sit. If graphic elements are created on the same canvas, then it is much easier to move them together.

You can tell when the canvas is present by its thick shaded border and corner 'crop handles' (see below). You can move the whole canvas by dragging with the mouse on the border. Dragging on the corner 'crop handles' lets you resize the canvas area.

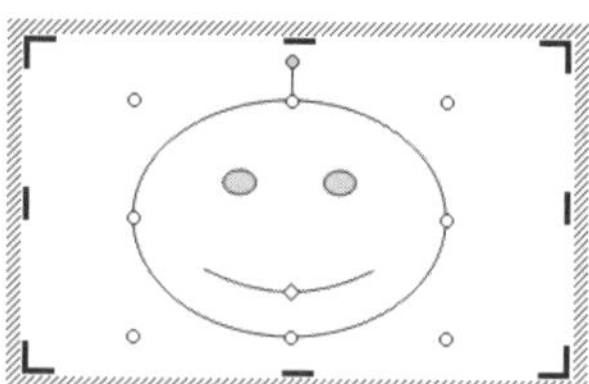

When you click on a graphic you'll see 8 blocks around it: 1 at each corner and 1 at the middle of each side. These are the graphic's control handles, which can be used to change its dimensions.

1. Click on the graphic to make its handles appear.

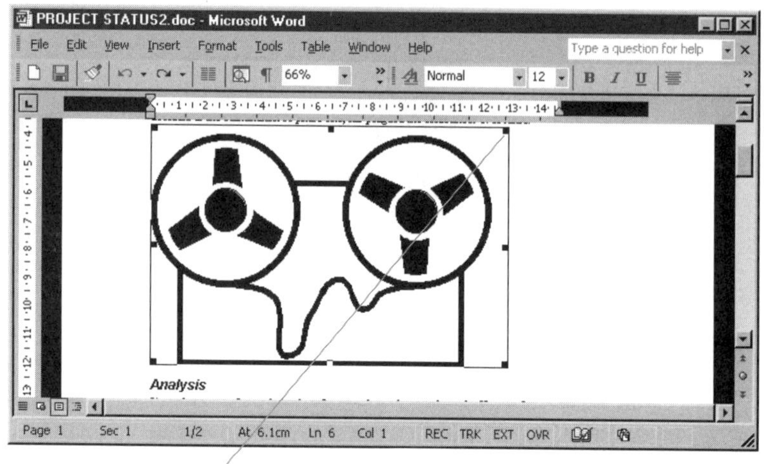

2. Drag on a handle to resize the picture.

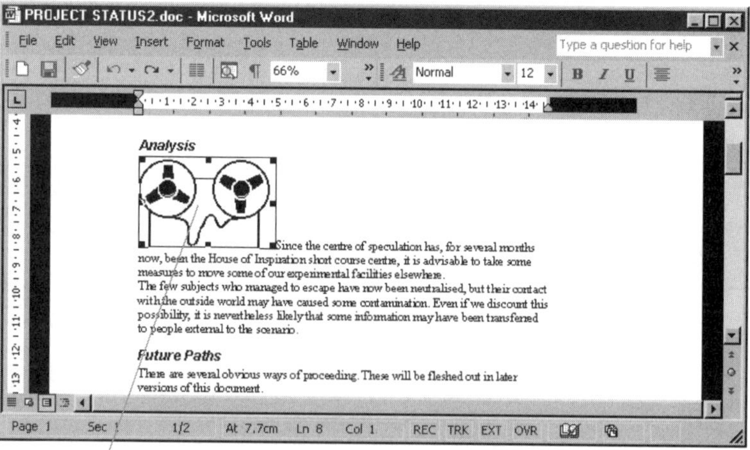

3. To move, drag anywhere within the object.

Note that the graphic is treated like a text item, so when you drag it to a new position, the surrounding text moves to make room.

The Picture Toolbar

The Picture toolbar appears when you insert a picture into a document and provides an easy way of making a wide range of changes to your pictures. Use it for the following functions:

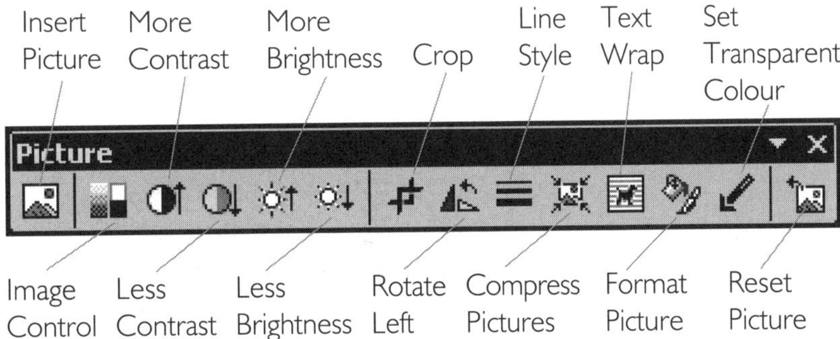

Cropping a Picture

If you want to display only part of an image in your Word document, you should crop it. This cuts away a part of the picture from any of its four sides.

1. Select the image.

2. Click on the Crop icon.

Cropping is non-destructive. This means that you can restore the rest of the picture by dragging the edges back with the Crop tool, or by clicking on the Reset Picture icon.

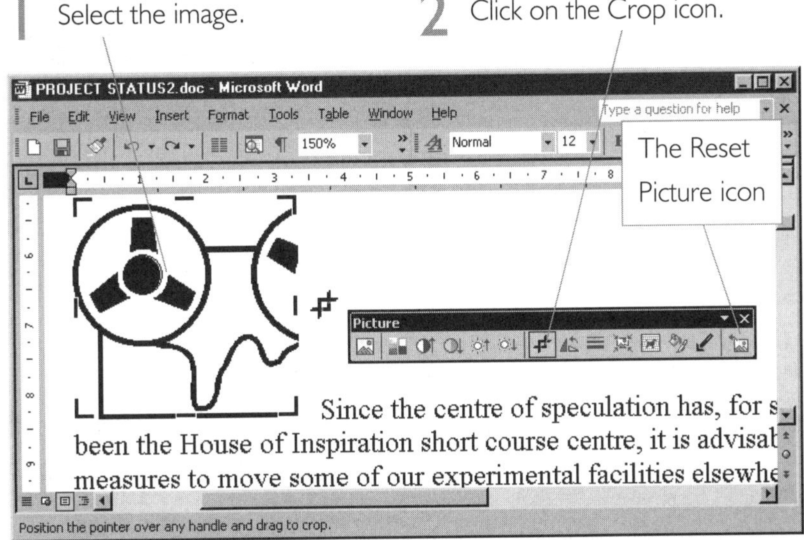

3. Rest your cursor over any of the picture's control handles, then drag the edges to where you want them.

Editing an Imported Picture

Most normal clip art that you import will be in vector format (they'll usually have the .WMF extension), which means that they can be broken down into simple, individual elements which can be edited separately. To edit a vector clip art image, do the following:

1 Right-click on the image and choose Edit Picture.

2 Click Yes.

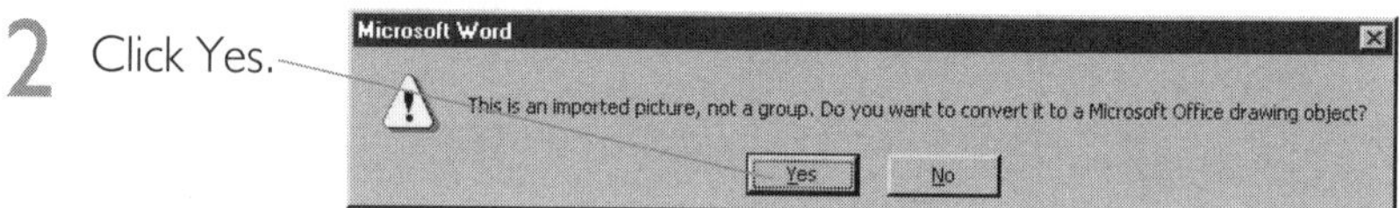

3 The clip art is composed of several different objects which can be selected individually. Click on one then try stretching or deleting it.

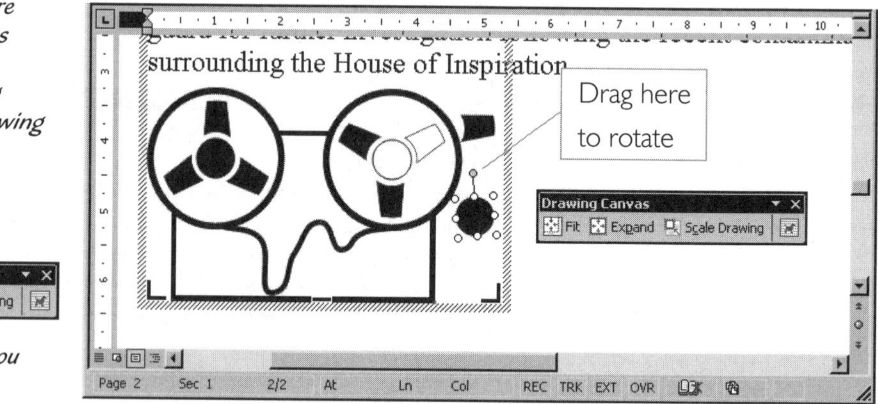

HOT TIP

If you extend the picture beyond its normal bounding rectangle, do the following to reset the picture boundary.

Click here

This also applies if you reduce it in size.

Wrapping Text Around Graphics

When a graphic is inserted into a Word document, it is placed into the text by default as a simple object, on a new line. However, you can very easily change this, so that text wraps around the image in any of a number of ways.

1 Select the picture.

2 Click on the Text Wrap icon in the Picture toolbar, and select how you want the text to wrap around the image.

If the Picture Toolbar is not visible, select Toolbars from the View menu, and choose Picture.

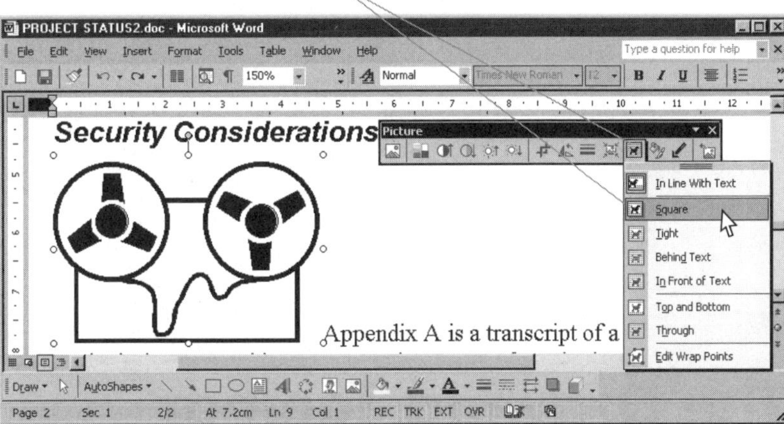

The text now wraps around the image. This is 'Square' wrap: the text wraps around a rectangular area that borders the graphic.

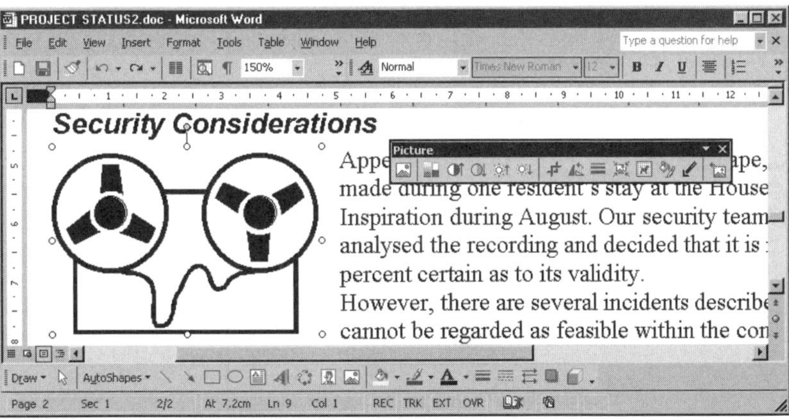

The Format Picture Dialog

From here you can numerically change all the properties of a graphic, including its size, position, text-wrap properties and crop parameters.

1 Select the picture.

2 Choose the Format Picture icon from the Picture toolbar:

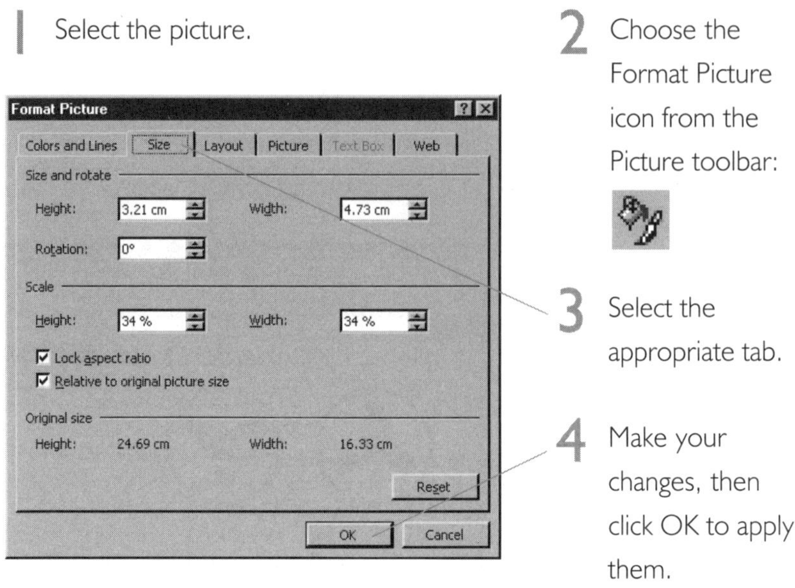

3 Select the appropriate tab.

4 Make your changes, then click OK to apply them.

The Drawing Toolbar

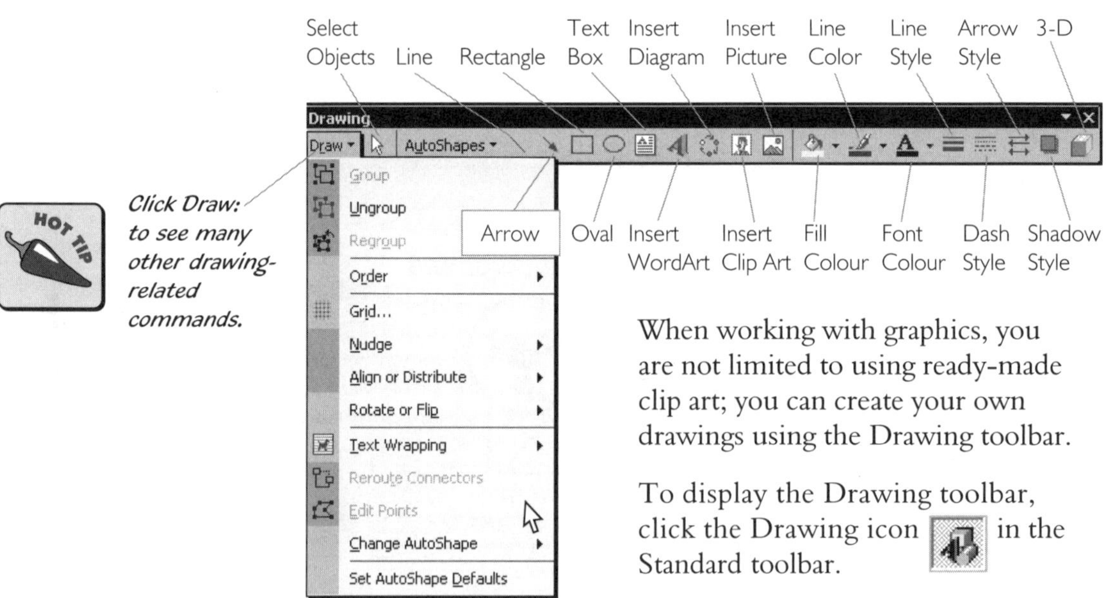

Click Draw: to see many other drawing-related commands.

When working with graphics, you are not limited to using ready-made clip art; you can create your own drawings using the Drawing toolbar.

To display the Drawing toolbar, click the Drawing icon in the Standard toolbar.

Creating Shapes

1 Select the appropriate shape tool.

2 Click and drag within the document to create the shape.

Re step 2 – for lines, drag from one end-point to the other; for boxes and ovals drag diagonally from one corner to the other.

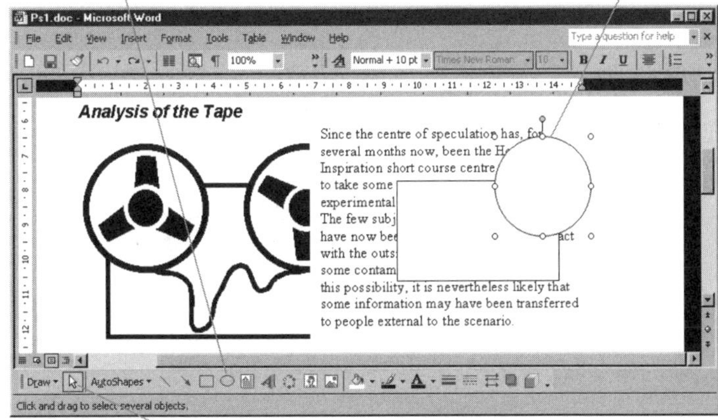

3 Click on a shape with the pointer to select it. Then drag it to another location or resize it by dragging directly on a handle.

Lines and Fills

Click on a shape then use the Fill and Line drop-down menus to select colour, shading and line patterns.

Click on the arrow to the right of the icon to produce the menu.

Click here to add special effects to the object's fill.

These properties can also be changed using the Format AutoShape dialog box: right-click on a shape, then select Format AutoShape from the drop-down menu.

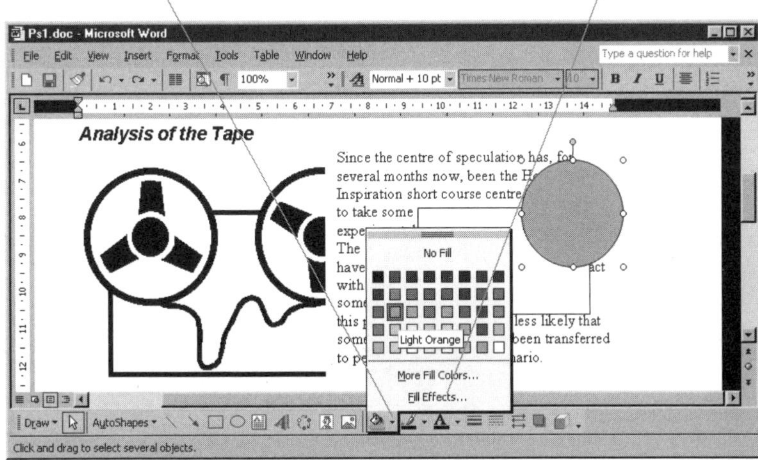

AutoShapes

AutoShapes let you insert common shapes which otherwise might take some time to draw. To insert an AutoShape, do the following:

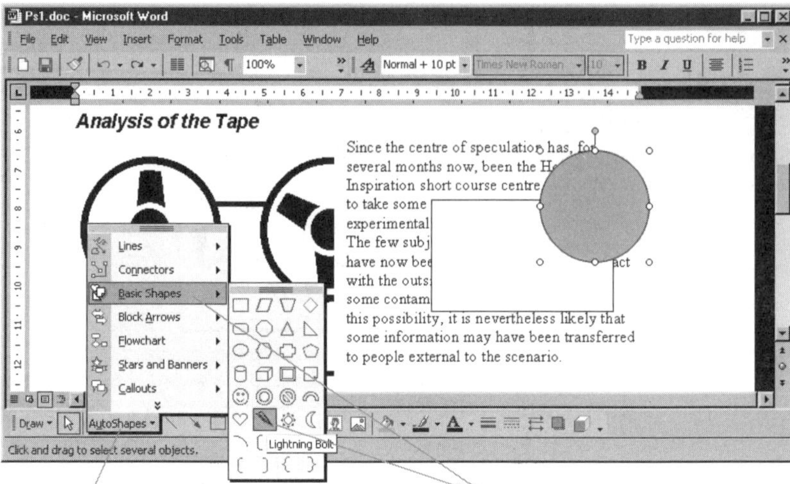

1. Click on the AutoShapes button.
2. Select an AutoShapes category, then click on a specific shape.

If you plan to use several AutoShapes in one session, you can simply drag one of the submenu palettes away from the main menu, to create a floating palette. It will then stay on-screen when the AutoShapes menu disappears.

3. Click in the area of your document where you want the AutoShape to appear.

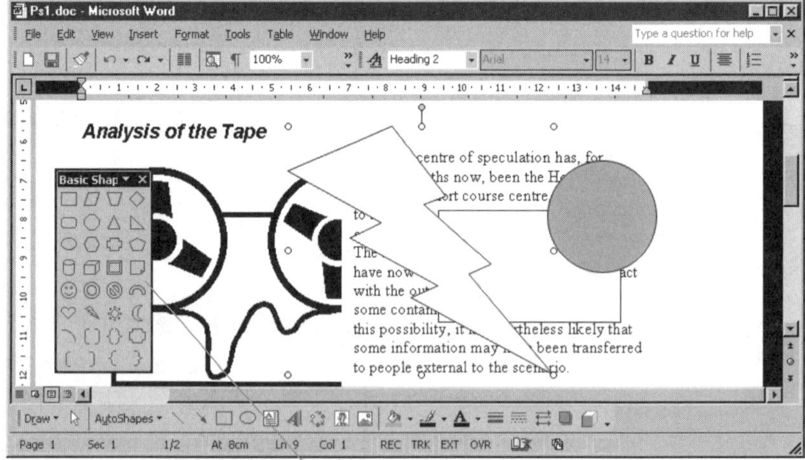

Free-floating Shapes palette

Formatting Shapes

Many objects properties can be amended by accessing the drop-down menus in the Drawing toolbar. However, by right-clicking on a shape you can summon a dialog box that allows you to change many of these properties straightaway. Right-click on the AutoShape whose format you want to change, choose Format AutoShape from the drop-down menu, then select the appropriate tab.

To set the properties for more than one shape, you should first select all the shapes you want to change. To do this, you have two options:

- *click successively on each object while holding down the Shift button, or:*
- *click in the document area and drag a selection box around all of the objects.*

Once all the objects are selected, change the properties as you would for a single object (e.g., right-click on any object, then select Format AutoShape from the drop-down menu).

The Colors and Lines Tab

Use this to set the shape's fill and line attributes.

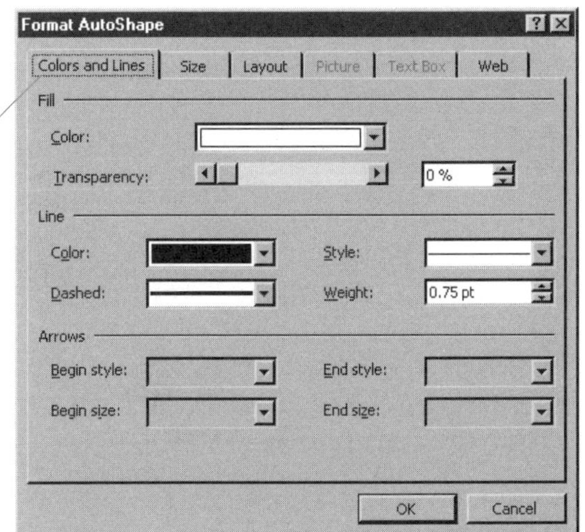

The Size Tab

Use this to set the shape's dimensions, scale properties and rotation value.

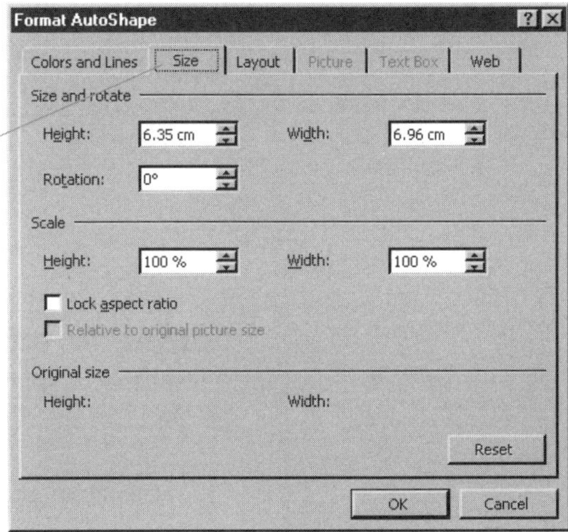

The Layout Tab

From here you can control the way text wraps around the AutoShape.

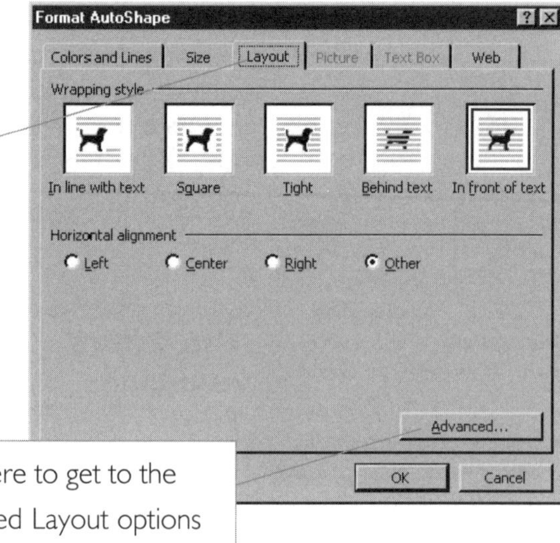

Click here to get to the Advanced Layout options

Advanced Layout

Here you can set the coordinates used to determine the object's precise position on the page.

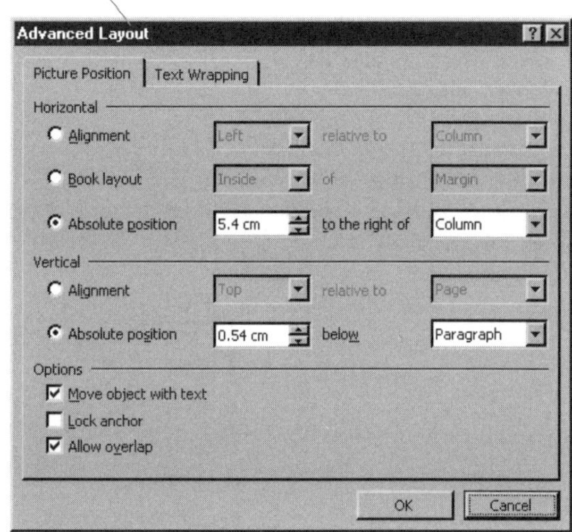

Setting AutoShape Defaults

To set the properties that all AutoShapes will have when they are created, do the following:

1. Format an existing AutoShape using the Drawing toolbar or the Format AutoShape dialog.
2. Right-click on the shape, then select Set AutoShape Defaults.

Changing Object Order

When you place a new image or shape in a document, it appears in front of all the other objects. To change the relative order of objects subsequently, select the object(s) to move, then...

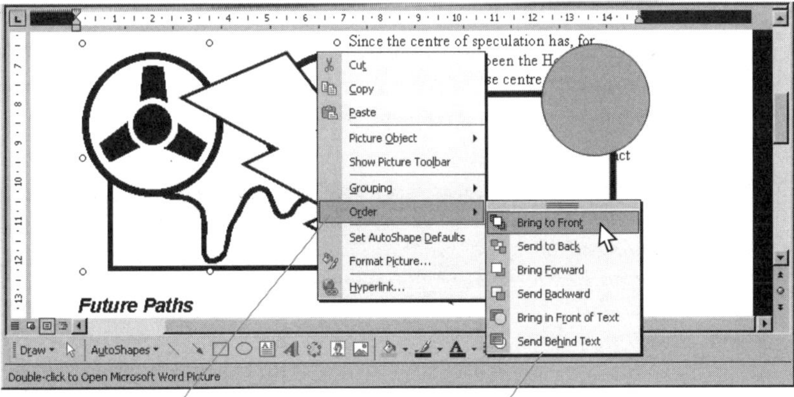

1 Right-click on a shape and choose Order from the drop-down menu.

2 Choose to send the object in front of or behind all other objects, or to move it just one step.

Sending Objects Behind the Text Layer

By default, all graphic objects appear in front of the text in your document. However, you can send objects behind the text by selecting Send Behind Text from the menu shown above.

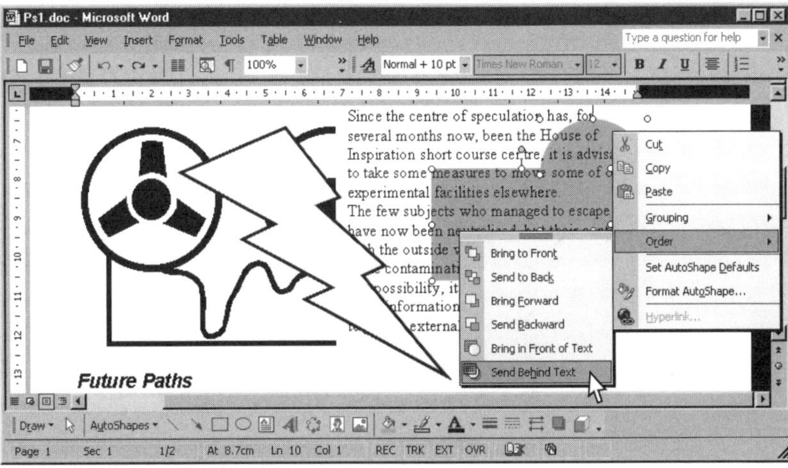

Grouping and Ungrouping

Once you have placed several objects in your Word document, you may no longer need to treat them separately, but might benefit from treating them as a single object which can be moved and modified easily. To do this, you can group the objects, as follows:

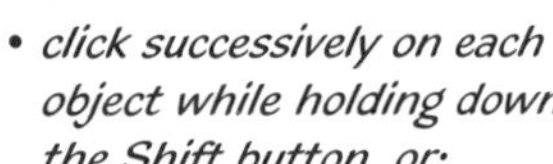

There are two basic ways of selecting a series of objects:

- *click successively on each object while holding down the Shift button, or;*
- *click in a vacant part of the document area and drag a selection box around all of the objects.*

1 Select all of the objects that you want to be grouped together.

2 Choose Group in the Draw menu in the Drawing toolbar.

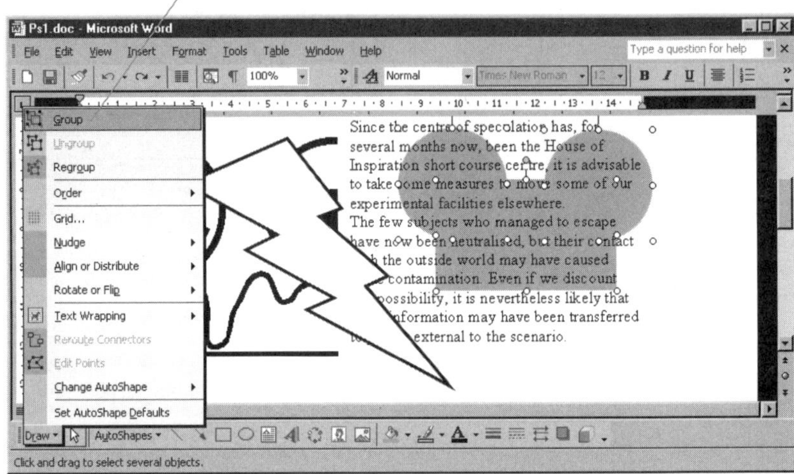

Any changes to the group are applied to all the grouped objects:

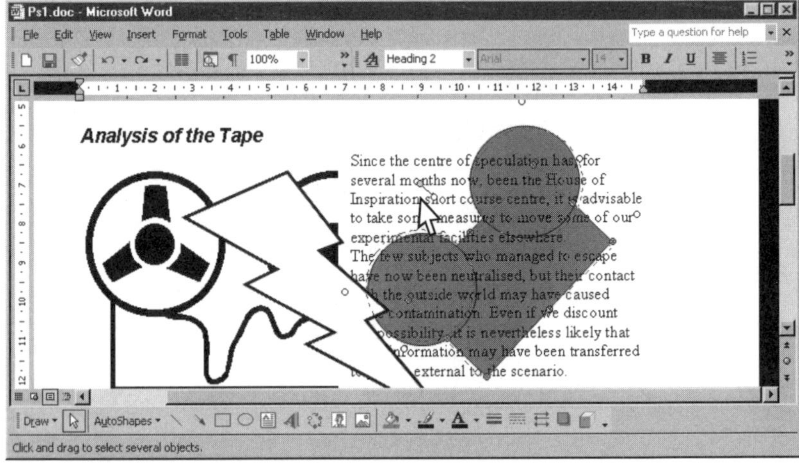

WordArt

WordArt is a tool you can use to apply a wide range of special graphical effects to text that you use in your Word documents. The objects created by WordArt are treated not as plain text but as drawing objects, so they can be manipulated further with the tools from the Drawing toolbar. To use WordArt, do the following:

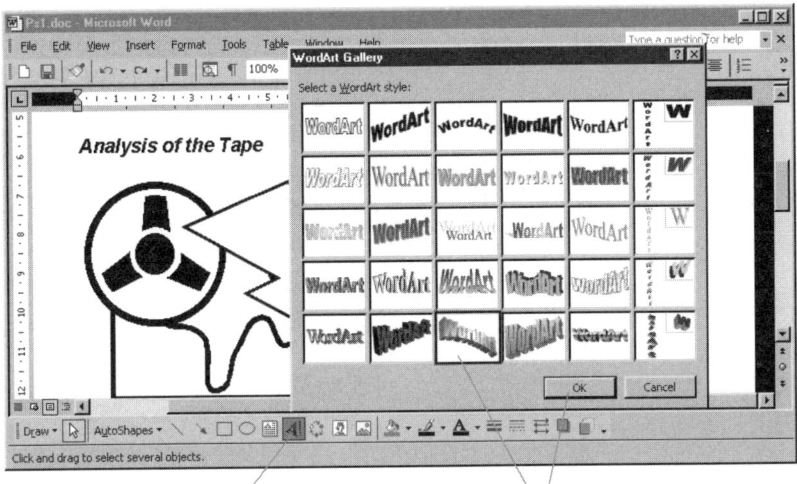

1 Click on the WordArt button in the Drawing toolbar.

2 Select a style (you can change it later) then OK.

3 Enter your text here, then click OK.

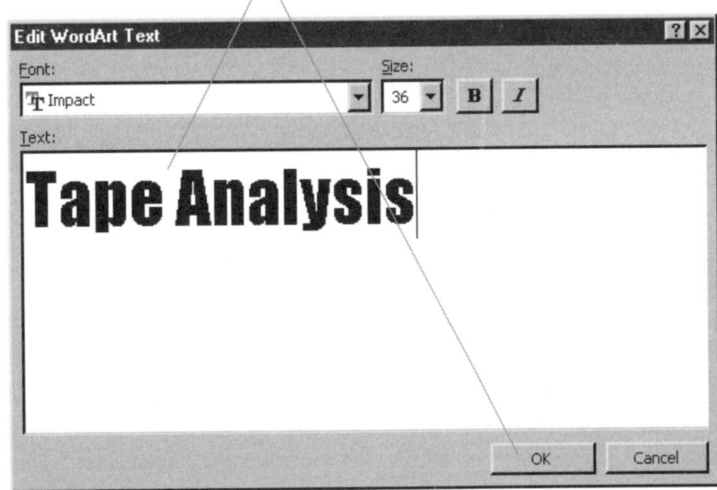

The WordArt object is placed, and can now be edited:

4 Click on the text and drag it to the desired position.

5 Drag on the text's control handles to resize it.

6 Drag the yellow handles to alter the effect's attributes.

The floating WordArt toolbar appears whenever you select a WordArt object. You can use it for the following functions:

When you select the Change shape icon, you are presented with a palette containing 40 different text shapes. This offers a wider range of shapes than the Gallery:

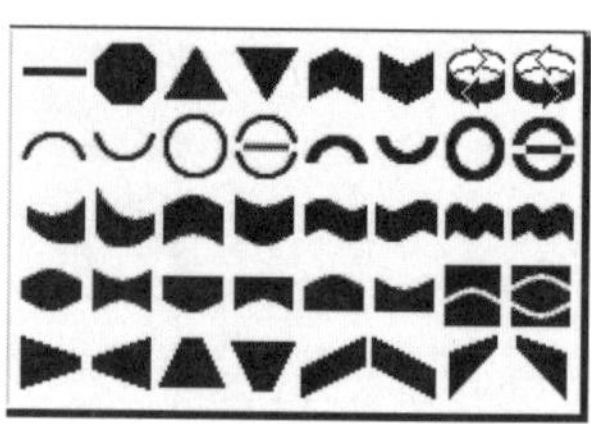

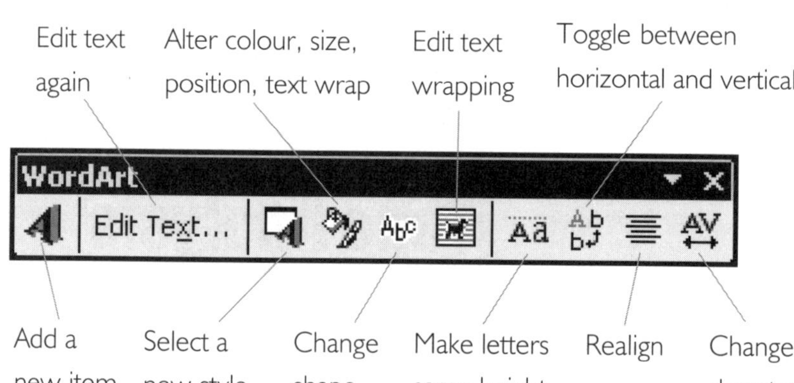

Tables and Charts

Tables allow you to organise and manage text in rows and columns. Charts provide a valuable way of presenting numeric table information in pictorial form, making statistical information much easier to understand.

Covers

Chapter Eleven

Inserting a Table

If you want to insert a simple table with more than five columns or four rows, select Insert Table from the Table menu. This will summon a dialog box, where you can specify the table's dimensions.

If you want to insert a simple table of no more than five columns and four rows you can use the Table icon in the Standard toolbar.

1 Place the insertion point on a blank line in the document.

2 Click on the Table icon in the Standard toolbar and, in the drop-down table box, drag downwards and to the right.

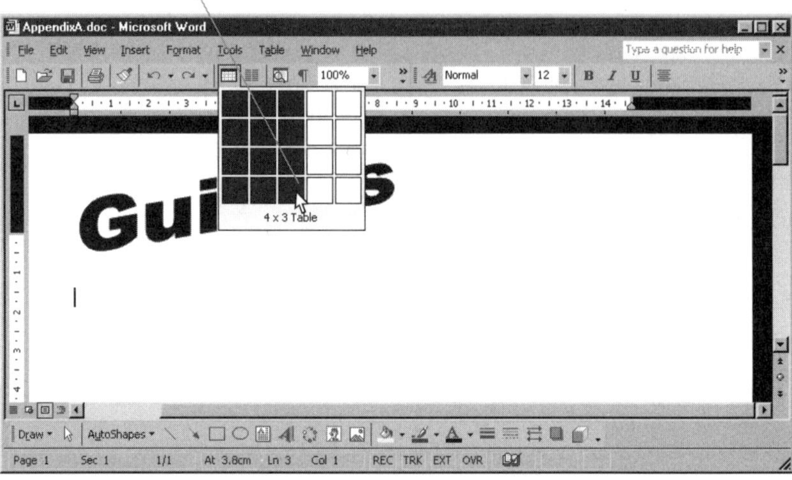

You can resize a column by moving your mouse pointer to the border between the columns: it will turn into a black double-headed arrow:

You can resize rows in the same way.

The further you drag, the larger the table. In this case a table of 4 rows and 3 columns is being created. The table is inserted into your document:

Hold down the Alt key while dragging a column or row to see the measurements in the ruler.

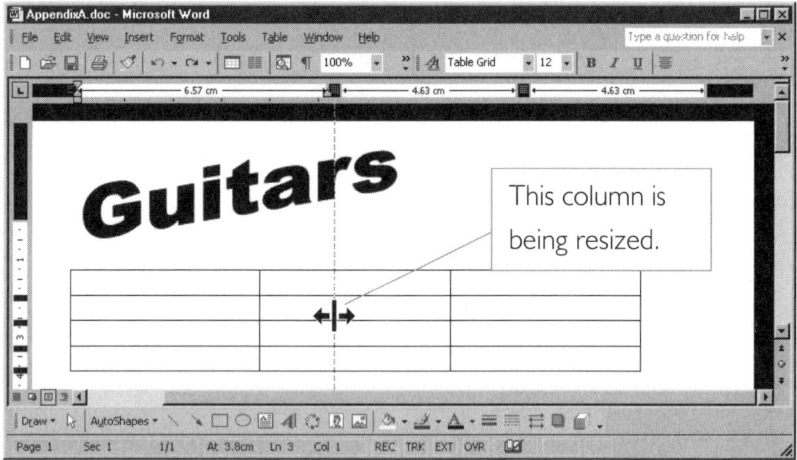

Drawing a Table

Word 2002 offers an alternative method to create tables. The Draw Table tool lets you draw a table directly into your document without using dialogs or drop-down boxes.

1 Select Table>Draw Table to run the Tables and Borders Toolbar

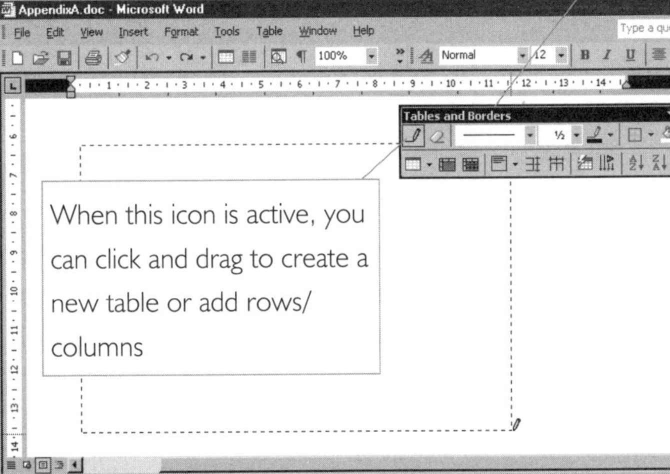

There is an alternative way to begin drawing a table and specify the width of its columns visually: in normal text-entry mode, enter a line using plus and minus symbols, like this:

---+------+------+

When you press Return, Word will automatically convert this into the first line of a table, the plus signs becoming column boundaries.

If this doesn't work, select Tools>AutoCorrect, choose the AutoFormat As You Type tab, and check the Tables box.

2 Your pointer will turn into a pencil shape (if not then make sure that the Draw Table tool is active). Drag an initial shape for the table within your document.

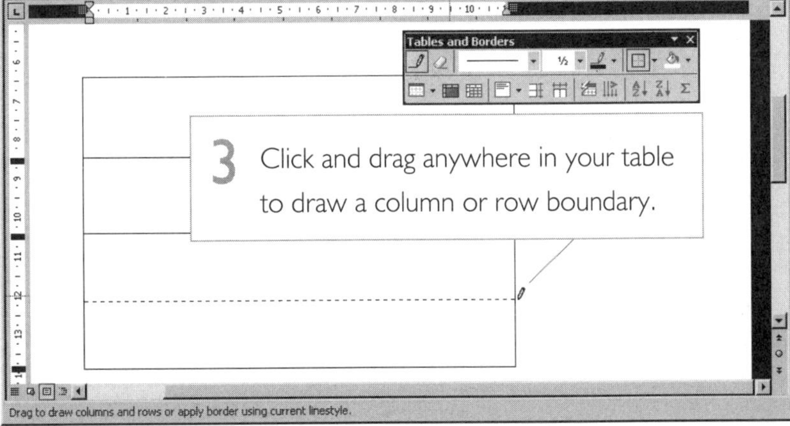

Drawing Diagonal Table Lines

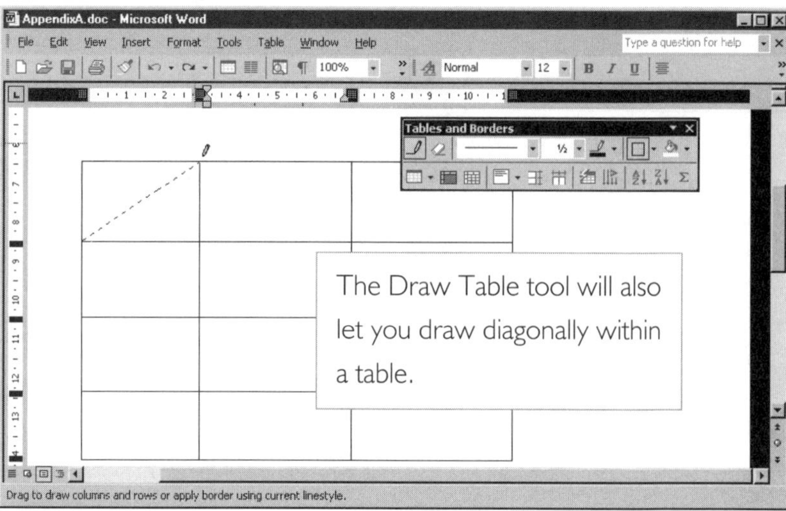

Erasing Table Lines

1 Click on the Eraser tool in the Tables and Borders palette. Your cursor turns into an eraser shape.

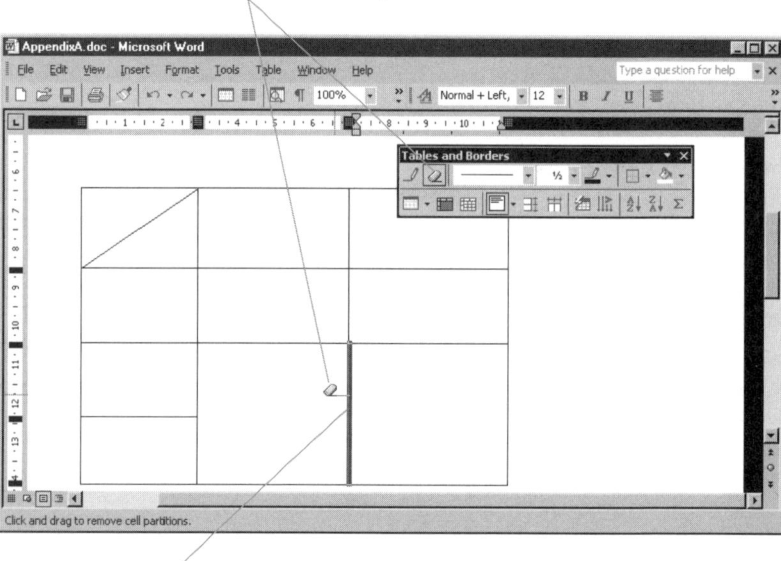

2 Click directly on a line within the table to make it disappear.

Creating Irregular Tables

The table drawing tools make it easy to create irregularly structured tables.

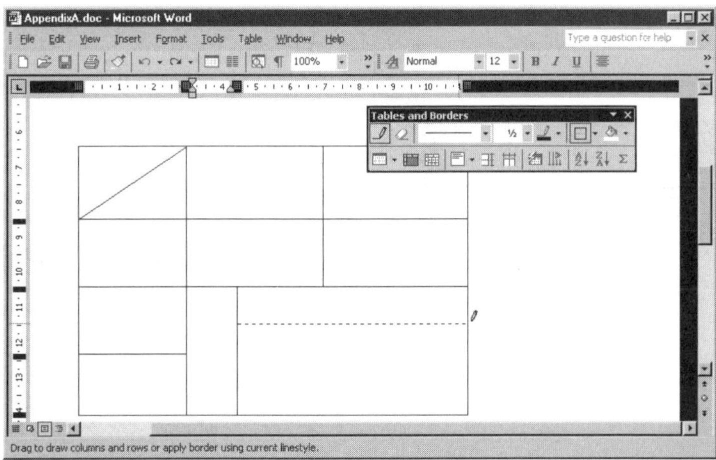

Entering Text

You can add text to your table by clicking in each cell in turn. All the normal formatting commands still apply.

If you actually need to enter a Tab character within a table's cell, press Control+Tab.

A quick way to get to the next cell is to press Tab. Shift + Tab takes you back to the previous cell.

You can have more than one line within each cell. The Table row will expand to accommodate any extra text.

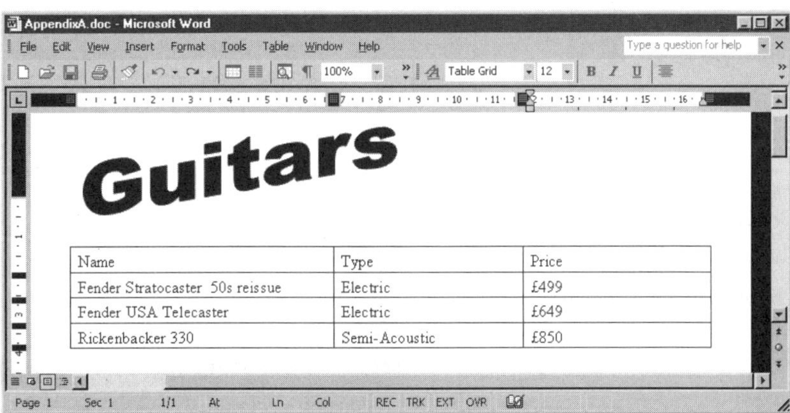

Formatting

You can format the contents of a whole row or column – or several rows or columns – at once. To select a row, drag across it, or click in the space just to its left.

The same applies to columns. To select, click slightly above the top cell of the column.

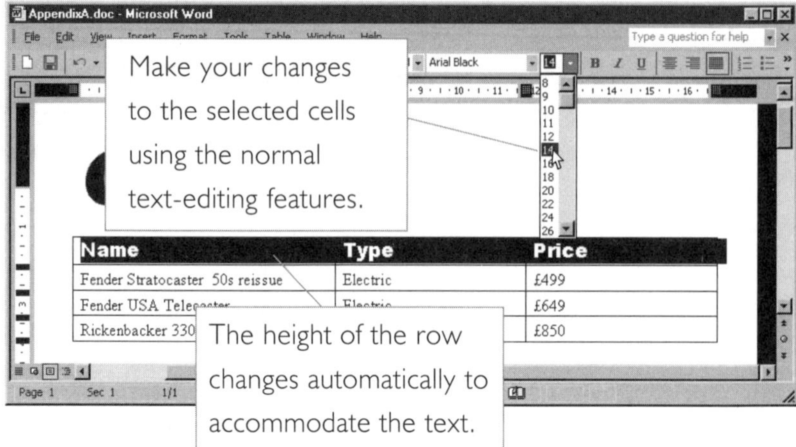

Inserting a Row/Column

To insert a row into an existing table, do the following:

To add a column, first select the column to the right of where you want to insert.

1. Select the line below where you want the new row.
2. Click the right mouse button on the selected row, and choose Insert Rows from the drop-down menu.

To insert multiple columns or rows, select the amount of columns/rows you want inserted before right-clicking.

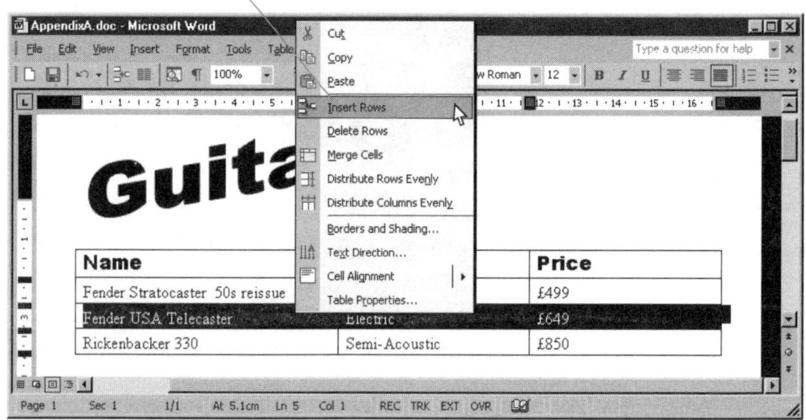

Cutting and Pasting

1. Select the row/column or cells.

2. Right-click on the selected cells and choose Cut from the drop-down menu.

3. Select the destination row/column or cells.

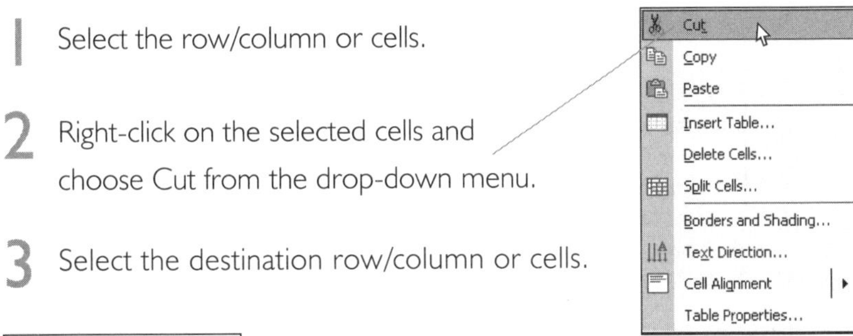

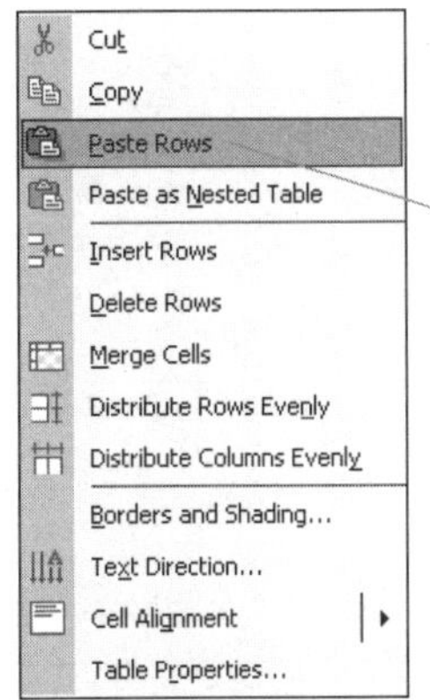

4. Right click on the selected cells and choose Paste... from the drop-down menu.

The text is pasted back into the table, immediately above the selected row, or to the left of the selected column.

Merging Cells

Any number of adjacent cells can be merged to create a single cell. Select the cells and then choose Table>Merge Cells.

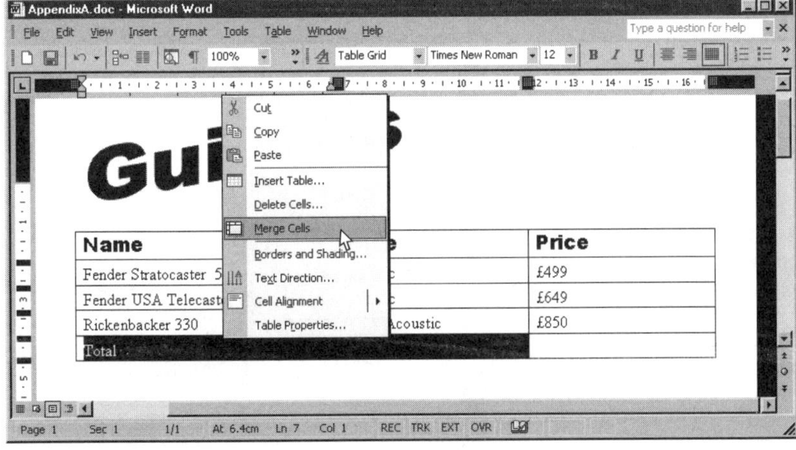

Controlling Height and Width

To select an entire table, choose Select, then Table from the Table menu, or type Alt + Numeric keypad '5' with Num Lock turned off.

1. Select the cell(s) to change, or the entire table.
2. Choose Table Properties from the Table menu, or by right-clicking.
3. Click on the Row tab, then the Column tab to see all the options available.

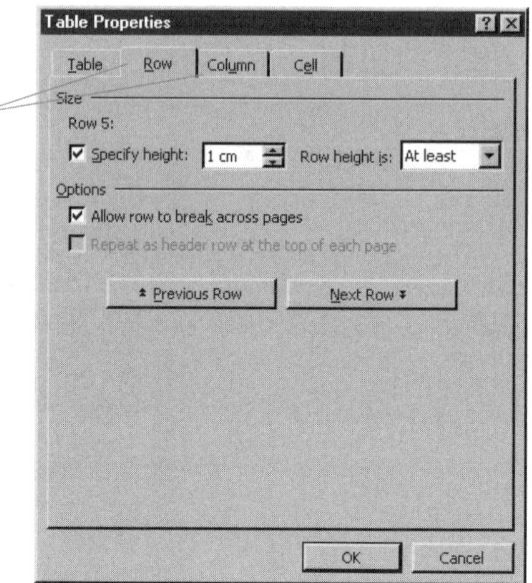

4. The Table Tab will let you set properties such as overall size, alignment and text wrap behaviour.

Nested Tables

It is also possible to insert a table within another table. You can draw the inner table in the normal way with the Draw Table tool:

Another way to create a nested table is to right-click on the destination cell and choose Insert Table. You can also cut, copy and paste entire tables.

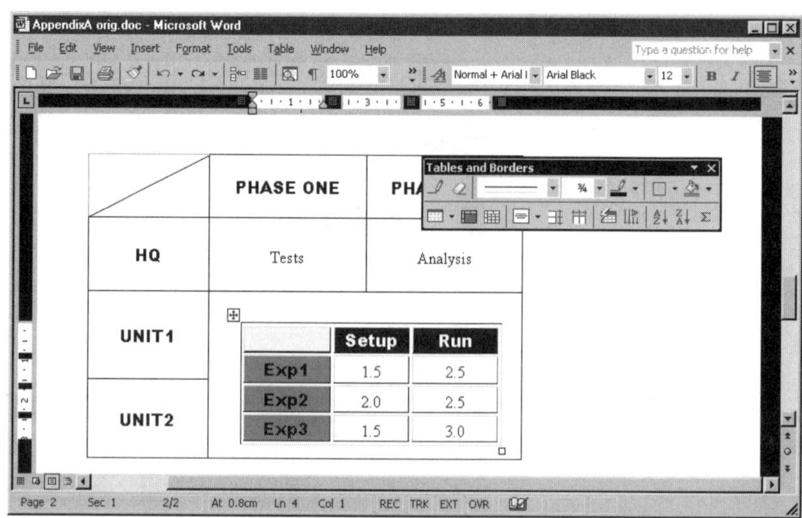

Formulae

If you want one cell of a table to display a number derived from a calculation (based on the numeric contents of other cells), Word can insert a code to perform this task automatically. Here, we want to total the price of the three guitars in the table.

For the Sum function to work properly, all rows above the current cell must have the same number of columns. If you merged the cells for the last example, you will need to split them again (choose Split Cells from the Table menu).

1 Click in the cell which is the destination for the calculation, and choose Formula from the Table menu.

2 Enter the formula or select from the list of Paste functions. Word correctly suggests the =SUM(ABOVE) function, which adds up the contents of the cells above the destination cell.

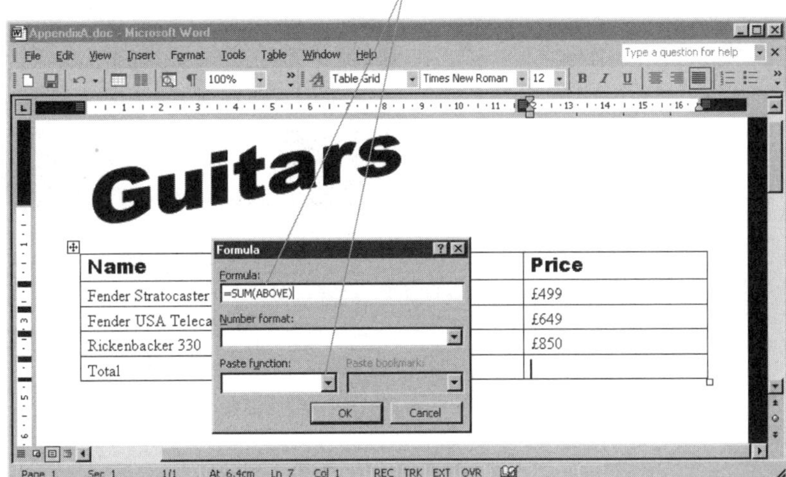

Unlike a spreadsheet (such as Excel), Word does not automatically update the contents of cells containing a formula when the values of cells used in the equation are changed. To update a formula, right-click on the cell and choose Update Field from the drop-down menu.

3 Click OK. The total is displayed in the destination cell:

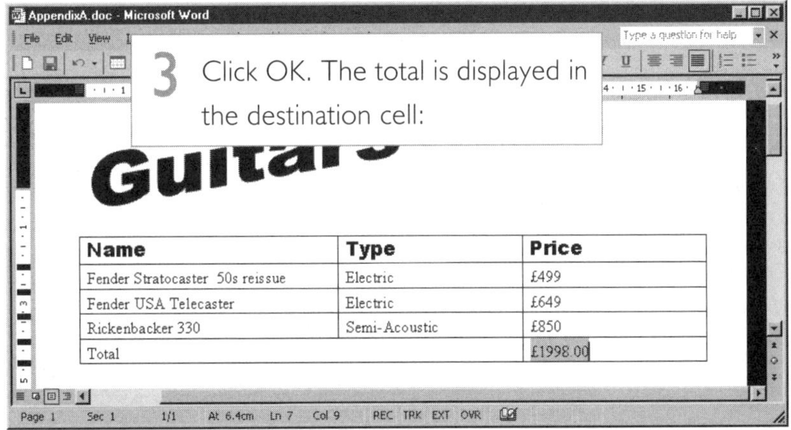

Borders and Shading

Word allows you to enhance your tables very easily using the Borders and Shading dialog. To use it, do the following:

1. Select either the entire table or just a range of cells.

2. Right-click on the selected cells and choose Borders and Shading from the drop-down menu.

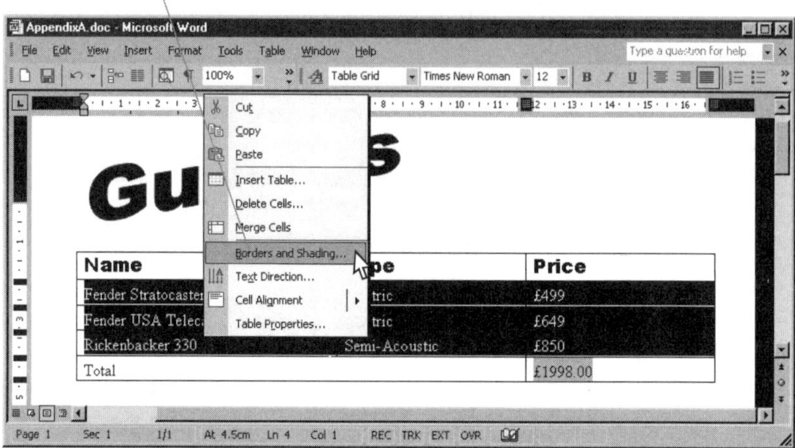

3. If necessary, activate the Borders tab and choose your borders options.

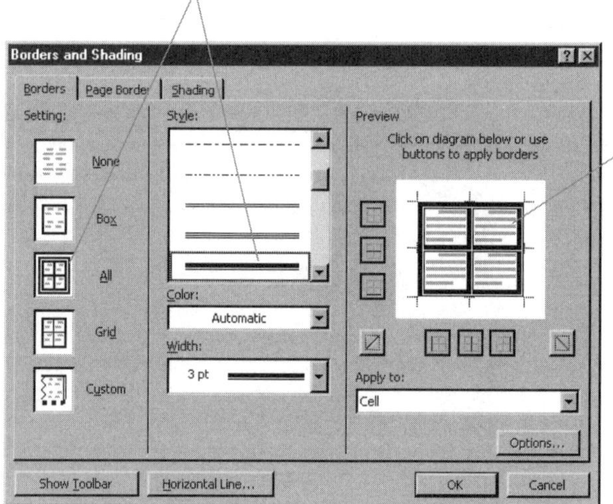

You can click various parts of this diagram to activate perimeter and internal lines.

4 Now click on the Shading tab and set your shading preferences.

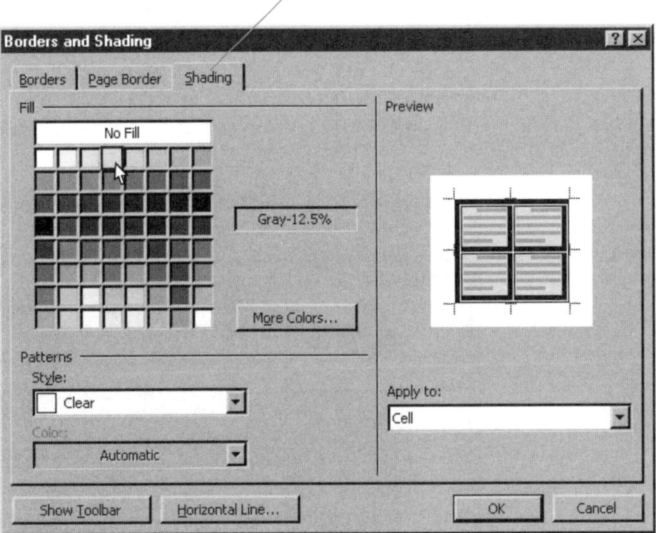

5 Click OK. Your selected cells now have a border and shading applied:

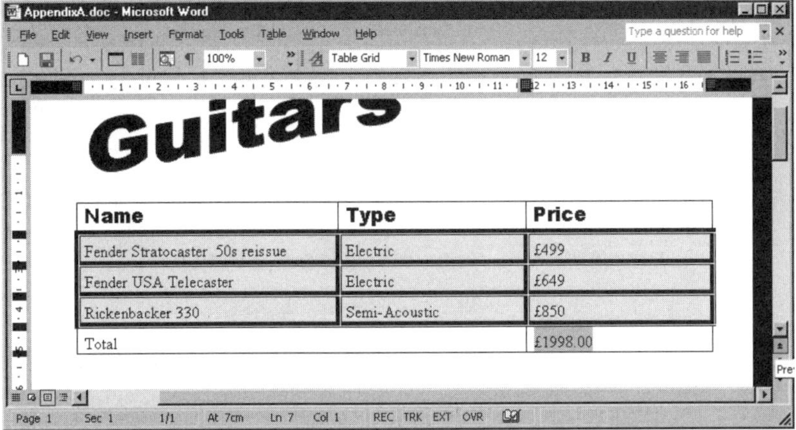

In the example above, the Borders and Shading dialog box has been used to alter the style of all the lines in the selected area, and to give those cells a fill of 12.5% grey.

Table AutoFormat

As an alternative to defining the format piece by piece (i.e. specifying the font, borders, shading, etc.), Word allows you to apply many different pre-defined formats to existing tables.

1. Select the table.
2. Choose Table AutoFormat from the Table menu, or click on this button:

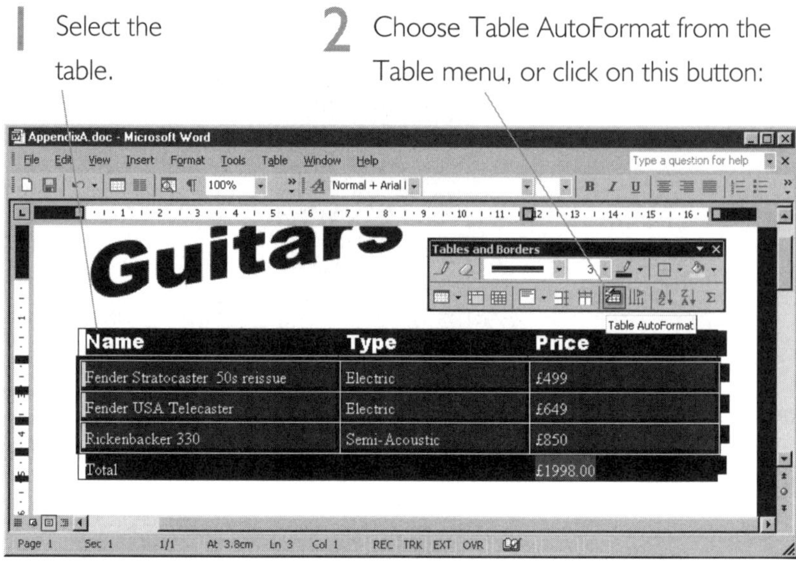

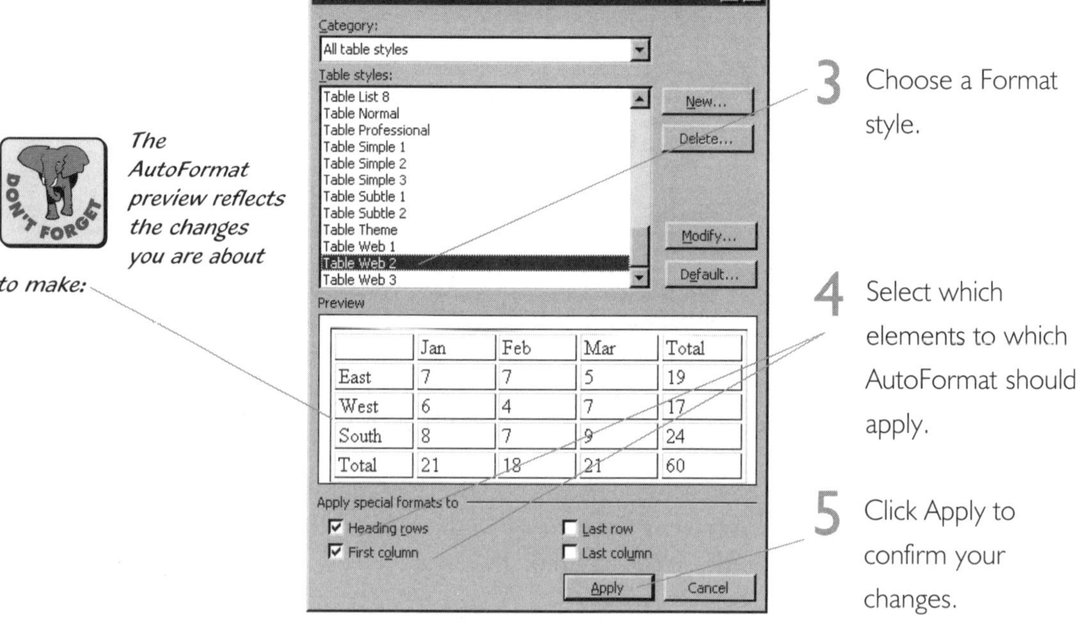

3. Choose a Format style.
4. Select which elements to which AutoFormat should apply.
5. Click Apply to confirm your changes.

The AutoFormat preview reflects the changes you are about to make:

The changes just specified are applied automatically to your table:

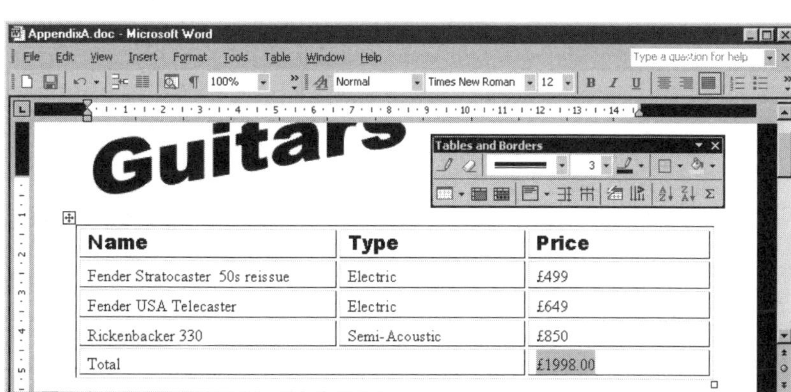

Name	Type	Price
Fender Stratocaster 50s reissue	Electric	£499
Fender USA Telecaster	Electric	£649
Rickenbacker 330	Semi-Acoustic	£850
Total		£1998.00

The Tables and Borders Toolbar

You can use the Tables and Borders toolbar to make many of the formatting changes that we have discussed earlier in this chapter. If it is not already activated, select View>Toolbars>Tables and Borders, or click on the appropriate icon in the Standard toolbar:

The Tables and Borders toolbar offers the following functions:

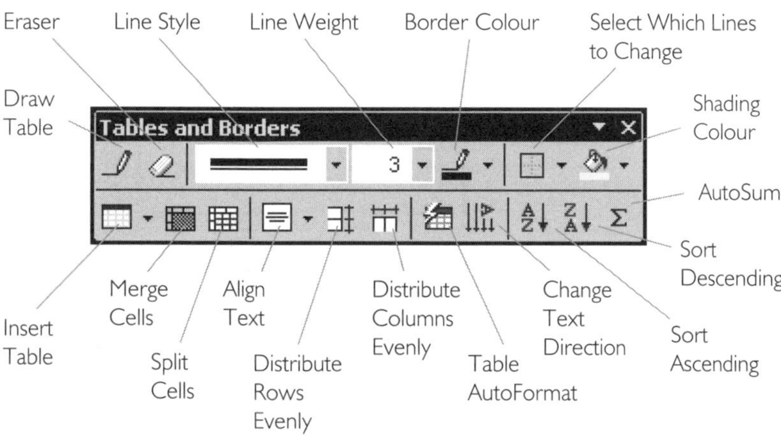

Graphics within Tables

With Word you can paste or insert graphics directly into cells. Once there you can right click on the graphic and choose Format Picture to control properties such as text wrap. In the example below text and graphics coexist within the same cell.

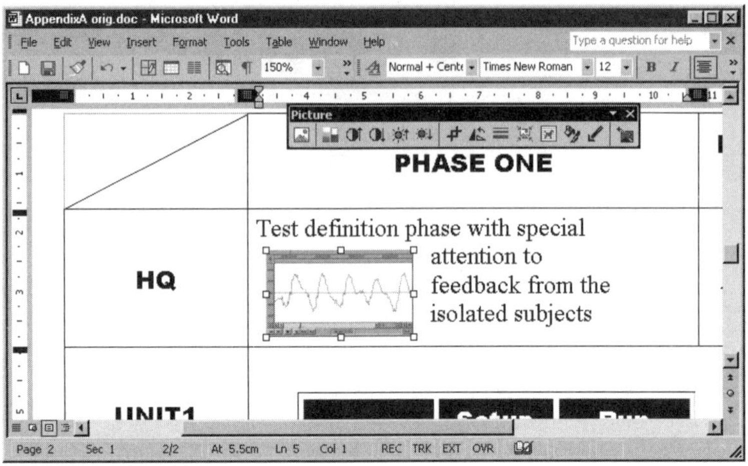

Text Wrap around Tables

If you right click on a table and choose Table Properties, you can control how text wraps around the table itself. In the example below a text wrap setting of Around allows the table to be included within the main text area.

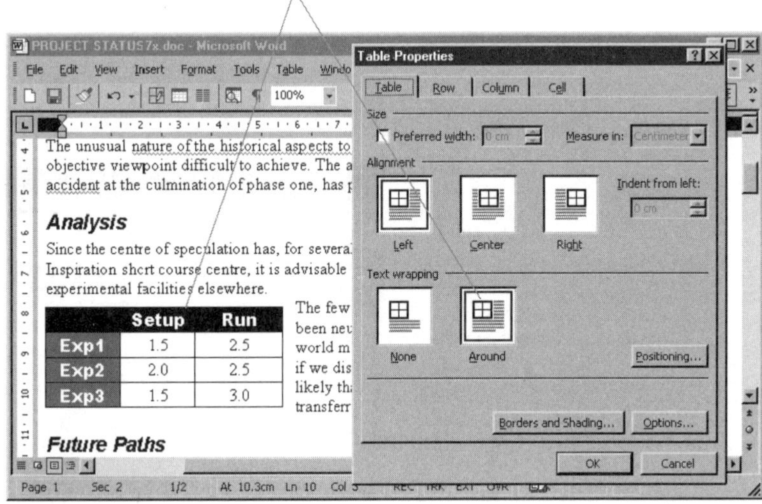

Creating a Chart from a Table

You can use the Microsoft Graph feature to convert a table you have created into an attractive chart.

1 Select the data in the table.

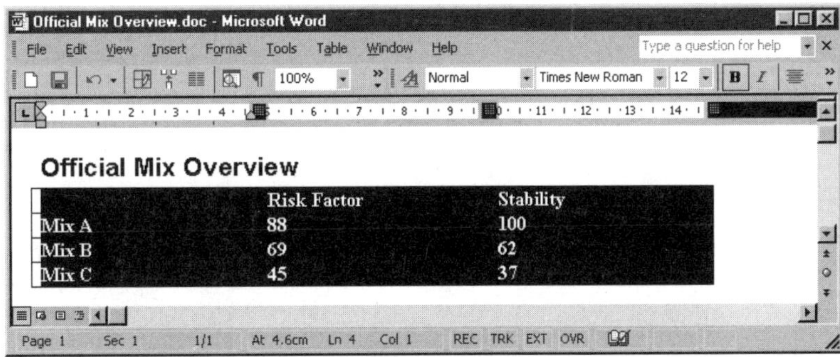

2 Choose Object from the Insert Menu.

3 Choose Microsoft Graph Chart from the Create New tab of the Object dialog, then click OK.

Microsoft Graph automatically generates a suitable graph based on your data, and places it in your document:

You can also activate the Chart application by clicking on the Chart tool:

If this is not visible, then right-click on a toolbar and choose Customise. The Chart icon is available under the Insert category. From here you can drag it onto any toolbar.

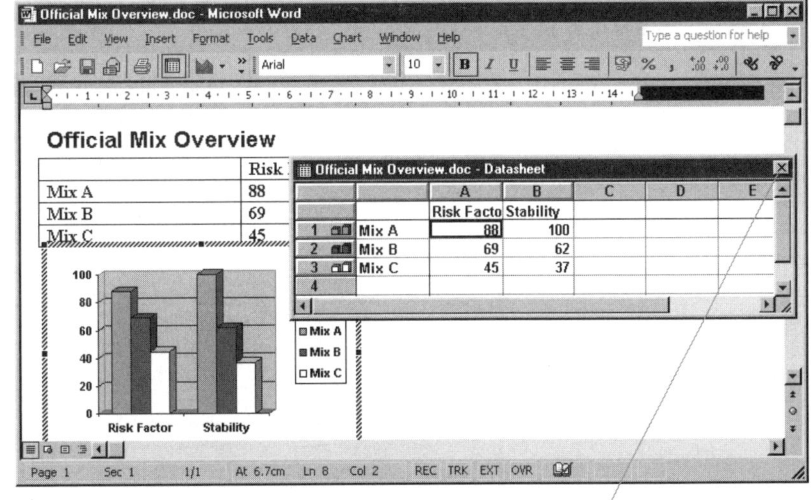

4 If you don't want to amend your data yet, close this window.

Formatting a Chart

Once your chart is in your document, you can very easily edit it to amend the format that Microsoft Graph applied by default.

1 Double-click on the chart to edit it. A striped border appears around it and special Microsoft Graph icons appear in the toolbar.

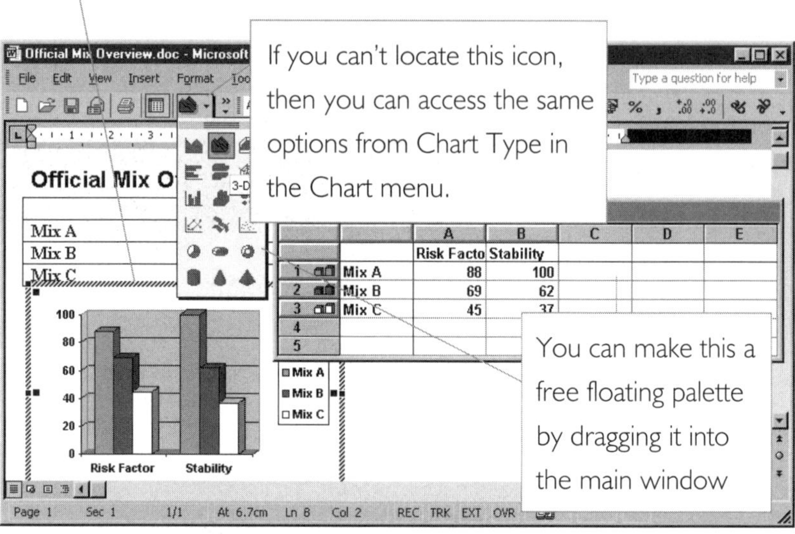

2 To change the type of chart, click on the arrow to the right of the Chart type icon and select an option from the palette.

Microsoft Graph uses two main windows, one for the data and one for the chart itself. You can turn the Datasheet on and off using the View menu, or the Datasheet icon on the toolbar:

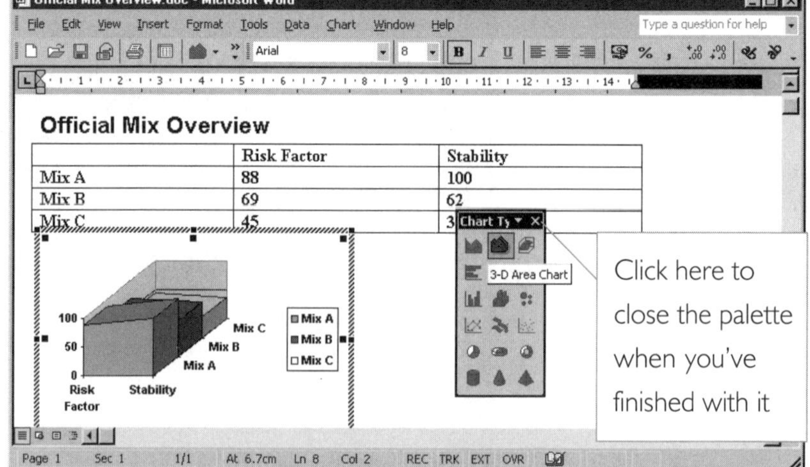

3 To change the properties of a 3D graph, rest your cursor over the chart area until the Chart Area bubble appears, then right-click.

You can change the number format of any of the data used in your chart. Simply select the relevant cells then choose Number from the Format menu.

4 In the drop-down menu that appears, select 3-D View.

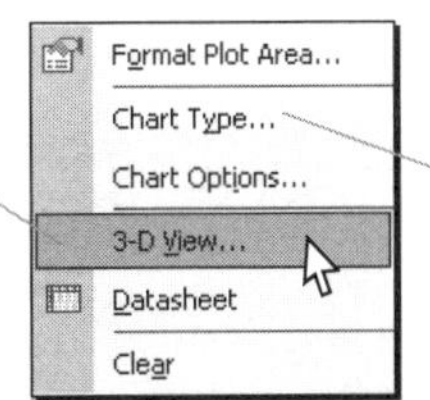

Clicking here would produce a dialog that offers an alternative way of selecting the chart type from the method in step 2.

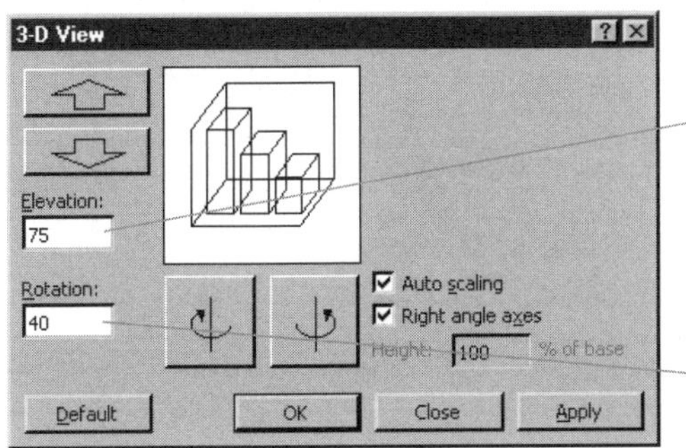

5 Type here to change the elevation of the view.

6 Type here to change the degree of rotation.

When changing the format of a chart, always use the bubbles that appear when you rest your cursor over a chart area. You can then be sure that you are about to format the area that you mean to, before you double-click or right-click on it.

7 To change the properties of a chart element, double-click on it. Here, the font properties of the axis legends are being changed.

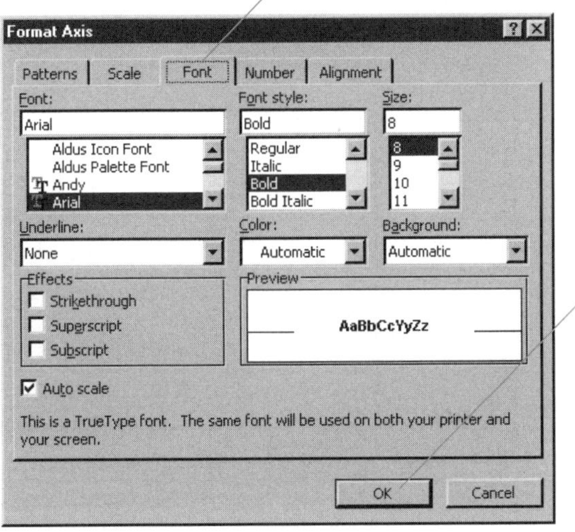

8 Click OK to apply your changes.

Importing Data into a Chart

If there is no striped border around the chart, then double-click directly on it. This will open the chart for editing.

To import data from an external source into a chart, make sure that it is open for editing (it will have a striped border around it, and the Microsoft Graph toolbar will be visible), then do the following:

1. Select Import File from the Edit menu.

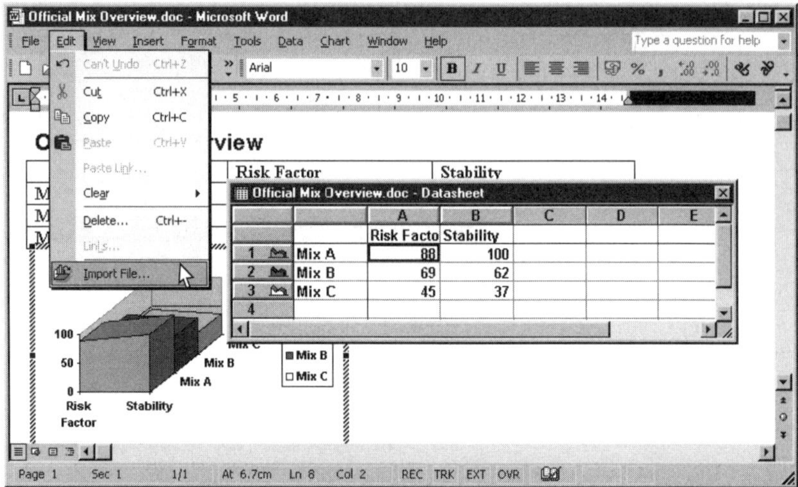

When you are working on a chart, you are effectively using the Microsoft Graph application. This means that the menu options and toolbar icons that you see are relevant only to Microsoft Graph.

To exit this mode and return to the normal Word environment, simply click your cursor anywhere outside the chart area; the Word toolbars and menu options will then return.

2. In the Import File dialog, select the file you want to import, then click Open.

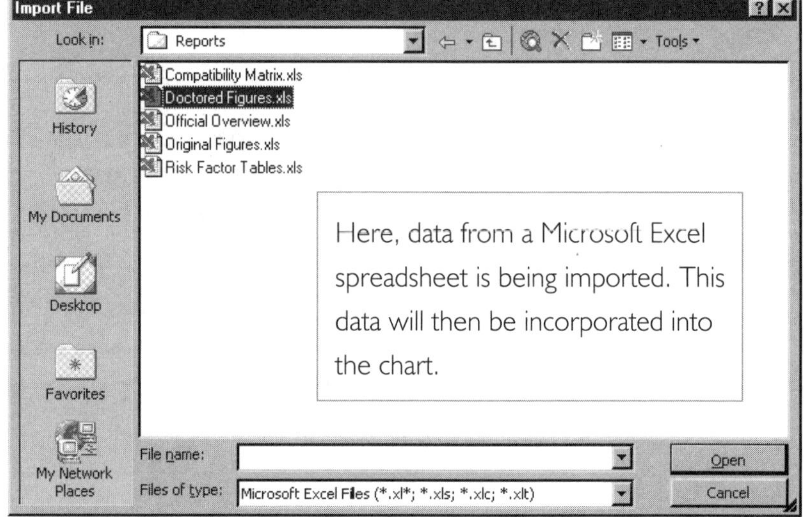

Web-based Documents

HTML is a native file format to Word 2002.

There are many new features relating to the Internet and documents intended for viewing online. Items normally present in web pages, such as hyperlinks, can be incorporated into standard Word documents allowing instant access to files stored locally or anywhere on the Internet. Word 2002 allows automatic editing of HTML web pages using an intuitive drag-and-drop interface.

The Web Page Wizard will even automatically set up a structure and basic functionality for your pages.

Covers

Chapter Twelve

Introduction

In the past, word-processors were used as tools for producing pure text documents and little else. Recent years have seen popular word-processors become embellished with new graphically-oriented features, which previously would have been found only in high-end desktop publishing packages.

Until recently, the aim of most people using a word-processor was to produce something that would ultimately be output on paper. However, the growing importance of the Internet and Intranet environments has seen a change in this situation. Communication which was once conducted on paper is increasingly being carried out in a purely electronic medium.

This electronic communication is carried out in a variety of forms. The World Wide Web is a vast resource containing endless linked pages, with text and pictures on virtually any topic imaginable. Until recently email had been restricted to text, and is essentially a means of communicating with a more restricted set of people.

However, these boundaries are beginning to be blurred. Word, for example, allows you to create an electronic document which is not simply text but which may contain:

- animations
- pictures
- sounds
- videos
- links to other documents or web pages

In fact, any document which you create in Word (or in any element of Office XP) may be placed on the web. You can even use Word as your primary means of composing/editing email messages.

Word also allows you to create web pages in the web's native format, HTML (HyperText Mark-up Language), without having to learn the many HTML codes. You can either use the Web Page Wizard to create a new set of HTML documents quickly and easily, or you can convert an existing Word document.

Using the Web Page Wizard

The Web Page Wizard is the most effective way to create a HTML document; it offers more control over the finished product than converting an existing document. To launch it, do the following:

1 Select New from the File menu. Click on General Templates in the Task Pane.

2 Select the Web Pages tab.

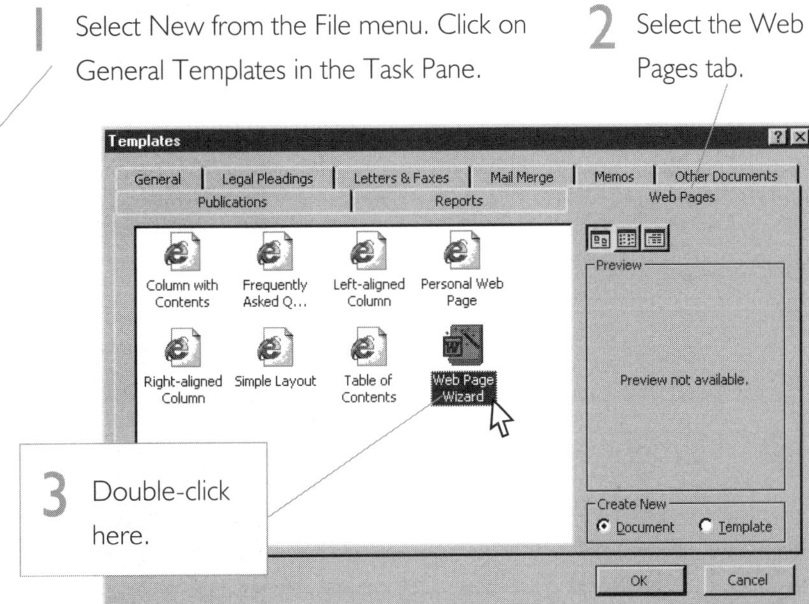

3 Double-click here.

The Web Page Wizard dialog appears. This will guide you through five steps, asking questions about your planned document.

You can jump to any page by clicking any chart icon. The green box tells you where you are.

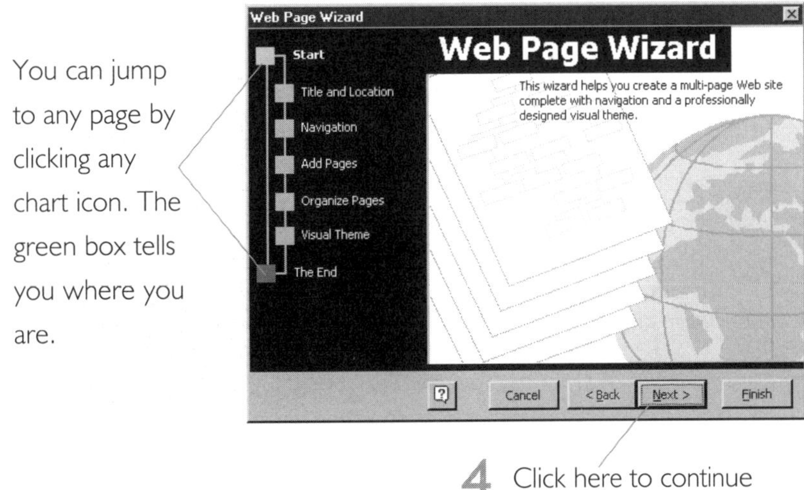

4 Click here to continue

5. Enter a title for your website then click Next.

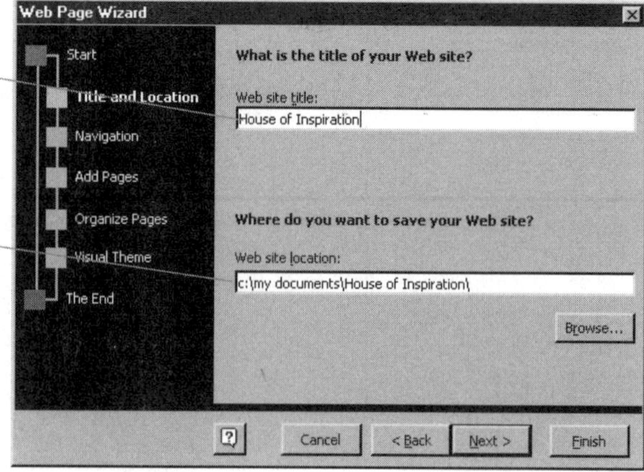

By default this title will be used as the directory for your web files, within 'My Documents'. However you can change it by editing this field.

6. Now choose a navigation model, then click Next.

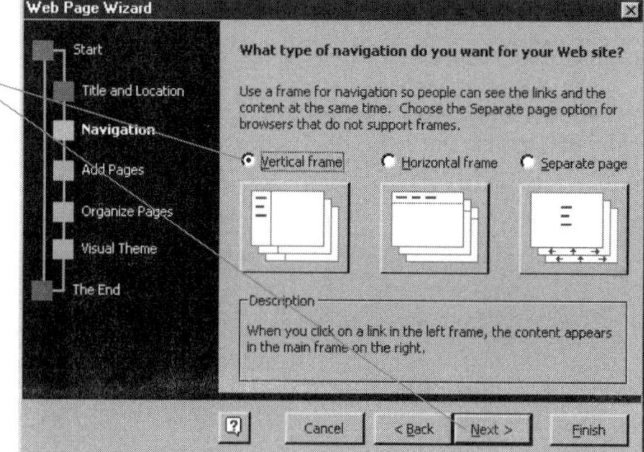

The frame options split the screen into two sections, one for navigation and one for content.

7. By default the Wizard creates 3 pages. Click here to add more then click Next.

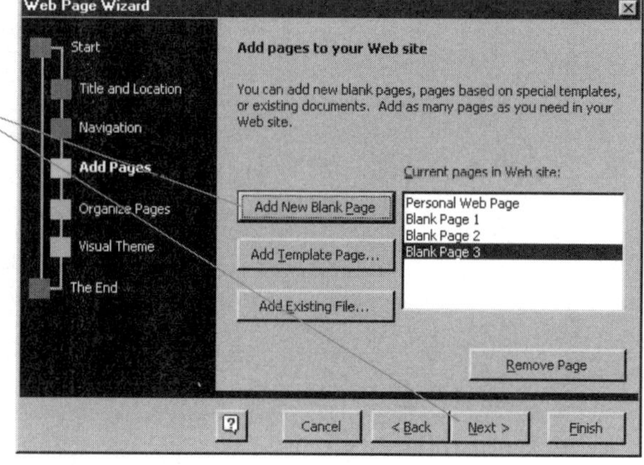

As long as the Wizard is still running, you can always return here to add or remove pages from the list.

8 You can now rename your pages and change their order.

Click Rename or double-click on the page name to edit

9 Finally, select a theme to give your web pages a consistent look/feel.

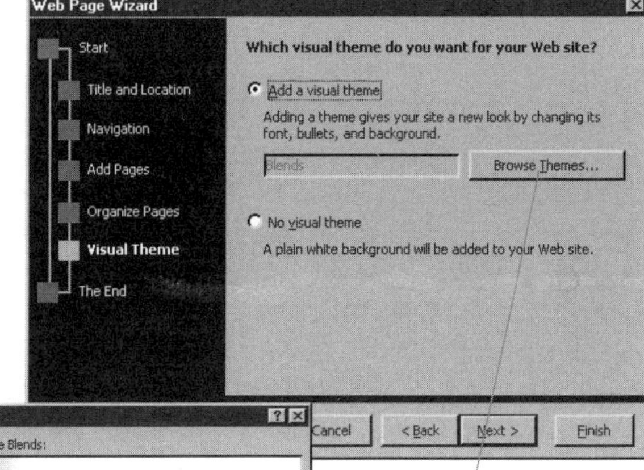

See Chapter 5 for more information about themes.

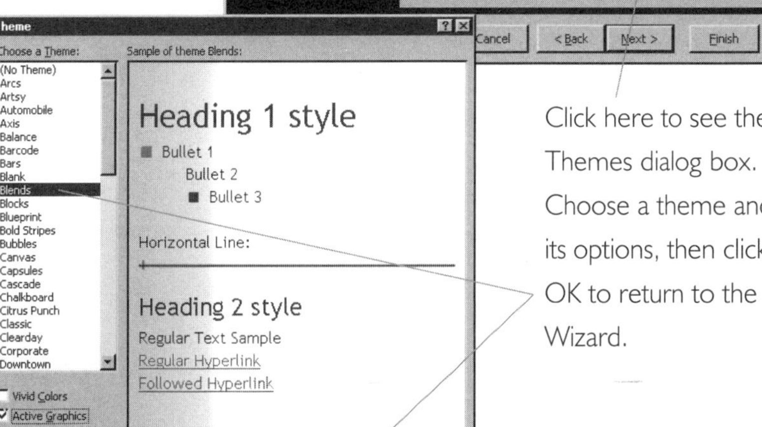

Click here to see the Themes dialog box. Choose a theme and its options, then click OK to return to the Wizard.

10 Now create your website. Click Finish.

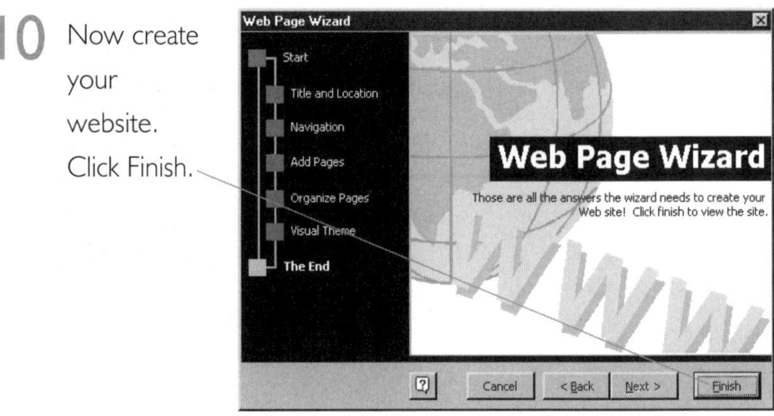

The Wizard now creates the necessary web pages, saved as .HTM files in the directory specified in step 5. You can view these directly in your web browser by choosing its Open file option. However, Word's Web Layout view will let you view and edit .HTM files.

The web pages are automatically connected using hyperlinks. For example, clicking the Overview link will cause the main content frame to load up the Overview.htm file

Main content frame

Now that the Wizard has set up the initial web document, it is up to you to edit the actual text to your own needs. Word has put placeholder information in each significant area of each page. You simply change and add to this sample text.

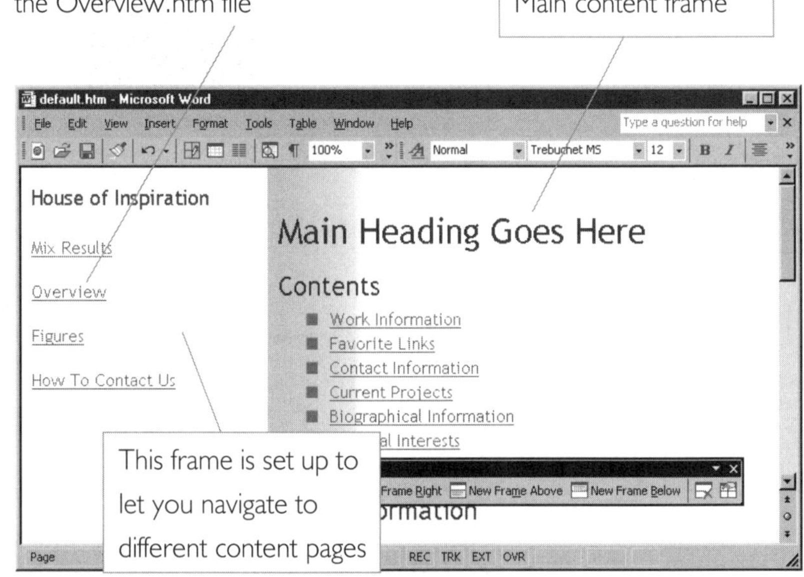

This frame is set up to let you navigate to different content pages

Frames

Frames allow you to divide your screen into rectangular areas, each of which can be used to view a different web page (or a different part of the same web page). In our example the Wizard has set up two frames: the left frame is used for navigation while the right shows the main content.

The Frames Toolbar appears automatically when the Web Page Wizard completes. However you can summon or dismiss it at any time using the View menu or by right clicking on an existing toolbar.

The Frames Toolbar

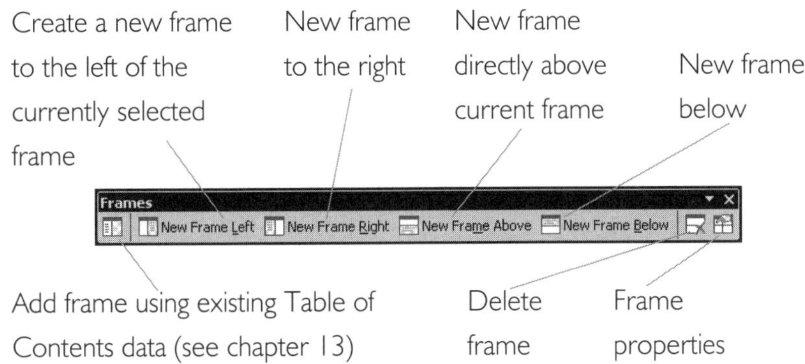

Adding a New Frame

Here we've clicked on the New Frame Above button to add a new frame along the top of the document. We'll use this to display a constant header for our pages.

The use of frames is not limited to web documents. Another useful tool for normal documents is the Text box (see chapter 13).

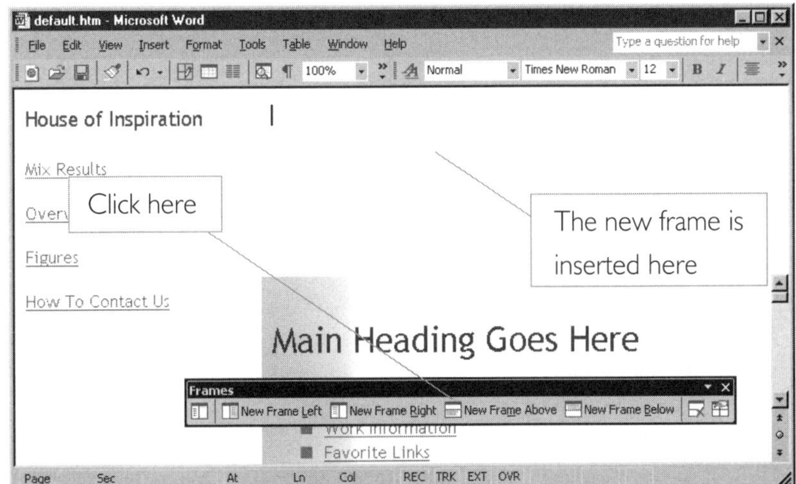

Adding Text and Graphics to a Frame

Once you've added a frame it behaves like an independent document: you can add/edit text or other objects as normal.

In the example below we've inserted a picture from a file and also incorporated some WordArt.

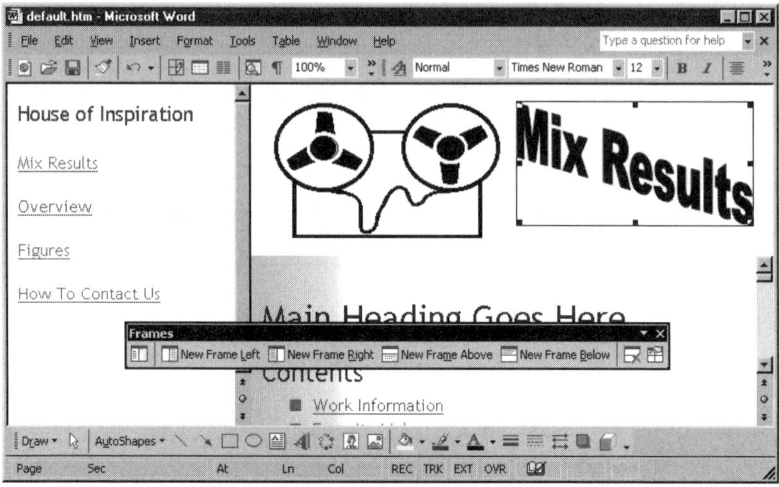

The Frame Properties Dialog

1 Make sure your insertion point is somewhere inside the relevant frame.

2 Click on the Frame Properties button in the Frames toolbar.

3 From the Frames Tab you can set the name, size and web page. From the Borders tab you can switch on the Frames border, allowing users to resize the frame.

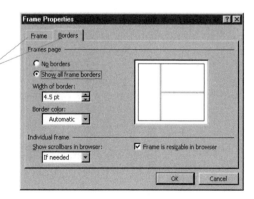

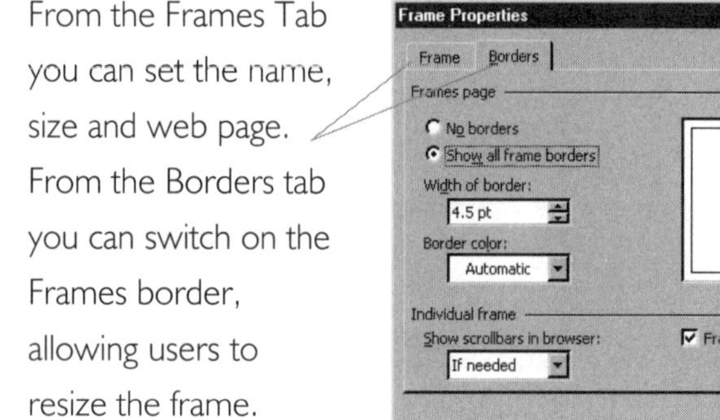

You can also access this dialog box by right-clicking inside a frame and choosing Frame Properties.

4 Click OK. In this example the user can now resize the frame by dragging directly on the border.

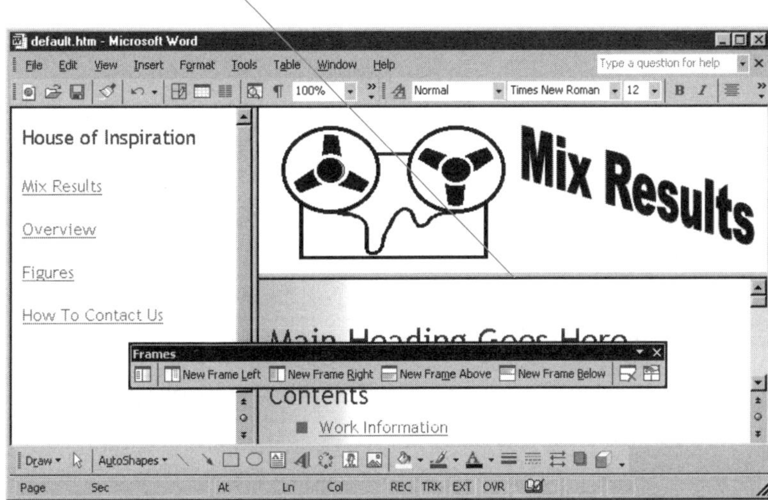

Alternative Text

Remember that some web browsers do not display graphics. Also, because graphics take much longer to download from the web, a user may decide to switch off a graphic display preference. In these cases, you can set text to be displayed as an alternative.

Alternative text also displays while a picture is loading. You may want to include the graphic's file size to give your users an idea of how long the loading process will take.

1 Right-click on the graphic and choose Format Picture from the drop-down menu.

2 Click on the Web tab and enter the text.

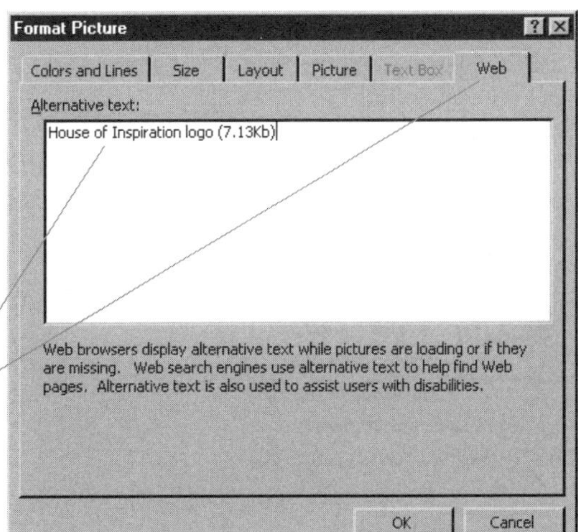

The Web Tools Palette

Word 2002 provides you with a powerful set of tools to enhance your web pages. This can be activated just like any other palette (either use the View menu or right-click on an existing Toolbar).

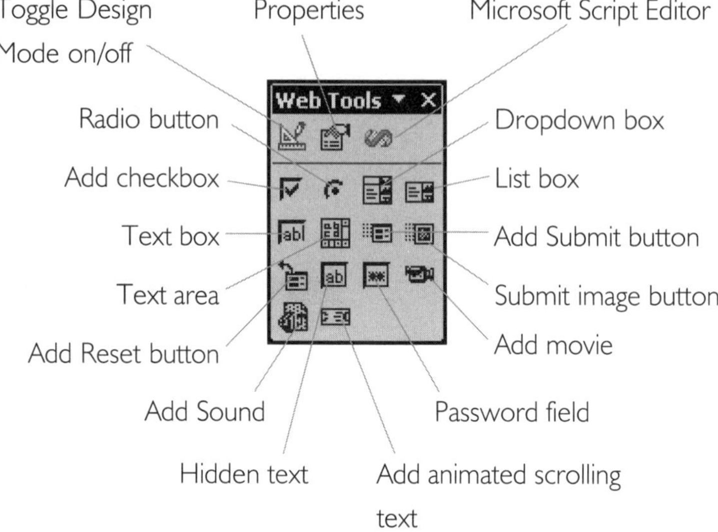

See page 183 for an example of adding sound to a web document.

As soon as you select one of the tools for adding objects to your web page, Word automatically activates Design Mode.

Design Mode

When Design Mode is active you can add, edit or delete objects such as radio buttons or text boxes.

When Design Mode is inactive you can test out your objects. Clicking on a check box, for example, will switch its checkmark on and off.

Microsoft Script Editor

This allows you to add functionality to your web page by adding scripts written in Microsoft Visual Basic® (scripting edition) or JScript® (Java Script).

For more details about how to write and edit scripts, refer to the Microsoft Development Environment online Help.

Adding Video Clips

Most web pages are a collection of text, images and links to other pages. However, as the multimedia capabilities of PCs increase, other types of media are becoming ever more common on the web. For example, you can place video clips on your web pages.

1. Place the cursor where you want to insert your video.

2. Click on the Add Movie button in the Web toolbar.

You can add a movie to a normal document by choosing Object from the Insert menu.

3. Click Browse next to the Movie field, then select the video file you want to insert.

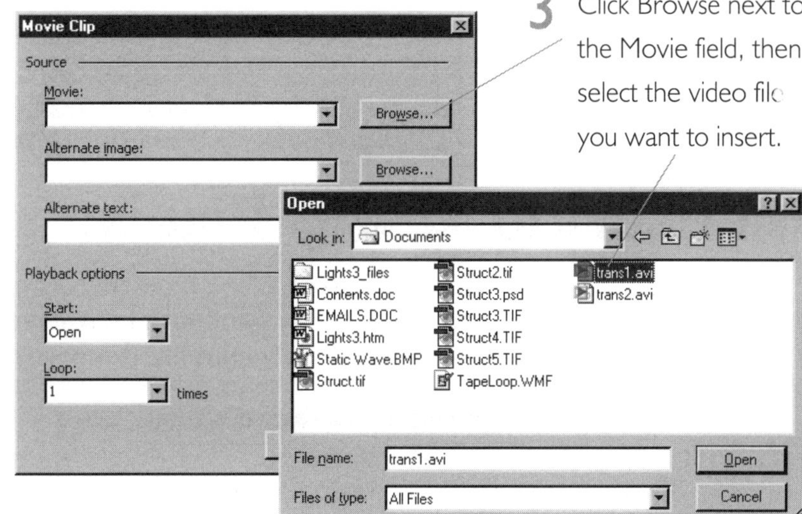

4. You can set an alternate image to be displayed if the browser doesn't support video playback, or if it is disabled by the user.

5. Set the Start and Loop options then click OK.

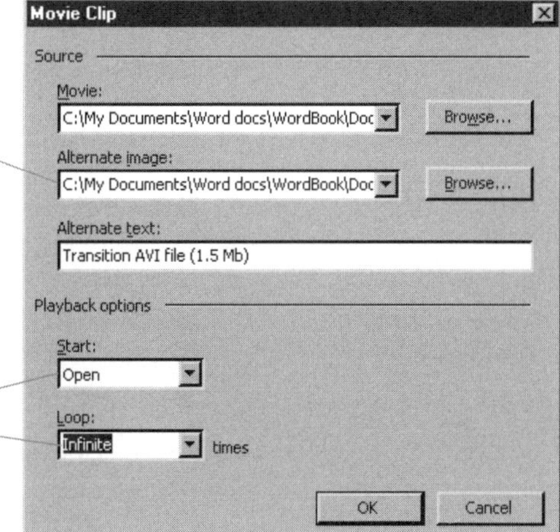

The video clip appears at your insertion point.

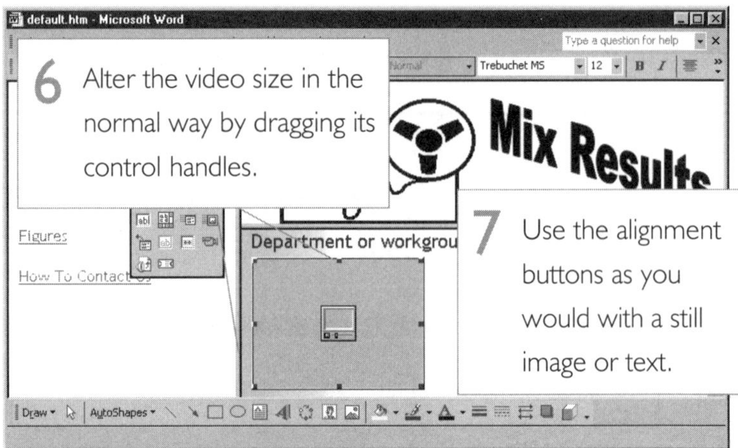

6. Alter the video size in the normal way by dragging its control handles.
7. Use the alignment buttons as you would with a still image or text.

Measuring Using Pixels

When working with web pages, the computer screen is the primary output device. It is thus much more convenient to measure objects in pixels rather than units like centimetres, inches or points.

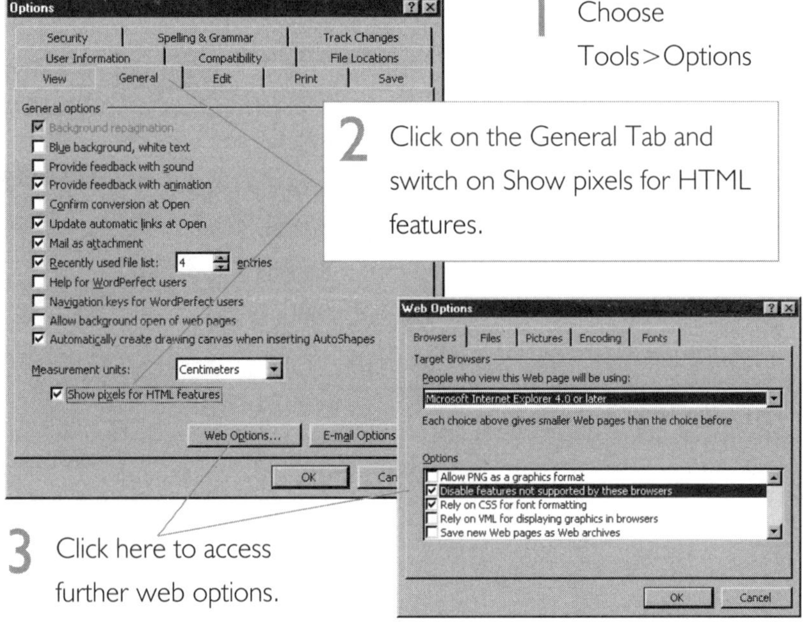

1. Choose Tools>Options
2. Click on the General Tab and switch on Show pixels for HTML features.
3. Click here to access further web options.

Hyperlinks

If Word doesn't convert link addresses like this to hyperlinks by underlining them and changing their colour, you may need to change your AutoFormat settings. Choose AutoCorrect from the Tools menu, then select the AutoFormat As You Type tab. Make sure the Replace... Internet and network paths with hyperlinks option is checked.

In an earlier topic ('Using the Web Page Wizard'), hyperlinks were used to provide a method of moving between one HTML document and another. With Word you are not restricted to using hyperlinks in HTML pages. You can place them in any normal Word document to link to another place in the same document, to another Word document on your hard drive/local network, or even to a file anywhere on the Internet/Intranet.

AutoFormatting Hyperlinks As You Type

By default, Word's AutoFormat feature will automatically convert any piece of text that looks like an Internet address or other file location to a hyperlink. These addresses must be in the standard URL format, with which you will be familiar if you have any experience of using a web browser:

Click on these arrows to move backwards and forwards through documents and web pages you have visited recently.

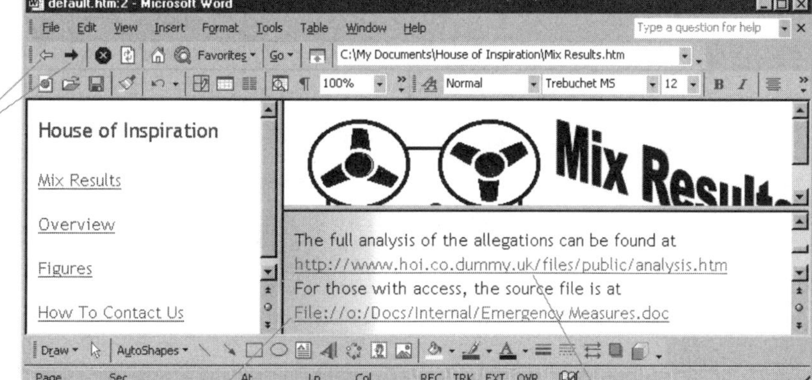

This is a link to a Word file on a hard drive accessible from the current PC. Note the prefix 'File://' (minus the quotes) is needed for Word to recognise this as a file location.

This is an Internet URL, linking to a website. In general you must be connected to the Internet for this link to work.

Inserting Hyperlinks Manually

The AutoFormat method is fine for converting actual Internet addresses and file locations to hyperlinks, but many hyperlink markers do not take this format; instead the hyperlink is represented by some more meaningful text, or even an image. You can use Word to make either of these into a hyperlink.

1. Select the text or image that the user will click on to jump to your linked file or website.

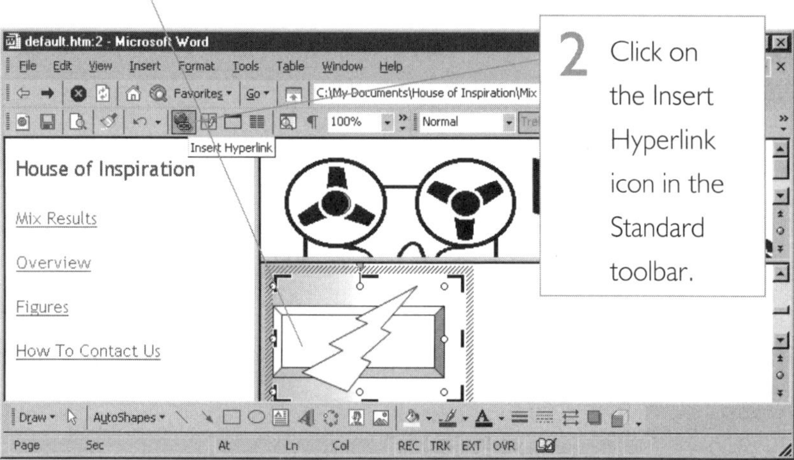

2. Click on the Insert Hyperlink icon in the Standard toolbar.

3. Type or select the name of the file you wish to link to (a file or a web page). Use the browsing buttons to search a specific location.

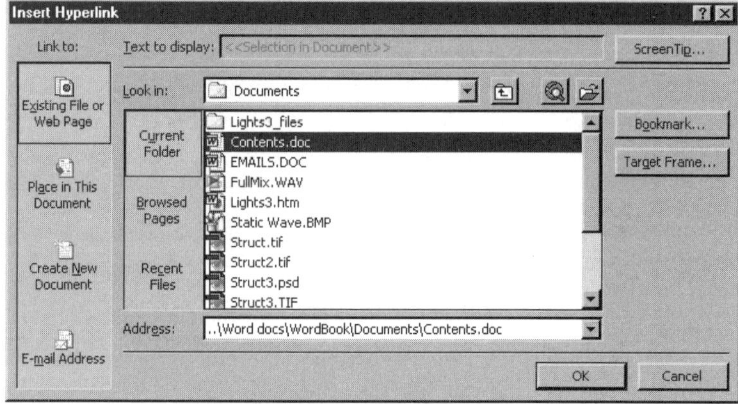

Saving HTML Files

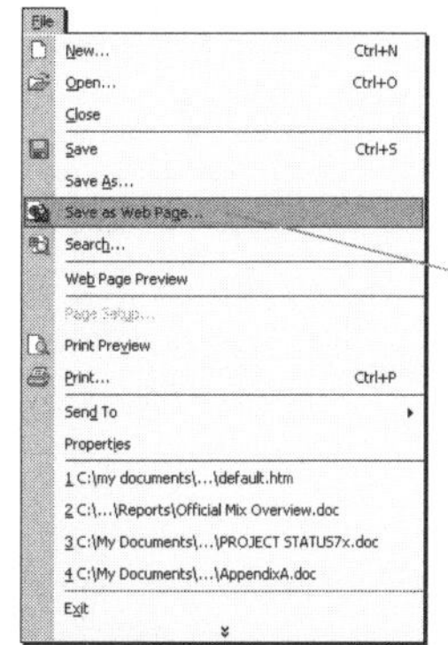

HTML is a native file format for Word. This means that you can open, edit and save in .HTM format just as easily as the .DOC files more traditionally associated with Word.

If you have just created some web pages from scratch, you will need to choose Save as Web Page from the File menu.

The option to save as type Web Page (.htm or *.html) is also available in the standard Save dialog.*

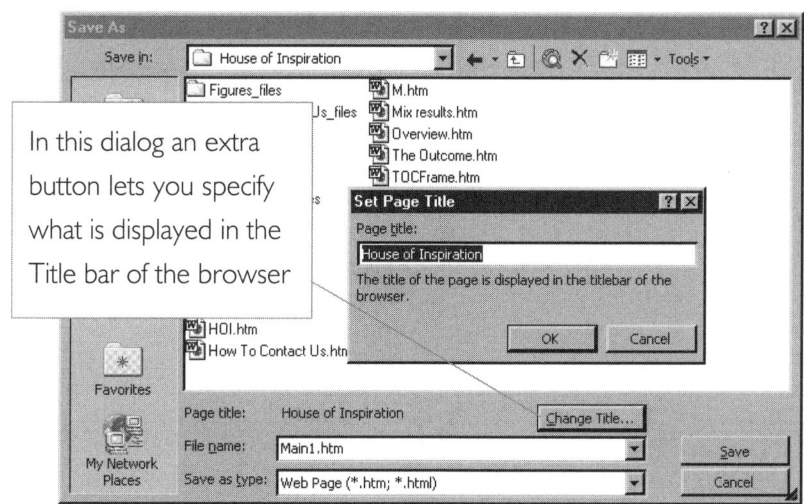

In this dialog an extra button lets you specify what is displayed in the Title bar of the browser

Editing Existing HTML Files

Some specialist programs such as Microsoft FrontPage allow you to design web pages using advanced effects like animated buttons. You can still take the files produced by FrontPage and edit them using Word.

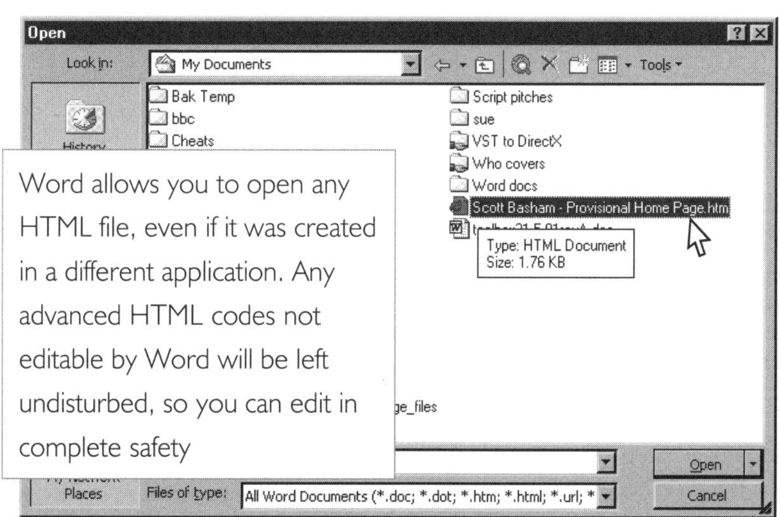

Word allows you to open any HTML file, even if it was created in a different application. Any advanced HTML codes not editable by Word will be left undisturbed, so you can edit in complete safety

Here we've opened a file created by a separate web design package. We can now edit its text, graphics and even the hyperlinks.

If you have been editing a file which has already been saved in .HTM format, you don't necessarily need to use the Save as Web Page option. A simple Save will suffice.

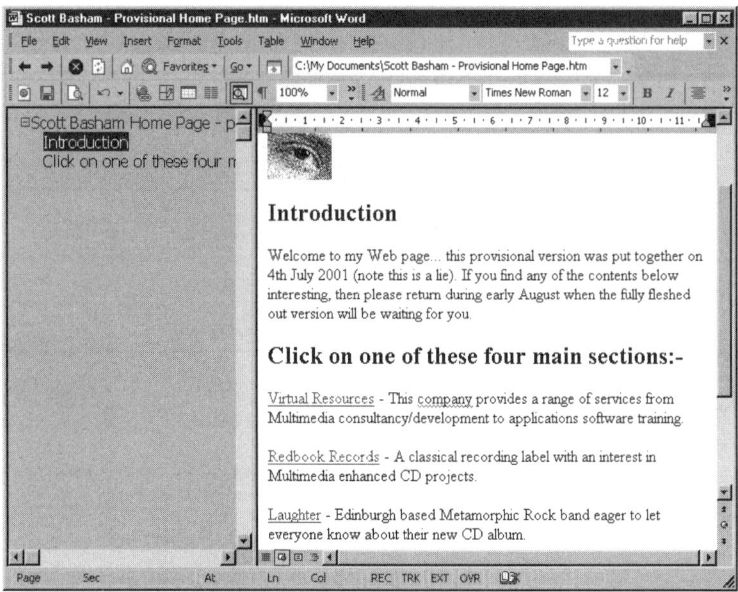

View HTML Source

This tool scores over a straight text editor in a number of ways. It allows you to see an organised view of your web pages, and also uses a colour coding system to help you distinguish the syntax.

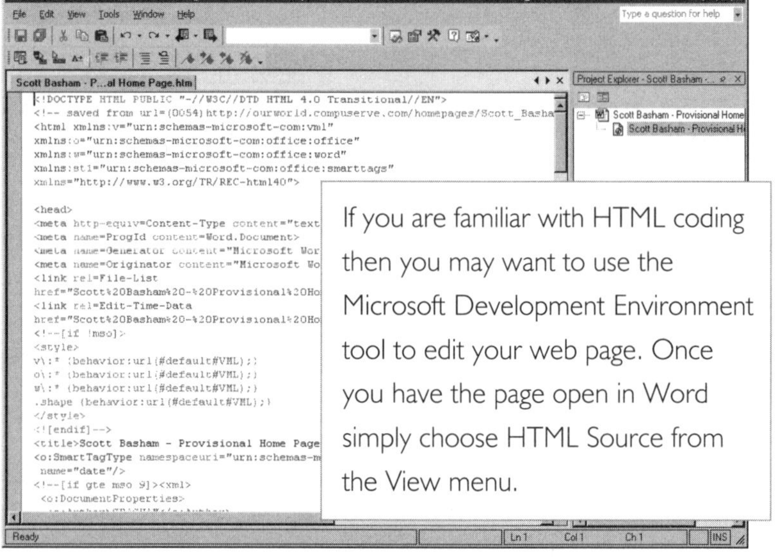

If you are familiar with HTML coding then you may want to use the Microsoft Development Environment tool to edit your web page. Once you have the page open in Word simply choose HTML Source from the View menu.

Using Word 2002 for Email

Using Word as Your Email Editor

If you use Microsoft Outlook or Exchange, your email composition can be enhanced by many Word features such as spelling and grammar checking, version tracking and the use of tables.

To set up Word as Email Editor from Outlook

1. From Microsoft Outlook, open the Tools menu and choose Options.
2. Select the Mail Format tab and click on Use Microsoft Word to edit email messages.
3. The next time you create or view an email message, Word will be activated.

The first time you use Word for email editing, the Office Assistant (if enabled) may launch with help on setting up an autosignature or stationery. These will be discussed on the next page.

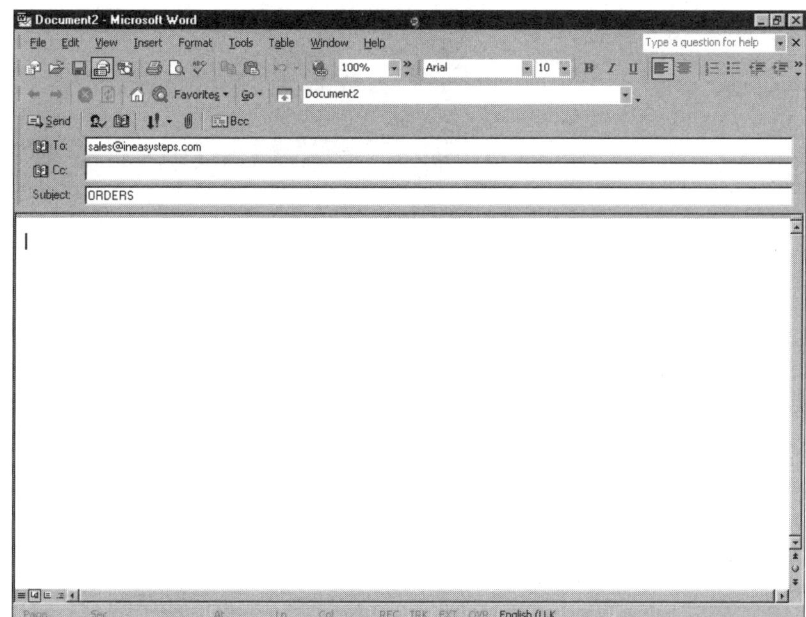

Email Signatures

A signature can be automatically added to the end of any email message. This can contain text (including hyperlinks) or graphics.

1. Go to the Tools menu and choose Options. Select the General tab and click on the E-mail Options button.

From the Personal Stationery tab you can choose a theme for your messages. You can also set a specific font for new messages, and a separate font for replies or forwarded messages.

2. Enter a name for your signature.
3. Type in its text. You can click on the Insert Picture or Insert Hyperlink buttons to add graphics or references to other pages.
4. Click on Add.

The signature will now be available for any new messages you may send.

Advanced Topics

Word 2002 has many advanced features. Some are designed to generally make life easier while others allow you to enhance your documents with comments, Tables of Contents or even to compile an index.

Covers

Chapter Thirteen

The Reviewing Toolbar

Animated text is another feature you can use in online documents: refer to the topic 'The Font Dialog Box' in Chapter 3.

Word incorporates several sophisticated features that allow you to review documents clearly, and track the various stages of these reviews. The Reviewing toolbar contains icons that allow you to access these features easily. It can be displayed in the normal way from the View menu.

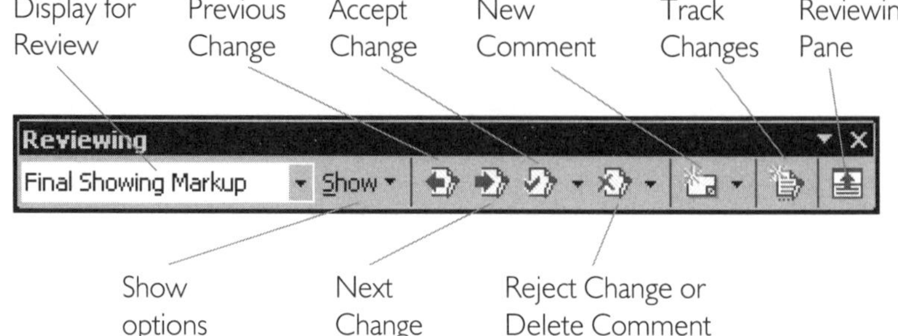

Inserting Comments

To insert a comment on a section of your document:

1. Highlight the text on which you wish to comment.

2. Click the Insert Comment icon.

If you rest the mouse over text with a comment attached for a few moments, the comment itself will appear in its own box:

Scott Basham:
Commented - Is this the correct official title?

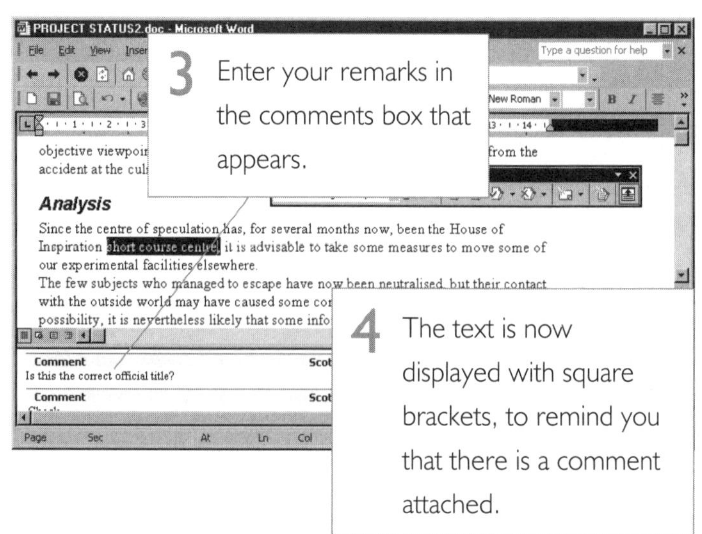

3. Enter your remarks in the comments box that appears.

4. The text is now displayed with square brackets, to remind you that there is a comment attached.

Highlighting Text

If you want to mark a piece of text without adding additional notes, you can highlight it, just as if you were using a real Highlighter pen on paper. To do this, follow either of the steps below:

If you use the Highlighter icon's drop-down menu, then you can choose from a range of colours. Selecting None will remove the highlight altogether.

1 Select your text with the cursor tool, then click on the Highlighter icon (in the Formatting toolbar).

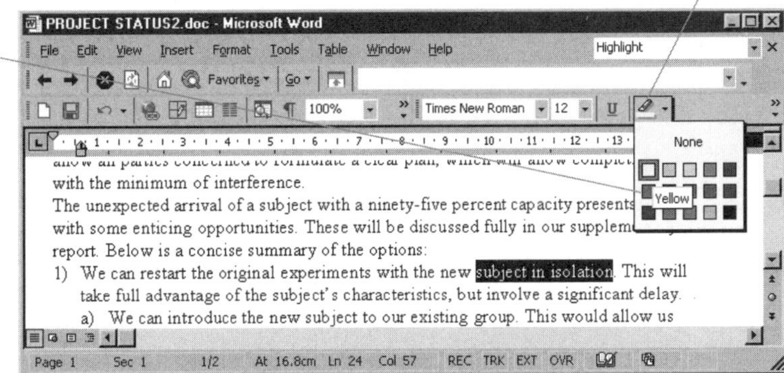

2 Alternatively click on the Highlighter icon first, to enter Highlighter mode, then highlight as many different pieces of text as you want. To return to normal editing mode, click the Highlighter icon again.

Versioning

You can save the various stages of a document, allowing you to see how it has developed and (if relevant) which authors have made which changes. To save a new version, do the following:

After step 2, enter comment text for the new version and click on OK.

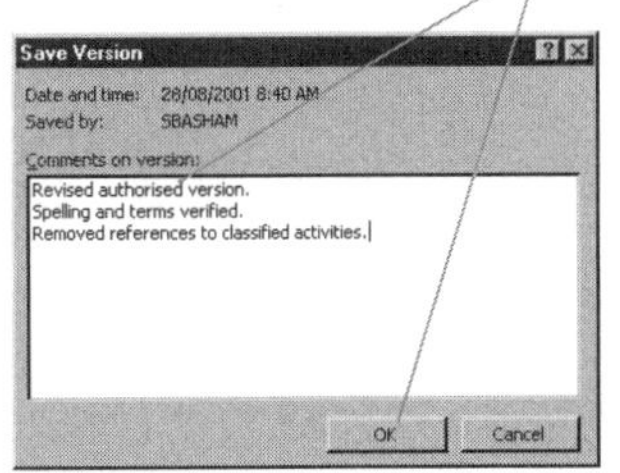

1 Go to the File Menu and choose Versions....

2 Click on Save Now.

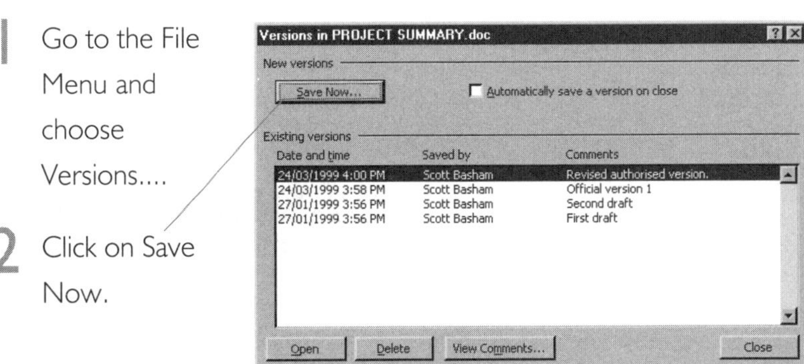

To review the different versions of a document, follow these steps:

1 Select Versions from the File menu.

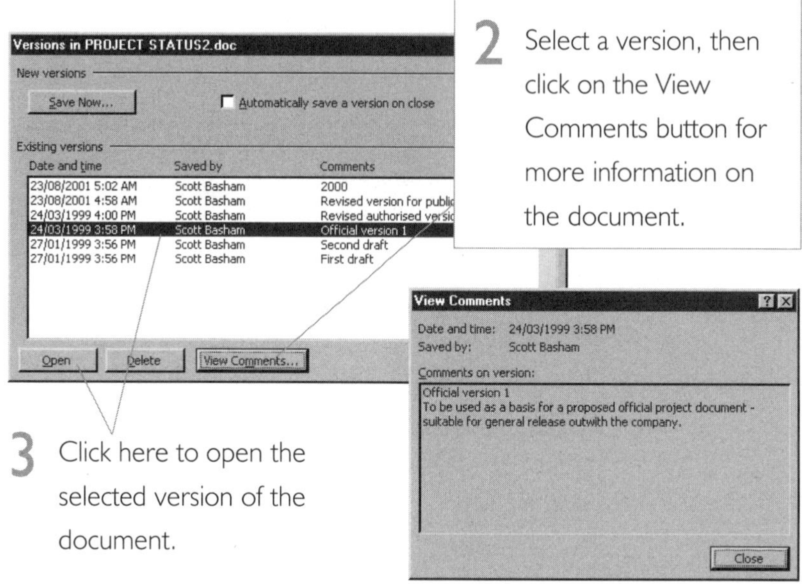

2 Select a version, then click on the View Comments button for more information on the document.

3 Click here to open the selected version of the document.

Macros

Macros are recordings of common activities. You can record your own macros, and play them back whenever necessary.

Recording a Macro

1 Go to the View menu, choose Toolbars and make sure that the Visual Basic Toolbar is active.

You can also access macro recording and playback by opening the Tools menu and choosing Macros.

This gives you access to two buttons for recording and replaying macros.

Macro names must begin with a letter and can contain up to 80 letters and numbers. Spaces or special characters are not allowed.

2 When you click the Record Macro button the following dialog box appears. Enter a name for your macro.

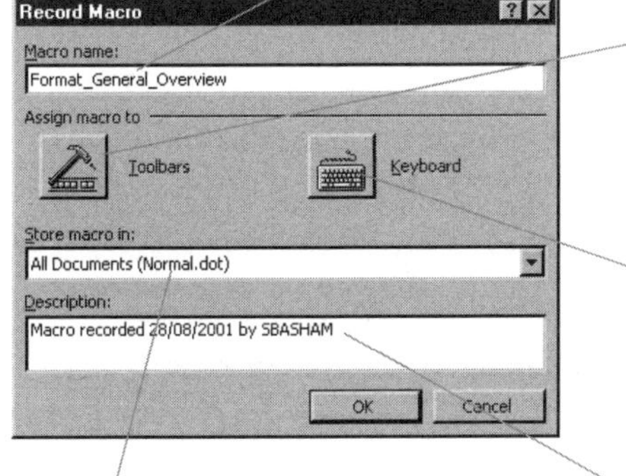

3 Click here to assign your new macro to a toolbar.

4 Click here to assign your new macro to a keyboard shortcut.

5 Select the template where you want to store the macro.

6 Enter a description for your macro.

You can also stop macro recording by opening the Tools menu and choosing Macros.

7 When you click OK recording becomes active. You can now walk through the commands you wish to be included in the macro. During this time your cursor takes the form of a pointer with a cassette tape attached. There is also a small toolbar which allows you to pause or stop recording:

8 When you have finished recording, click the Stop icon.

Running a Macro

You can run a macro from a toolbar icon or keyboard shortcut if you chose either of those options when creating the macro.

1 To play back a macro, click the Play button and choose your macro from the dialog box.

2 Click Run.

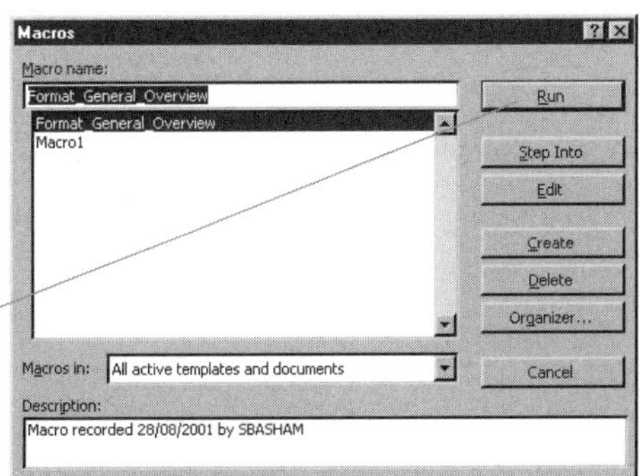

Collaborating on Documents

If each of the different reviewers of a document works from a different computer, which is used by he or she alone, then there should be no need to alter the reviewer information as this should have been established when Word was installed. However, if a computer is shared by a number of people to review documents, then the user information should be changed whenever a reviewer begins, so that it is clear who made which comments.

1 Select Options from the Tools menu.

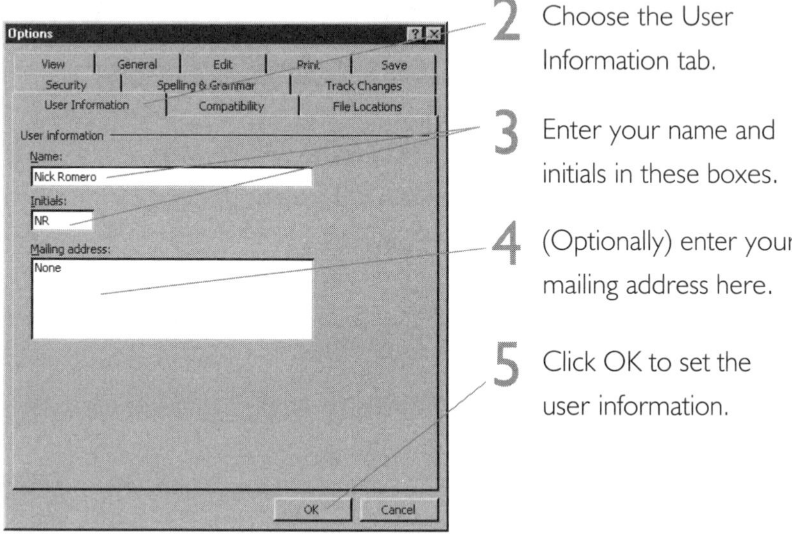

2 Choose the User Information tab.

3 Enter your name and initials in these boxes.

4 (Optionally) enter your mailing address here.

5 Click OK to set the user information.

Merging Documents

If a number of reviewers have been working together on the same document by updating the same Word file, then the sum of all their efforts is collected in the most up-to-date version of the document. However, if different reviewers have made changes to a document and saved the results as a different file (e.g. to take the document away to work on at home), it is possible to merge the files back into one document

1 With one of the files open, select Tools>Compare and Merge Documents.

2 In the file dialog that appears, double-click on the file to merge.

Text Boxes

Text boxes give independent control over text flow/positioning.

Inserting a new Text Box

1. Click on the Text Box icon in the Drawing Toolbar. Your cursor will turn into a cross symbol.

The first thing you'll probably want to do is apply Text Wrap to the new text box. To do this right-click on one of its edges and choose Format Text box. Activate the Layout tab.

2. Click and drag diagonally to create the Text Box.

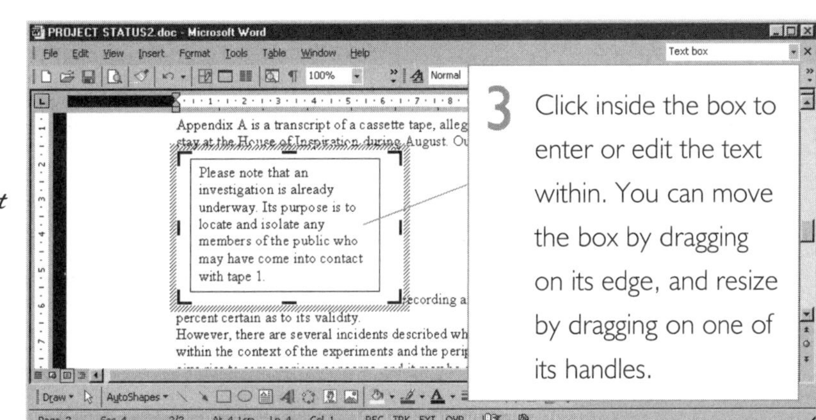

3. Click inside the box to enter or edit the text within. You can move the box by dragging on its edge, and resize by dragging on one of its handles.

The Text Box Toolbar

The Text Box Toolbar gives you access to additional text box options.

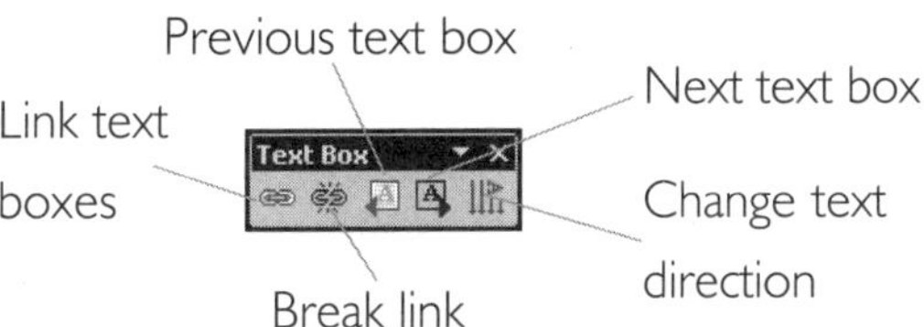

To link text boxes click on the first box, then the Link button in the toolbar, then on the second box. Any text which doesn't fit in the first box will now flow automatically into the second.

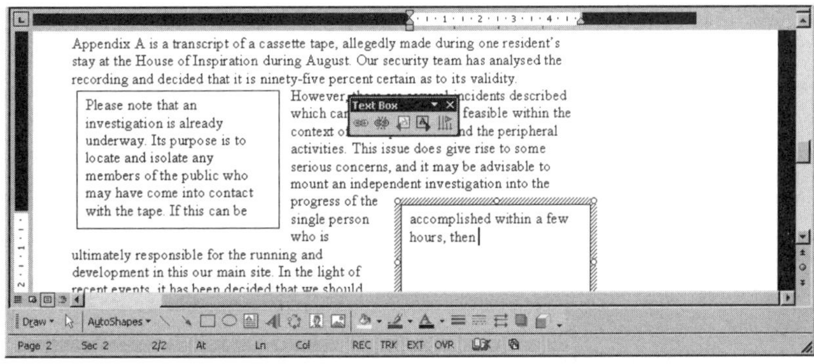

Footnotes and Endnotes

Word allows you to add footnotes (which appear at the bottom of a page), or endnotes (which appear at the end of your document). These reference text on the main page, usually using a superscript number.

1 Select the text which will reference the footnote or endnote, then choose Footnote from the Insert menu, Reference submenu.

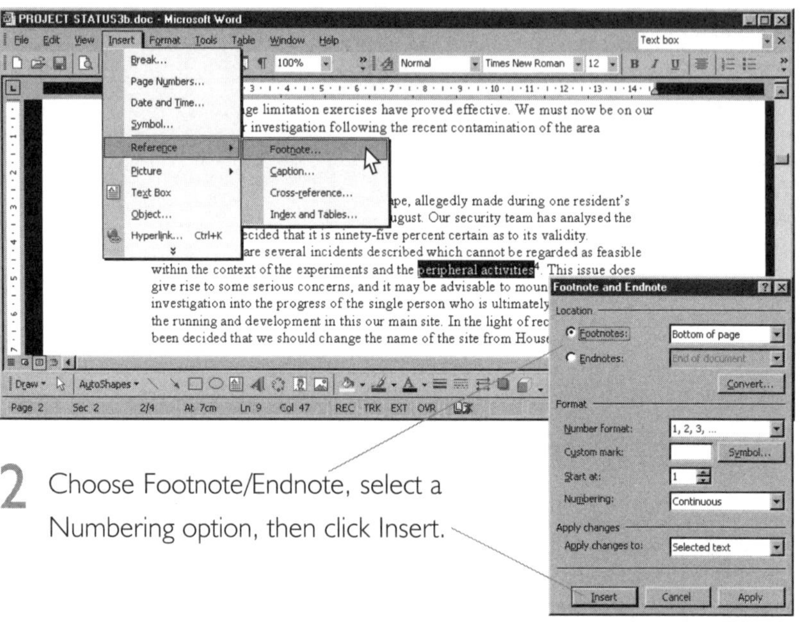

2 Choose Footnote/Endnote, select a Numbering option, then click Insert.

Existing footnotes or endnotes are renumbered automatically each time you insert another.

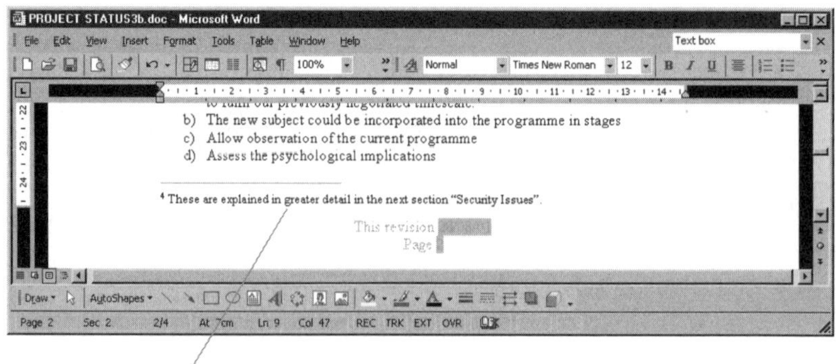

3 You can now enter the text for your footnote or endnote.

Tables of Contents

You can automatically create a Table of Contents by asking Word to look for instances of particular styles, or entries that you create manually. Word will track each entry's page numbers.

Creating a new Table of Contents

1. Place your insertion point at a suitable location for your Table of Contents.

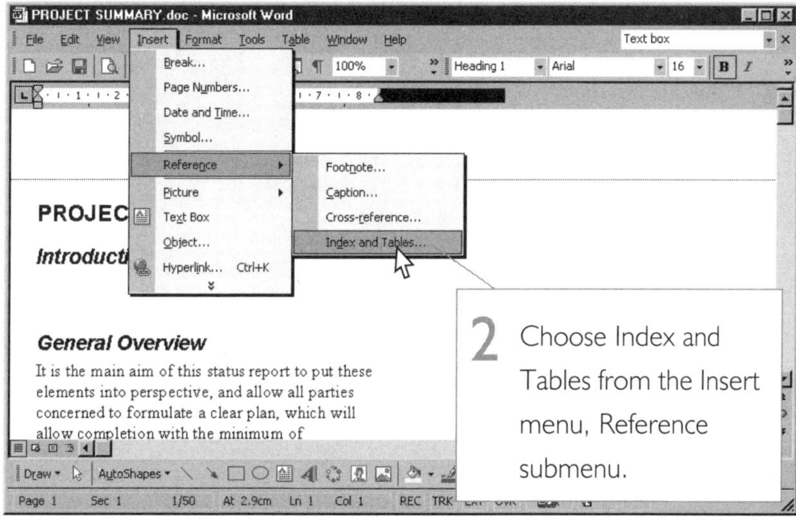

2. Choose Index and Tables from the Insert menu, Reference submenu.

3. Make sure the Table of Contents tab is active.

4. Set the page and tab options.

5. Apply a style from the Formats drop-down list then click OK.

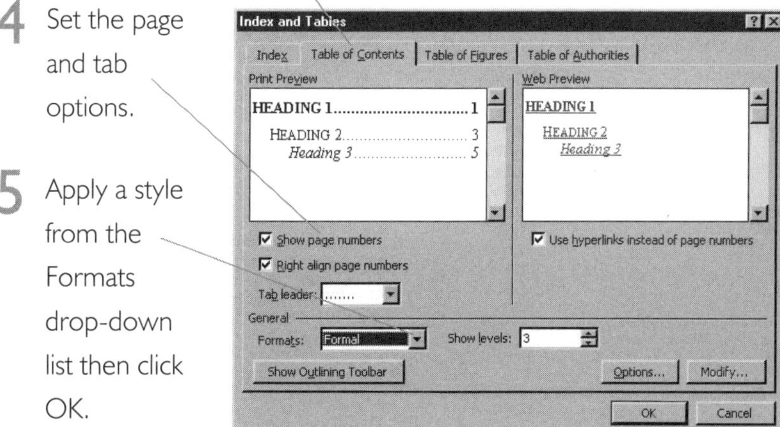

By default Word will use instances of the styles Heading 1, 2 and 3 to build the Table of Contents. You can change this by clicking on the Options button.

Word scans through your document for instances of different heading styles, and creates the Table of Contents.

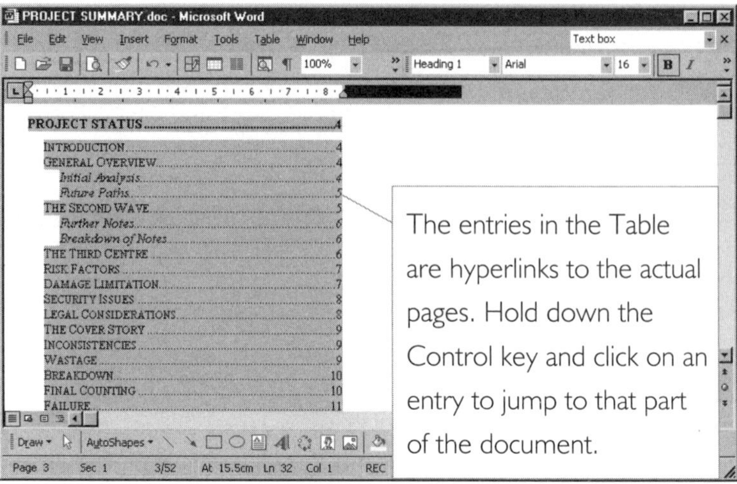

The entries in the Table are hyperlinks to the actual pages. Hold down the Control key and click on an entry to jump to that part of the document.

Updating a Table of Contents

The grey background on the Table of Contents indicates that you're looking at a Word Field. Fields contain text which Word automatically generates. The background doesn't print, but you can change it by selecting Options from the Tools menu. Click on the View tab and choose a different option under Field shading.

If you have added new headings, or edited your document so that the page numbers are different, then you'll probably want to update the Table of Contents to reflect the changes.

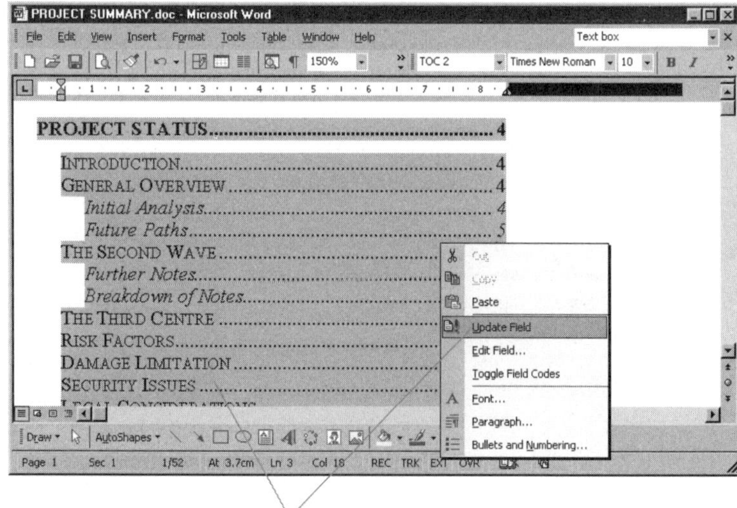

Right-click on the Table of Contents and choose Update Field from the drop-down menu.

If you have added or removed headings or Table of Contents entries, then you will need to choose Update entire table.

2 Decide whether to update just the page numbers or to rebuild the whole table.

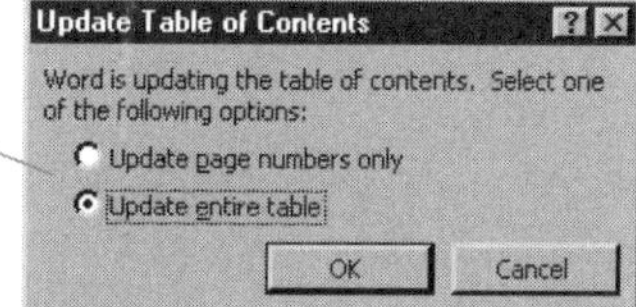

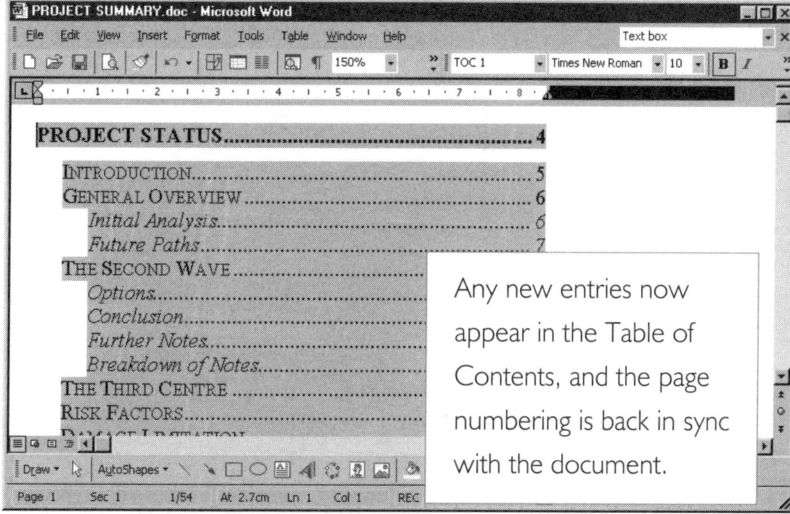

Any new entries now appear in the Table of Contents, and the page numbering is back in sync with the document.

Altering the Appearance of the Table of Contents

Entries in the Contents Table use special styles which have been set up automatically (they are named 'TOC' plus a level number).

Any formatting changes you make normally affect these styles. This means that the new formatting will be retained even if you rebuild the Table of Contents.

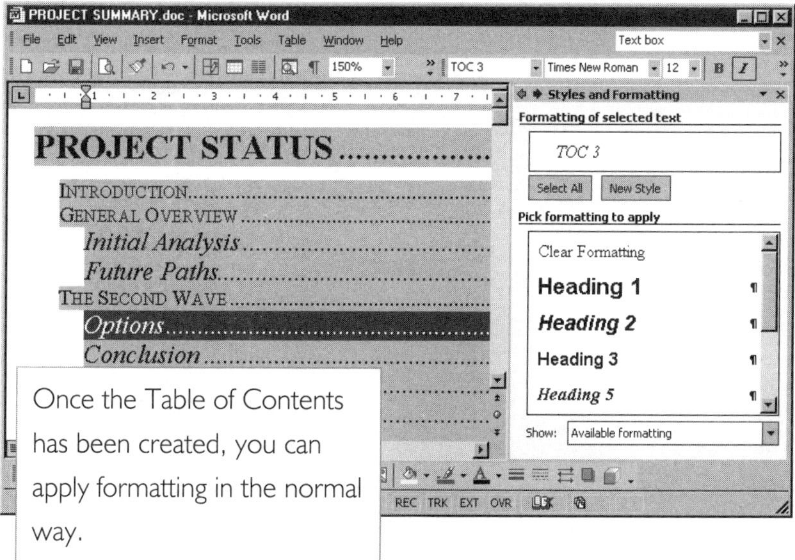

Once the Table of Contents has been created, you can apply formatting in the normal way.

Adding a Manual Entry to the Table of Contents

Sometimes you may want to add an entry which does not use one of the Heading styles.

1 Click in the relevant part of the document.

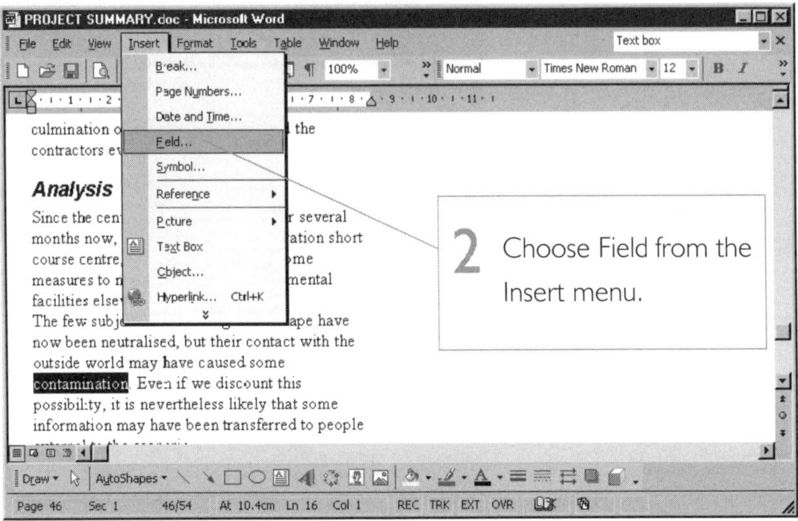

3 Under Categories, choose Index and Tables.

4 For field names choose TC.

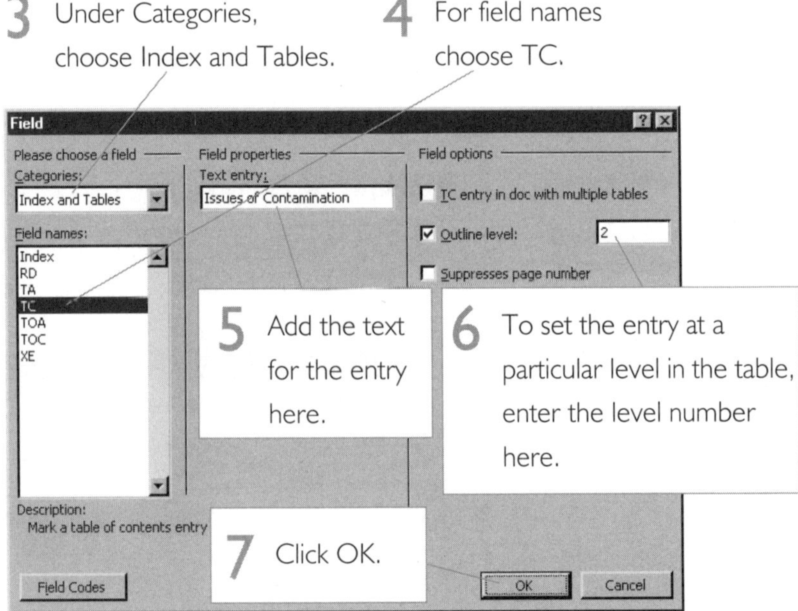

The field for the TOC entry is added to your document.

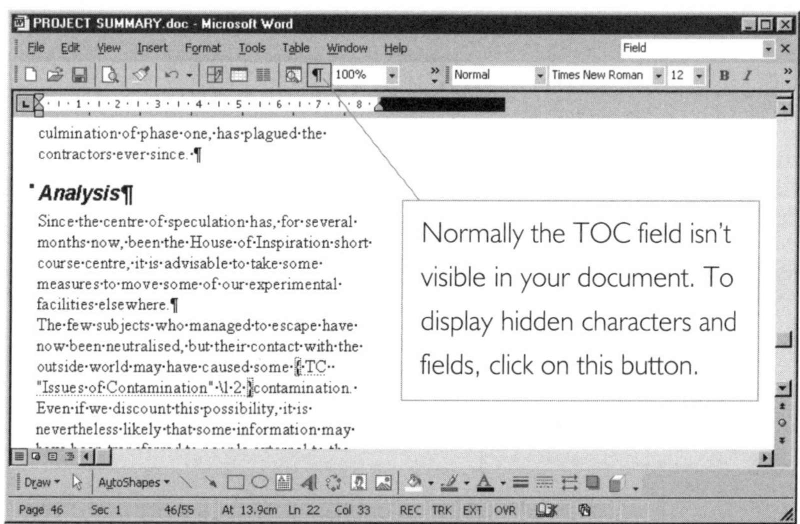

8 To rebuild the Table of Contents, click to select your existing table, then choose Insert>Reference>Index and Tables.

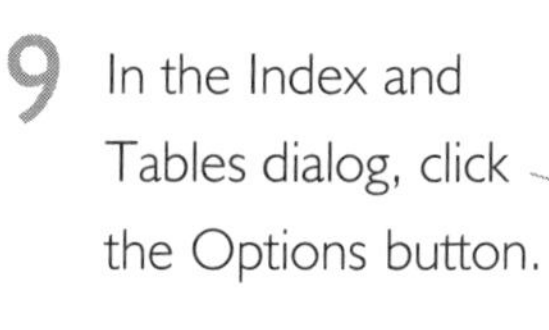

9 In the Index and Tables dialog, click the Options button.

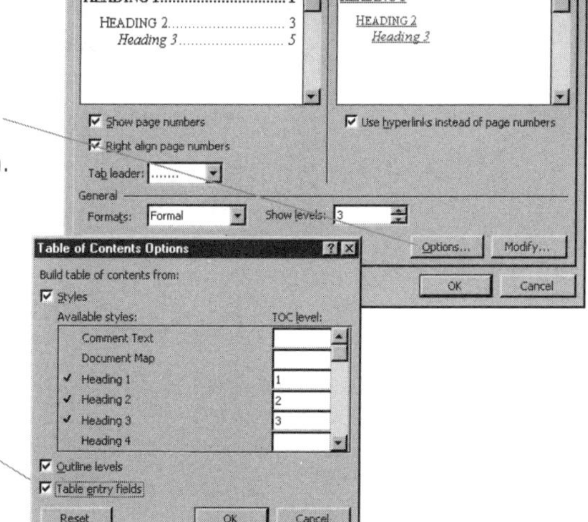

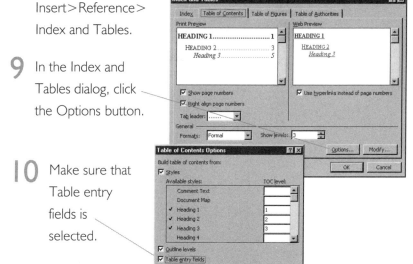

10 Make sure that Table entry fields is selected.

11 Click OK when asked if you want to replace the current Table of Contents.

Bookmarks

A Bookmark can help you keep track of a location in your document.

Bookmarks can be used to let you specify a range of pages when creating an index entry. *See page 182 for more details.*

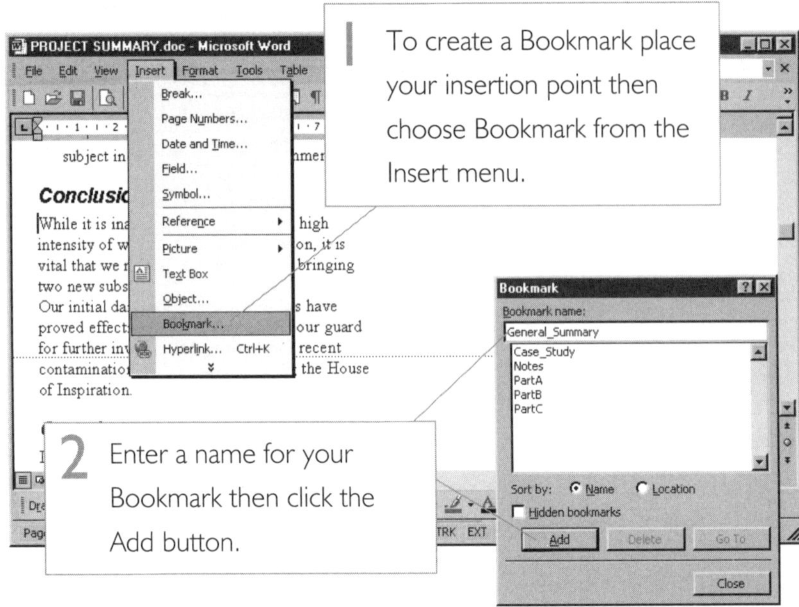

1 To create a Bookmark place your insertion point then choose Bookmark from the Insert menu.
2 Enter a name for your Bookmark then click the Add button.

Indexing

Word makes the process of creating an index fairly straightforward.

Adding an Index entry

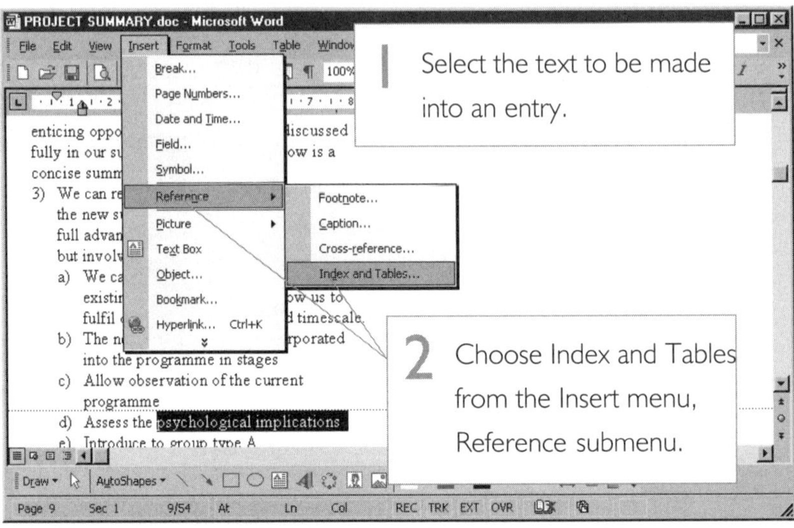

1 Select the text to be made into an entry.
2 Choose Index and Tables from the Insert menu, Reference submenu.

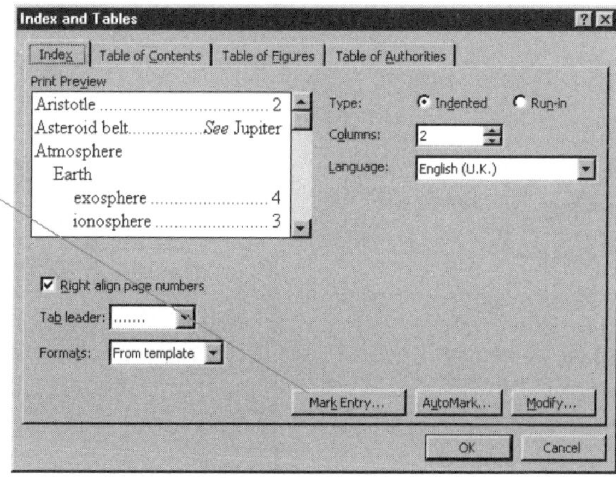

3 Click on the Mark Entry button.

The Mark Index Entry dialog stays open even after you've clicked the Mark button. This means that you can determine another index entry (by scrolling through your main document) then clicking the Mark button again, without having to go through the menus.

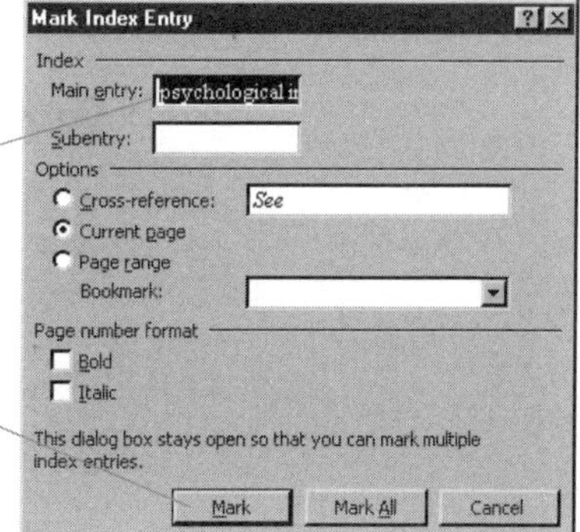

4 If necessary, edit the text inserted in Main entry.

5 For a simple entry, leave the options set at Current Page and click on Mark.

Topics and Subtopics

Most entries will probably only need to have text in the Main entry part of this dialog box.

See the next page for an example of subtopics in an actual index.

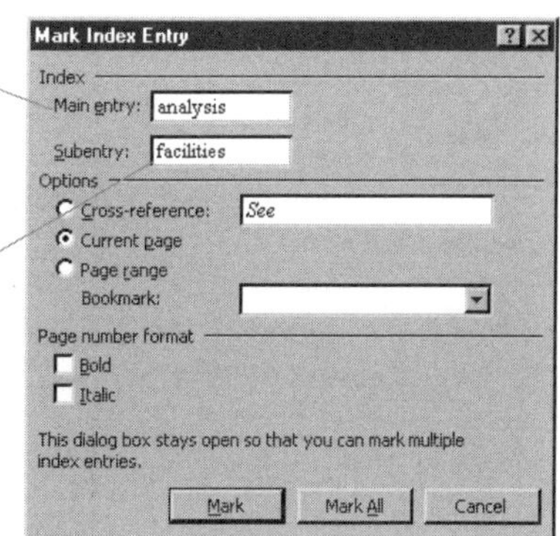

However, if you want an index which includes topics and subtopics, then fill in the main topic under Main entry, then the subtopic under Subentry.

Specifying Ranges of Pages

For most index entries you'll want just a single page number to appear. If you want a range of pages:

You can also create cross-reference entries. Click on the Cross-reference option and type in the relevant text for the entry.

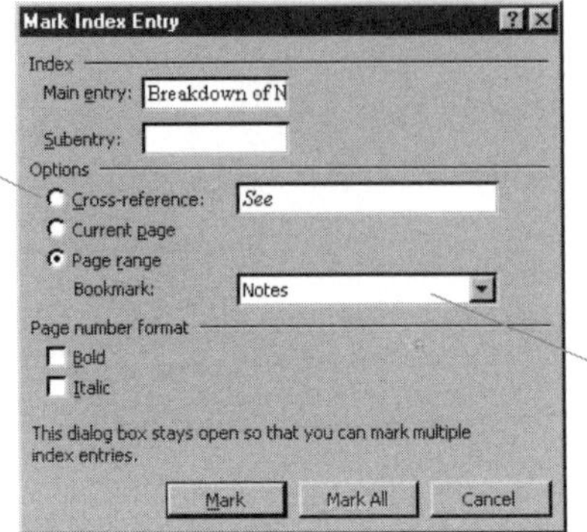

1. Move to the end of the topic and create a bookmark (see page 180).
2. Locate the start of the topic and mark the index entry. Set the Options to Page range, and select your bookmark from the drop-down list.

Generating the Index

1. Click where you'd like the Index to appear. Go to the Insert menu and choose Index and Tables.
2. Make sure the Index tab is active.

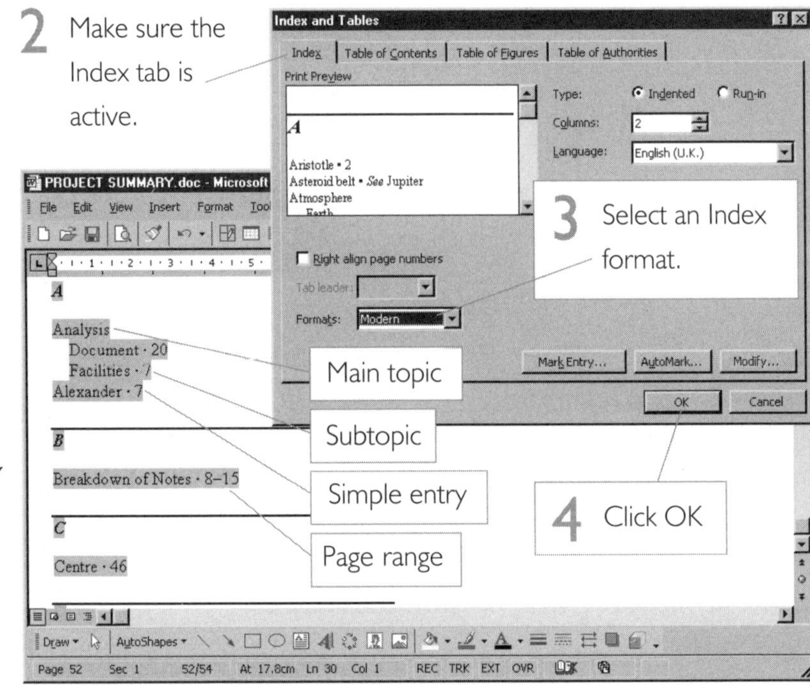

As with the Table of Contents, you can rebuild the index at any time, or change its formatting by editing the styles (each is named 'Index' followed by a level number).

Adding Sound

You can add background music or sound recordings to a web page document just as easily as adding the video clip (see Chapter 12).

Word allows you to use files in a number of formats including WAV and MIDI files. Whenever someone accesses your page, this file is played providing the browser allows background music, and also if a suitable driver for the type of sound file has been installed.

If the Web Toolbar is not visible, go to the View menu, choose Toolbars then Web Tools.

1 Click on the Sound icon in the Web toolbar:

2 Select the required sound file then click Open.

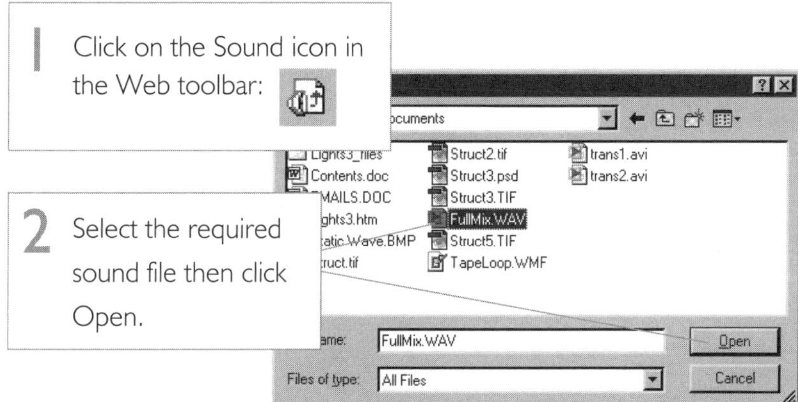

3 Set the looping option then click OK.

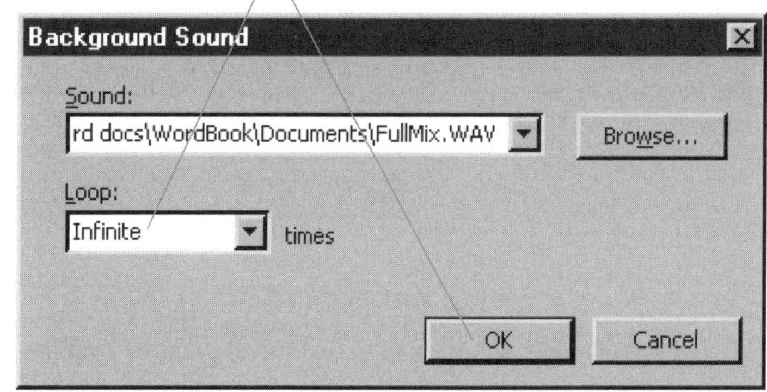

Note that you can add a sound file to any Word document by choosing Object from the Insert menu:

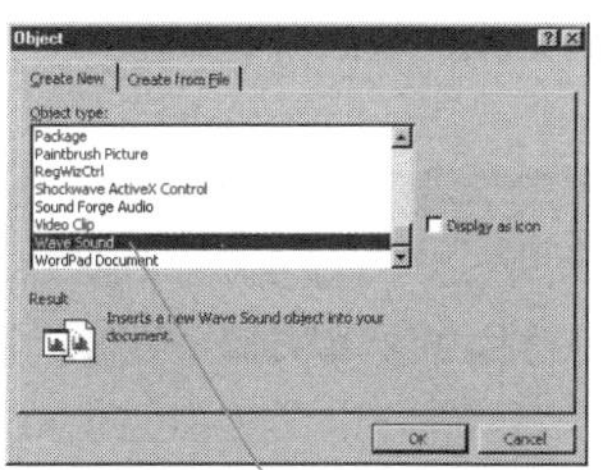

Wave Sound and MIDI sequence are just two examples of the files you are able to import

In this example the file FullMix.WAV will play and repeat indefinitely as longs as the user is on the current web page.

Language Autodetect

If you have multiple languages installed, Word can automatically select the correct language based on what you're currently typing. This means that features such as the Spelling Checker and Thesaurus will use the correct dictionary.

If you only have one language currently installed, you will need to install at least one more for the Language Autodetect feature to work.

Installing Multiple Languages

1. Click on the Windows Start button, choose Programs>Microsoft Office Tools>Microsoft Office XP Language Settings.
2. To add a language, select it from the list on the left. Continue to select all the languages you require then click OK or Apply.

When you change the Microsoft Office Language Settings, Windows usually needs to shut down any Office Applications such as Word. A dialog box will appear offering to do this for you automatically.

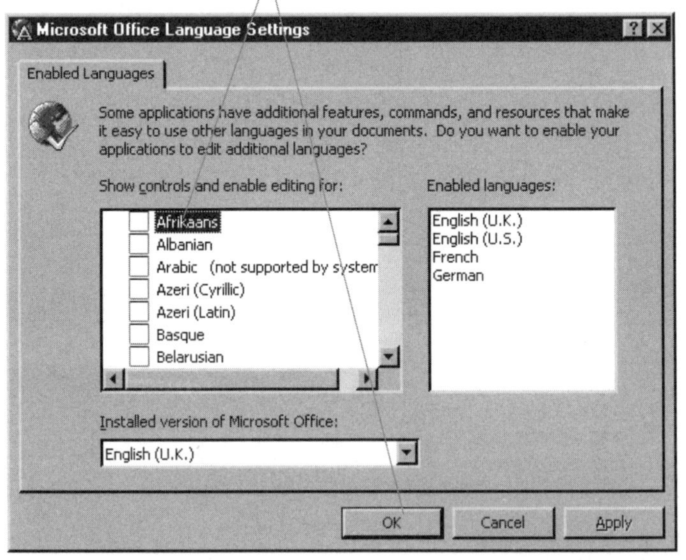

3. Back in Word choose Tools>Language>Set Language. Make sure that Detect language automatically is switched on.

You can also manually specify a language for any block of text. To do this simply select the text, then choose Tools>Language>Set Language then click on the desired language.

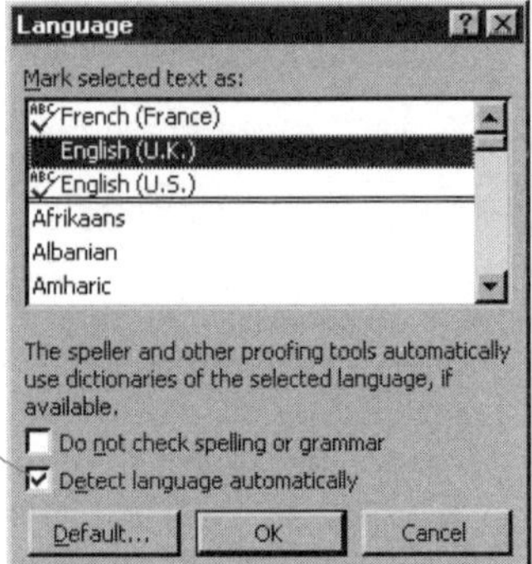

Automatic Translation

This is another feature new to Word 2002. If you have more than one language installed, you can see a translation of your text into another language.

1. Select the word(s) to be translated.

2. Choose Tools>Language>Translate.

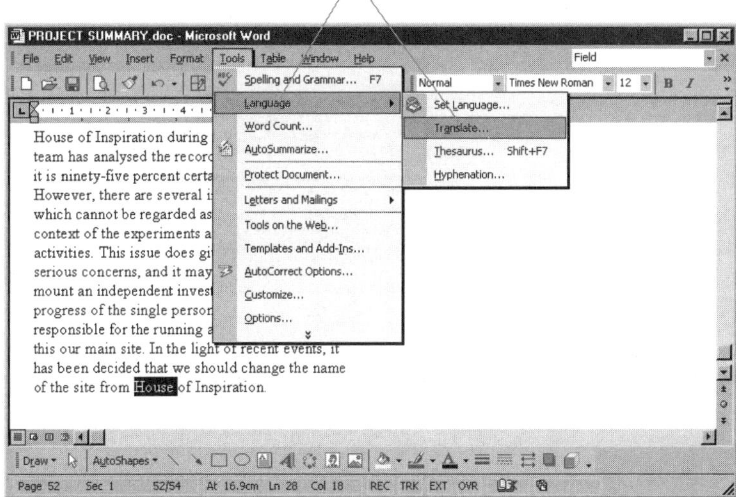

3. The Translate section of the Task Pane appears. Choose the destination language, then click Go.

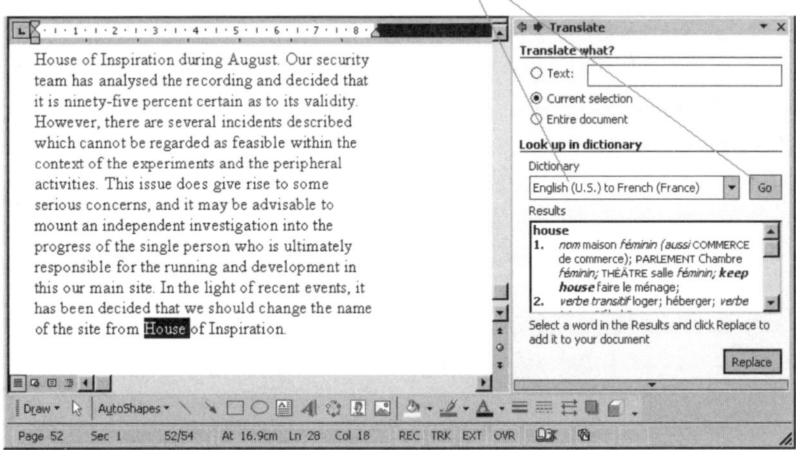

The translation feature works better on single words rather than whole sentences or paragraphs.

Compatibility Options

These settings only affect how Word displays a document which has been saved in a particular format. It does not permanently change its formatting.

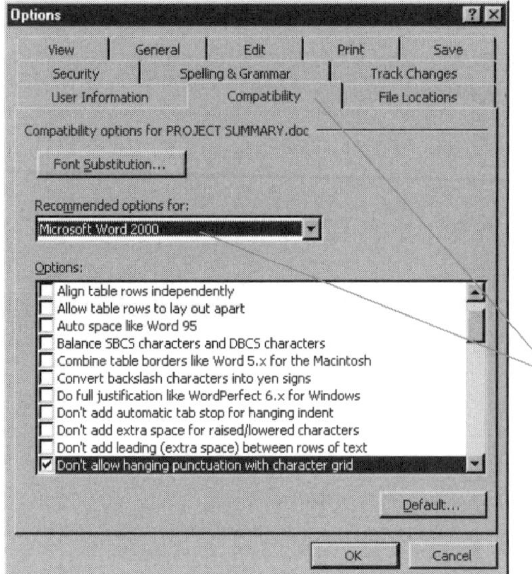

You can customise how Word displays documents which have been saved in another format.

1. Choose Options in the Tools menu.

2. Click on the Compatibility tab, select a format and view or change its options.

Installing Features

In order to conserve hard disk space, you can choose to include only the commonly used features when you first install Word. Later on, if you try to use a feature which isn't installed, Word will ask you if you want to load it there and then. If you answer Yes, you'll need to insert your original CD.

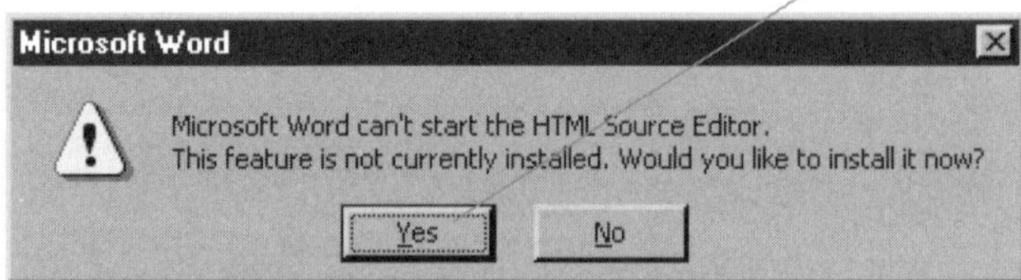

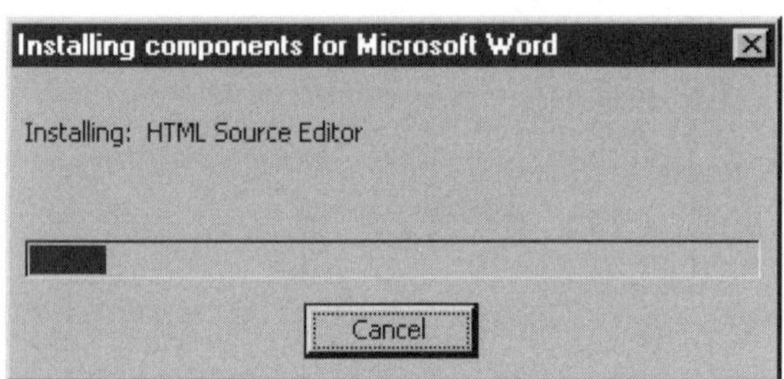

Index

E

G

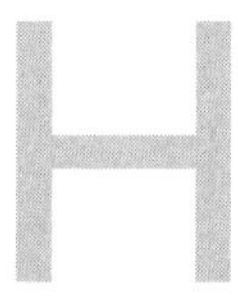

I

J

K

L

P

Q

R

S

T

U

Z